MODERNISM, MATERIAL CULTURE AND THE FIRST WORLD WAR

Edinburgh Critical Studies in Modernist Culture
Series Editors: Tim Armstrong and Rebecca Beasley

Available

Modernism and Magic: Experiments with Spiritualism, Theosophy and the Occult
Leigh Wilson

Sonic Modernity: Representing Sound in Literature, Culture and the Arts
Sam Halliday

Modernism and the Frankfurt School
Tyrus Miller

Lesbian Modernism: Censorship, Sexuality and Genre Fiction
Elizabeth English

Modern Print Artefacts: Textual Materiality and Literary Value in British Print Culture, 1890–1930s
Patrick Collier

Cheap Modernism: Expanding Markets, Publishers' Series and the Avant-Garde
Lise Jaillant

Portable Modernisms: The Art of Travelling Light
Emily Ridge

Hieroglyphic Modernisms: Writing and New Media in the Twentieth Century
Jesse Schotter

Modernism, Fiction and Mathematics
Nina Engelhardt

Modernist Life Histories: Biological Theory and the Experimental Bildungsroman
Daniel Aureliano Newman

Modernism, Space and the City: Outsiders and Affect in Paris, Vienna, Berlin, and London
Andrew Thacker

Modernism Edited: Marianne Moore and the Dial *Magazine*
Victoria Bazin

Modernism and Time Machines
Charles Tung

Primordial Modernism: Animals, Ideas, Transition (1927–1938)
Cathryn Setz

Modernism and Still Life: Artists, Writers, Dancers
Claudia Tobin

The Modernist Exoskeleton: Insects, War, Literary Form
Rachel Murray

Novel Sensations: Modernist Fiction and the Problem of Qualia
Jon Day

Hotel Modernity: Corporate Space in Literature and Film
Robbie Moore

The Modernist Anthropocene: Nonhuman Life and Planetary Change in James Joyce, Virginia Woolf and Djuna Barnes
Peter Adkins

Asbestos – The Last Modernist Object
Arthur Rose

Visionary Company: Hart Crane and Modernist Periodicals
Francesca Bratton

Modernist War Poetry: Combat Gnosticism and the Sympathetic Imagination, 1914–19
Jamie Wood

Abstraction in Modernism and Modernity: Human and Inhuman
Jeff Wallace

Modernism and Religion: Between Mysticism and Orthodoxy
Jamie Callison

Modernism, Material Culture and the First World War
Cedric Van Dijck

Forthcoming

Modernism and the Idea of Everyday Life
Leena Kore-Schröder

Sexological Modernism: Queer Feminism and Sexual Science
Jana Funke

Reading Modernism's Readers: Virginia Woolf, Psychoanalysis and the Bestseller
Helen Tyson

www.edinburghuniversitypress.com/series/ecsmc

MODERNISM, MATERIAL CULTURE AND THE FIRST WORLD WAR

Cedric Van Dijck

EDINBURGH
University Press

Edinburgh University Press is one of the leading university presses in the UK. We publish academic books and journals in our selected subject areas across the humanities and social sciences, combining cutting-edge scholarship with high editorial and production values to produce academic works of lasting importance. For more information visit our website: edinburghuniversitypress.com

© Cedric Van Dijck, 2023, 2025

Edinburgh University Press Ltd
13 Infirmary Street,
Edinburgh, EH1 1LT

First published in hardback by Edinburgh University Press 2023

Typeset in 10/12.5 Sabon by
Cheshire Typesetting Ltd, Cuddington, Cheshire

A CIP record for this book is available from the British Library

ISBN 978 1 3995 0786 8 (hardback)
ISBN 978 1 3995 0787 5 (paperback)
ISBN 978 1 3995 0788 2 (webready PDF)
ISBN 978 1 3995 0789 9 (epub)

The right of Cedric Van Dijck to be identified as the author of this work has been asserted in accordance with the Copyright, Designs and Patents Act 1988, and the Copyright and Related Rights Regulations 2003 (SI No. 2498).

CONTENTS

List of Figures	vi
Acknowledgements	vii
Series Editors' Preface	ix
Introduction	1
1 Guillaume Apollinaire's Curiosities	16
2 E. M. Forster in the Streets	50
3 Monuments in Virginia Woolf and Hope Mirrlees	88
4 Mulk Raj Anand in the Mud	128
Coda: At the Museum	164
Bibliography	174
Index	197

FIGURES

1.1	Apollinaire's apartment on the Boulevard Saint-Germain in Paris, René Giton, 1952–53. Médiathèque du Patrimoine et de la Photographie and Fondation Foujita (Sabam Belgium 2022).	20
1.2	Three Belgian soldiers in the 11th Line Infantry Regiment making trench art. Collection P. Vanleene, Ghent.	28
1.3	'1915' and 'Carte Postale' in *Case d'Armons*. Bibliothèque Nationale de France (RES P-YE-2442).	38
2.1	Men in the 5th Battalion travelling to the Suez Canal, Egypt, 1916. Australian War Memorial (A00089).	56
2.2	Restaurant sign, Egypt. Australian War Memorial (PS1275).	66
2.3	Billet room in Egypt, 1914–15. Imperial War Museum (Q 102963).	68
2.4	A page from *The Gnome*, 1916. The British Library (P.P.4039.wes).	74
3.1	Stanley Spencer, *Unveiling Cookham War Memorial*, 1922. Private Collection. Estate of Stanley Spencer, Bridgeman Art Library.	89
3.2	Soldiers stand as statues in France, 1915. Bibliothèque Nationale de France (Rol 44369).	91
4.1	Indian soldiers digging, September 1914. Bibliothèque Nationale de France (Rol 42667).	129
4.2	Hindu soldiers sorting the mail. Service Historique de la Défense, Fonds Rumpf, Vincennes.	150
5.1	Visitors at the new war museum at Crystal Palace, May 1921. Imperial War Museum (Q 17028).	168

ACKNOWLEDGEMENTS

I have been thinking about modernism and war for a decade now. It makes me happy finally to acknowledge the debts I have incurred along the way. In a sense, this book began its life as an MSc dissertation at the University of Edinburgh, in 2013, and then morphed into a doctoral thesis I submitted at Ghent University in the spring of 2018. I am grateful to Marysa Demoor, Sarah Posman and Birgit Van Puymbroeck for giving me my start and for welcoming me into the fold. Without them, I would never have written a thesis, nor revised it into a monograph. Virginia Woolf once reflected on this process, wondering how certain writers 'lay their facts out rather badly in the first version' and then go 'back and back and back' until there is a book. I simply could not have kept returning to this manuscript without the help of others: Maaheen Ahmed, Tim Armstrong, Rebecca Beasley, Gert Buelens, Marco Caracciolo, Koenraad Claes, Santanu Das, Eloise Forestier, Shannon Lambert, Jason Harding, Alex Houen, Delphine Munos, Richard B. Parkinson, Jasper Schelstraete, Phil Sicker, Randall Stevenson, Katie Trumpener, Patrick Vanleene, Debora Van Durme, Marianne Van Remoortel, Beatrijs Wille, my friends at the Blandijn, and my editors and reviewers at Edinburgh University Press. For all their kindnesses, I remain very grateful. I should like warmly to thank Huiying Yong for years of reading and editing my work all the way from Singapore. She will hate to see her name appear in print and I hope our friendship survives this reckless mention.

With much gratitude, I am indebted to the Research Foundation Flanders, the Belgian American Educational Foundation and the Historial de la Grande Guerre for their generosity in funding my project, and to the editors of *PMLA* and *Texas Studies in Literature and Language* for their permission to reproduce some of my initial thoughts on Apollinaire (on which Birgit Van Puymbroeck, my co-author in *TSLL*, has had a formative influence). The following institutions kindly welcomed me while I travelled with my manuscript: Ghent University, the University of Cambridge, the Netherlands-Flemish Institute in Cairo, Fordham University, Yale University, the Belgian Academy in Rome and the University of Brussels (VUB). So many people drifted in and out of my life in these places – I think of them often. At home, too, I feel fortunate to be surrounded by my friends and my family, especially my grandparents, aunts, uncles, cousins, nephew, niece and two brothers. The years I spent writing this book have been happy ones, and that is largely because of all of them, and because of Ruben, my twin, who has been in school for as long as I have. All this time, his belief in this book has been unwavering – *oud vertrouwen*, as he calls it. My parents have been unfailingly generous in their support of my education and for this they deserve my final thanks. Their encouragements continue to sustain me as the years fall away.

Schaarbeek, May 2022

SERIES EDITORS' PREFACE

This series of monographs on selected topics in modernism is designed to reflect and extend the range of new work in modernist studies. The studies in the series aim for a breadth of scope and for an expanded sense of the canon of modernism, rather than focusing on individual authors. Literary texts will be considered in terms of contexts including recent cultural histories (modernism and magic; sonic modernity; media studies) and topics of theoretical interest (the everyday; postmodernism; the Frankfurt School); but the series will also reconsider more familiar routes into modernism (modernism and gender; sexuality; politics). The works published will be attentive to the various cultural, intellectual and historical contexts of British, American and European modernisms, and to inter-disciplinary possibilities within modernism, including performance and the visual and plastic arts.

Tim Armstrong and Rebecca Beasley

INTRODUCTION

This book explores the modernist fascination with the material culture of the First World War – a focus that may seem counter-intuitive at first. Modernist authors were famously captivated by the ways the conflict unravelled the mind, recruiting experimental forms to capture this undoing in writing. At the same time, their texts were packed with monuments, gravestones, helmets, uniforms, shells, military signs, mud, war debris and shrapnel. The First World War had even prompted a way of thinking of these texts as objects in their own right, from books handprinted at the front to tattered letters and censored newspaper pages all uniquely shaped by the ongoing hostilities. What meanings convened around these objects and around these texts as objects? This book tells the story of that two-pronged question. It argues that modernist encounters with the things of war – equipment, museum pieces, souvenirs, paraphernalia, commodities, curiosities – served as a way to make sense of an extraordinary historical moment.

Each chapter centres around this dual question. The five authors featured in this study are Guillaume Apollinaire, E. M. Forster, Virginia Woolf, Hope Mirrlees and Mulk Raj Anand. In the years between 1914 and 1941, these writers represented and repurposed a great number of objects from the war world. Engagement with these objects figured as a response to some of the First World War's emblematic experiences. For instance, Guillaume Apollinaire's dispatches from the front, in which the French poet humorously reinvented the use of the Adrian helmet as a shopping basket, read as an attempt to grapple with the precarity of life in the trenches. These dispatches appeared in trench publications that were peculiar material records of their wartime surroundings: printed in the war zone on poor-quality paper, affected by paper shortages and censorship, stained, annotated by hand or wrapped in pages from army newspapers. Apollinaire's modernist texts, then, reflected on the war through staging visceral encounters with the material culture of conflict, and were themselves encountered as such affectively charged objects, with their physical contours serving as unique witnesses to the poet's precarious existence at the front. The chapters that follow will turn to *other* writers and *other* things: Forster's shop signs, Woolf's monuments, Mirrlees's gravestones and Anand's mud-stained bodies. In ways still little understood today, the war's characteristic moments, from the failure to capture its horror in words and the feeling of impotence in the trenches to the overwhelming sense of grief at home, were mediated through these objects.

Across four chapters and a coda, a new vision of the shaping influence of the First World War on modernism will emerge. For a long time, the traumatised mind has been integral to investigations into the relationship between this historical event and the experimental aesthetic that gathered momentum in the 1910s and early 1920s. The impressions and experiences at the heart of my close readings – death, linguistic crisis, loss and power imbalance – have been well-rehearsed in modernist scholarship, where they are typically discussed as the prerogative of the (traumatised) mind. However, this is only part of the story. By examining how centrally tangible objects such as helmets, shop signs, monuments and mud-stained bodies featured in responses to these experiences, this book will bring to light what the war meant to the modernists. My account foregrounds agency instead of endurance. The things of warfare were far from dead matter, and the modernist relationship with these things was creative and productive, despite the conflict's destructive powers. Not only were objects ingeniously introduced at key turns in modernist narratives to address the ongoing hostilities, some experimental features of these narratives themselves emerged as creative responses to the conflict's changed material realities. As a result, modernist writing became an indispensable part of the material culture of war – a physical record of its exceptional moment in history.

The Material War

Four months after the Armistice, in March 1919, Virginia Woolf sat down to assess the state of modern literature for the *Times Literary Supplement*. Her essay, 'Modern Novels', targeted three established novelists, H. G. Wells, Arnold Bennett and John Galsworthy. For Woolf, these men were 'materialists', a term she used with some reproach.[1] Their best-selling novels were packed with houses full of furniture and characters in elaborate dress, drowning readers in the kind of details needed to create a semblance of reality.[2]

Literature, Woolf felt, suffered under the weight of these details and in the process failed to capture something more significant – the mind at work. The author would rehearse this point in essays that spanned her writing career. In 'Mr Bennett and Mrs Brown', published in 1923, the Edwardian novelist was accused of providing too many specifics in his depiction of a house simply so as to 'hypnotise us into the belief that, because he has made a house, there must be a person living there'.[3] 'Phases of Fiction', from 1929, compared the Edwardian novel to a thin-blooded catalogue, an inventory of facts that fell short of illumining 'the mind within, rather than the world without'.[4] In Woolf's accounts, modernist novelists redeemed these shortcomings, moving away from the minutiae of the fictional environment and into the 'dark region of psychology' instead.[5]

The antagonistic divide Woolf set up in the *Times Literary Supplement* – the mind within rather than the world without – went on to define the priorities of modernist scholarship for decades, even though this distinction was never as clear-cut as the modernists would have it.[6] Under the auspices of the New Modernist Studies, we have begun to witness a profound shift in focus.[7] In *Solid Objects: Modernism and the Test of Production*, Douglas Mao charted how writers such as Virginia Woolf, Wyndham Lewis, Ezra Pound and Wallace Stevens began 'to lose patience with subjectivity' and turned to the object world for its 'impermeability to mind'.[8] Mao's prompt, and that of thing theory more broadly, which from the outset has been especially devoted to modernist literature, opened the field to readings of modernism's material cultures.[9] This gradual expansion of the field of modernist studies has a special relevance for the question of the impact of the First World War on modernism. For a large part, this question is still approached through modernism's well-rehearsed commitment to interiority. Woolf's call for a turn to the 'dark regions of psychology' in the *Times Literary Supplement* was published only a few months after the guns had fallen silent, and it serves as a good example of the shaping influence of the war in this debate. 'Modern Fiction' shared copy, in April 1919, with advertisements for such books as Edward Randall's *The Dead Have Never Died*, Victoria De Bunsen's *The War and Men's Minds* and Arthur W. Marchmont's *The Man Without a Memory*. This is more than a mere accident. Woolf's advocacy for a kind of writing that prioritises, and formally mimics, mental processes coincided with the fresh memory of the ravages the First World War had wrought on the mind. To this day, the relationship between this major geopolitical event and a concomitant period of aesthetic experimentation is often viewed as causal.[10] While scholars have more recently cautioned against such easy links, claims of causality persist, perhaps in large part due to the fact that they hold some veracity in individual cases.[11] '[I]t is only after the "shattering experience" of the war', a study on Ford Madox Ford suggests, 'that the mind moves to centre stage in Ford's fiction.'[12] For Ford, 'technical and stylistic inventiveness went hand in hand with the recovery of his ability to write at all and especially to write about the war and to register its effect on the mind'.[13]

The association between what one scholar terms 'the newness of modernist form' and 'the striking unfamiliarity of broken men and male minds' is old and practised.[14] This is the shellshock paradigm: shells shocked modernism into a newfound relevance.[15] As latter-day diagnosticians, scholars compulsively return to modernist writing in search of characters undone by traumatic war memories: Septimus Smith in Virginia Woolf's *Mrs Dalloway*, Chris Baldry in Rebecca West's *The Return of the Soldier*, Christopher Tietjens in Ford Madox Ford's *Parade's End* and the narrator in 'Arms and the Mind', Lord Marchmain in Evelyn Waugh's *Brideshead Revisited*, the drunk expatriates in Ernest Hemingway's *The Sun Also Rises*, the 'men whose minds the Dead have ravished' in Wilfred Owen's 'Mental Cases', the autobiographical protagonist in HD's *Bid Me to Live*, the figure in Conrad Felixmüller's *Soldier in a Madhouse*, Egbert in D. H. Lawrence's 'England, My England', Larry Darrell in W. Somerset Maugham's *The Razor's Edge* and the speaker in one of Siegfried Sassoon's poems, among many, who goes 'stark, staring mad because of the guns'.[16] 'We talk of shell-shock', observes the protagonist in Richard Aldington's *Death of a Hero*, 'but who wasn't shell-shocked, more or less?'[17] For Gertrude Stein, the affliction spanned an entire generation of young men – mad, numbed, restless, lost.[18] While sweeping, these claims have a truth behind them. In the British army alone, more than 80,000 soldiers on the Western Front suffered from war neurosis, and many more are likely to have been undiagnosed. In all, between 200,000 and 300,000 Frenchmen were affected and in Mulk Raj Anand's Punjab 327 'military insanes' arrived home between 1916 and 1933.[19] If the war had an inescapable effect on modernism, as these examples illustrate, then such an effect is found precisely in the way the conflict accorded a newfound relevance to modernism's interest in interiority and introspection. By this account, its experimental strategies – including stream of consciousness, fragmentation and disrupted chronologies – emerged from, or were felt to be particularly receptive to, a historical attempt to capture and contain the war's traumatic experiences in writing. '[T]he dislocations of war', Allyson Booth has argued in this vein, 'figure centrally in modernist form.'[20]

What image of modernism's relationship to armed conflict comes into view if we shift our focus not inward but outward? What impact did the war's material realities have on modernism? In which ways did objects and print artefacts from the war world help make modernism? These questions, which have remained largely unresolved, shape this book. To be sure, I do not mean to invalidate the agonies war brings to bear on the psyche, and in no way do I seek to uphold a subject/object, mind/body divide. Rather, while scholars have long favoured mental over material realities in their account of the modernist war, my aim is to shift the focal point in what was always already an *entangled* experience. In 'Mr Bennett and Mrs Brown', a follow-up to 'Modern Fiction', Woolf imagined her protagonist, Mrs Brown, 'in a seaside house, among queer ornaments: sea-urchins, models of ships in glass cases. Her husband's medals were on the mantelpiece.'[21] What if we enter modernism not so much through the 'dark regions of psychology', as the essay suggests we should, but through these military medals on the mantelpiece? To be sure, the years between 1914 and 1918, and their legacy, prove to be a particularly appropriate context to study modernism's unfolding engagement with material culture at work.[22] The armed conflict witnessed the invention, or widespread use, of a host of objects new to the modernist imagination: trench coats, teabags, grocery cars, Adrian helmets, wristwatches, Vermorel sprayers, stainless steel, stretchers, gas masks, identity discs, zeppelins, duckboards, mosquito nets, passports, air raid sirens, shells, shrapnel, tanks, nurses' uniforms, front souvenirs and subsidised bread. 'It was in the trenches', the French avant-garde artist Fernand Léger tellingly revealed, 'that I really seized the reality of objects.'[23]

At the same time, armies brought destruction in their wake. As the first industrial conflict, a *Materialschlacht*, the war introduced weaponry that devastated the material world on an unprecedented scale and created a new intimacy with its raw materials, including stone and rubble from debris, soil in the trenches, metal from shells, and the granite and marble out of which war memorials were sculpted. Economies collapsed. Mulk Raj Anand remembered how prices had soared in Amritsar's local bazaars; the price of a cup of coffee, in E. M. Forster's Alexandria, was likewise raised.[24] In a letter dated in early February 1919, Virginia Woolf commented on war inflation and the strikes that followed: 'You can't conceive what existence is like without trains or tubes, a heavy snow falling, no coal in the cellar, a leak in the roof which has already filled every possible receptacle, and probably no electric light tomorrow.'[25] Stuck across the border in Munich, and across a political divide, the Austrian poet Rainer Maria Rilke lost most of his belongings from his Parisian apartment, including keepsakes and manuscripts auctioned off, as enemy property, to cover rental debts.[26] T. S. Eliot's *Coriolan* turned an inventory of war *matériel* lifted from General Ludendorff's *The Coming War* – '5,800,000 rifles and carbines, / 102,000 machine guns, / 28,000 trench mortars' – into the occasion for a poem.[27]

Anecdotes from the lives and writings of the modernists, like Woolf, Rilke and Eliot, abound. Little is known, however, of the powerful hold war objects and realities had over the modernist imagination. In the recent surge of interest in modernist material culture, the war has remained out of scope.[28] In fact, the scholars who have most productively engaged with the material culture of conflict are historians and archaeologists.[29] Two early exceptions are Trudi Tate's *Modernism, History and the First World War* and Allyson Booth's *Postcards from the Trenches*. As Tate points out, in a chapter on the tank, 'military objects sometimes occupied an important place in the social and intellectual context in which writers such as Woolf, Ford, Lawrence and HD lived and worked'.[30] Taking its cue from Tate and Booth, this book brings a collection of war objects newly into view: Apollinaire's helmets and trench art, Forster's shop signs and monument inscriptions, Woolf's statues, Mirrlees's gravestones and Anand's mud-stained bodies. It argues that modernist literature played around with the social, cultural and political meanings of these things, staging engagements with the war's physical world in an attempt to make sense of certain aspects of the war experience, from epistemological crisis to personal loss.

Such close contact with the physical environment was often visceral. My readings revolve around affectively charged moments of handling a shell, of crawling through mud, of touching the cold stonework of a grave, or of picking up a memorial volume from the shelf. Touch, as Santanu Das influentially argued, lay at the heart of the war experience.[31] If we interact with things through our lived bodies, then the war provides a compelling context for studying this interaction: the body at war is always at risk of becoming itself thing-like. This is a fear to which modernist writers responded en masse. 'It is all just matter – all humanity,' Ford Madox Ford protested, writing from the Ypres Salient in September 1916; 'one with the trees, the shells by the roadside, the limbered wagons, the howitzers and the few upstanding housewalls.'[32] 'Of course we must be materialists,' observed E. M. Forster in a similar vein. 'Let us look after bodies that there may be a next generation which may have the right to look after the soul.'[33] In fact, the body – sleeping in close quarters, wounded in a hospital bed, lifeless in a ditch, made to move at zero hour – is perhaps *the* object from the material culture of war that has received most scholarly scrutiny, ever since Elaine Scarry's landmark *The Body in Pain*.[34] While I draw on some of this work, my engagement with affect and the sensing body is far from theoretical; instead, my aim is to show these historical moments of encounter at work. From this embodied contact with the material world, a sense of agency emerges – neither the object nor the body that picks it up are ever mere dead weight.[35] If modern warfare fundamentally altered what Margot Norris termed the 'locus of agency', so that survival in the war zone was not a matter of competence but of blind chance, then engaging with the objects of the conflict, in and around the modernist text, offered a way of critically diagnosing such a suspension of agency, and, in rare, profound cases, a way of restoring it.

THE MATERIAL TEXT

The First World War was a critical moment in the history of the book. On 30 May 1918, the *Egyptian Mail*, a colonial newspaper published in Cairo, brought the story of an odd artefact that had just arrived in Manchester:

> In a limp and sodden package which has had the misfortune to have been in a torpedoed ship and the luck to have been rescued, a copy of the 'Palestine News' has reached Manchester, writes the 'Manchester Guardian'. This is a weekly paper newly started by the British troops in Palestine, and is printed at Cairo. It is published at G.H.Q., and is more sober and austere in its aspect than are most of the jovial publications edited by the men themselves. A good deal of space is devoted to war happenings on other fronts and to the local interest of regimental concerts, church parades, and a mounted brigade's race meeting near Gaza. But to us, adds the 'Guardian' at any rate, its value lies chiefly in its little, awkwardly worded impressions of their surroundings which are written by one or two soldiers.[36]

It is hard to imagine a less newsworthy moment in those extraordinary times. With so much to report on in the spring of 1918, why did the *Manchester Guardian* advertise the *News*'s arrival in Britain? Why did the *Egyptian Mail* lift the short notice, almost verbatim, on to its own pages a few weeks later? In two ways, the *Palestine News* was a curious document. Founded in March 1918, the weekly army publication constituted a relatively new phenomenon for most readers at the time – and it had travelled far, published on Cairo's Kasr-el-Nil street, on the banks of the Nile, and arriving at the editorial office of the *Guardian* in Manchester. A regular contributor to the *Egyptian Mail*, E. M. Forster must have read the *Palestine News* at one point or other while living out his war years in Alexandria. T. E. Lawrence certainly did: a piece by his pen on the release of Damascus featured in an October 1918 issue of the *News*.[37]

Like the book, the periodical is not merely a vehicle for ideas, but an object in its own right.[38] In its physical form, the *Palestine News* was distinctively moulded by the ongoing hostilities. That is where the affective interest lay for readers of the *Guardian* and *Mail*. It was so unlikely that it should have arrived in Manchester at all. Limp and sodden, like the parcel in which it was mailed, the issue bore the traces of its wartime journey. 'The incoming mail has gone down in sight of our shores,' Forster wrote from Alexandria in July 1917. '[A] fortnight's letters, which means two from you, are lost.'[39] In fact, notices of mail 'lost through enemy action' appeared in the *Egyptian Mail* with a certain regularity.[40] But the *News* survived its ordeal and bore the mark of that survival in its material form. That the weekly paper was published, in due course, with Arabic and Hebrew supplements – جريدة فلسطين and חדשות מהארץ – must have called further attention to its materiality, for English readers at least. Had this waterlogged copy of the *Palestine News* been preserved (there is no way for me to find out if it has), then it is likely it would not have been a coincidence. At the time, the military newspaper already constituted a unique record of its historical moment in a curiously double way: its 'little, awkwardly worded impressions' about the war in the Near East as well as its tattered, 'limp and sodden' materiality.

In different respects, the war prompted modernist writers to view the text in this duality, exploring the interplay between the worded impressions and the material forms of a print artefact such as the *Palestine News*.[41] To do so is to firmly position the text within its historical moment. For the writers under consideration here, that moment was the First World War – a state of exception that imprinted, and left its physical marks, on artefacts in unprecedented ways. The period marked a sea change in the manner in which modernist writers and their contemporaries thought about the text *as object*. Across all warring nations, censorship was introduced, resulting in blacked-out passages in letters and newspaper columns. With overseas trade and importation in difficulties, paper was quickly in short supply in Europe. In Britain, a Royal Paper Commission was established, which curtailed paper use and prioritised the government in the allocation of paper.[42] As a result, the book business plummeted, from 12,379 titles published in 1913 to 8,131 in 1917.[43] Periodicals folded, or, in an attempt at survival, began to count fewer pages and to sport smaller type. Prices soared. In Forster's Alexandria the post office would only issue up to ten postcards per individual, and in Apollinaire's France the situation had become so dire by 1918, as the poet noted with some distress, that fellow countrymen started selling valuable historical documents to be made into pulp.[44] The French poet's experiments with collage as a creative response to these paper shortages, much like Virginia Woolf's inventions at the Hogarth Press, bear witness to the renewal of a sense of artistic agency. If stream of consciousness was felt to be a particularly appropriate strategy to capture the war's traumatic experiences, then a collage aesthetic was in tune with its more mundane, material realities.

At the same time, soldiers in the 1914–18 war were, in the often-repeated words of Paul Fussell, 'not merely literate, but vigorously literary' – producers and consumers of all manner of printed matter.[45] Comprising the first civilian army in modern history, soldiers wanted to keep in touch with the home front. The British postal service's Home Depot in London handled two billion letters and 114 million parcels across four war-ridden years.[46] On Christmas Eve 1914, Apollinaire received forty-two letters in the Nîmes barracks, a record high for all the regiments stationed there, more than 17,000 men in total.[47] Novels and newspapers were read, but also left unread, to be used simply as an object (for instance, by holding up a periodical, not necessarily reading it, soldiers or nurses living in close quarters created a moment of privacy).[48] Posters in the Parisian metro loom large in Mirrlees's *Paris: A Poem* ('CACAO BLOOKER', 'DEUIL EN 24 HEURES'); E. M. Forster composed pieces for the *Egyptian Mail* about the military signs erected in Alexandria and Cairo;

Mulk Raj Anand wrote about the use of bureaucratic documents, such as identity papers and land deeds. If scholars of material culture have mostly directed us to the novel and the short story – the latter 'thing-like', the former 'an exemplary portable property' – the 1914–18 conflict seems to ask us to open up the field to a range of writing objects with which the modernists gained a new familiarity at the time.[49] As war objects – mud-stained, censored, annotated, printed at the front, limp and sodden, patched together from a collage of other documents – these material texts elicited visceral responses. In my discussion of Virginia Woolf's *Jacob's Room*, for instance, I explore how characters grapple with the memory of loss through embodied encounters not only with the memorial statue, made from stone, but with the memorial volume, made from paper. A character in that novel, Sandra Wentworth Williams, often picks up a book she had received from a lover who fell in the war: doing so, 'her eyes would brighten (but not at the print)'.[50] Memory and loss were mediated through such intimate contact with the book as object.

Apollinaire, Forster, Woolf, Mirrlees and Anand

In Chapter 1, 'Guillaume Apollinaire's Curiosities', I explore the French poet's experiments with the material culture of the trenches, ranging from his articles and poems on war objects such as the Frisian horse, a military contraption he turned into a symbol of love and the butt of a joke, to the decorative items he carved out of war debris, such as a ring from a bullet. On and off the page, these experiments disarmed the deadly objects of an industrial conflict, turning them into peculiar products of everyday life at the front, which was at times precarious, at times dull. I argue that this reappropriating impulse also underwrote Apollinaire's engagement with the trench press: tattered magazines and shoddily produced booklets handprinted in the war zone. My reading focuses on two poems in his trench volume *Case d'Armons*, '1915' and 'Postcard', which take the monotonous yet perilous wartime everyday as their topic and affective circumstance. Through a collage aesthetic – both poems are linked by a military postcard glued into the volume – the poet playfully subverted the everyday and military connotations of this print artefact, making the volume as a whole into what he termed a 'bibliographical curiosity'.[51]

'E. M. Forster in the Streets' shifts the scene to the urban environments of wartime Egypt, a place the novelist found 'difficult to describe'.[52] Not just Egypt, but the war itself defied such easy description. The representational crisis posed by the conflict, I contend in Chapter 2, was keenly felt on a colonial front saturated with the babble of different tongues. I begin by examining the print artefacts that helped new arrivals in Egypt navigate and interpret this unfamiliar setting, including colonial newspapers, dictionaries and travel guides. Because of their layout and practical use – often dipped into in the streets of Alexandria rather than read consecutively at home – these documents drew attention to their status as print artefacts. As I go on to show, a concern with the materiality of language and print also developed into a preoccupation within these pages. In the *Egyptian Mail*, a colonial newspaper, and *Alexandria: A History and a Guide*, his travel guide, E. M. Forster staged encounters with shop signs and monument inscriptions as a way of grappling with the war's linguistic crisis. Ranging from spelling mistakes enlarged on English shop signs in Cairo to the indecipherable scripts on the ancient monuments of Alexandria, words on public display brought the material and visual qualities of language, rather than its referentiality, newly into view. For Forster, these objects of writing – censored papers, shop signs, monument plaques – were at the heart of his response to the conflict, developing into concretely tangible records of the war's epistemological crisis.

Chapter 3, 'Monuments in Virginia Woolf and Hope Mirrlees', leaps forward in time to what Samuel Hynes influentially described as a period of 'monument making'.[53] In modernist writing of the late 1910s and early 1920s, I argue, mourning the loss of the war dead was presented as a tangible process. Through embodied encounters with memorial objects such as gravestones, statues and commemorative volumes, memories of the fallen were evoked. My first case study is Virginia Woolf's *Jacob's Room*, which portrays its often-absent protagonist as a statue in a gesture anticipating his death on the battlefield. If solid stones come to occupy the place of ephemeral lives, then it is the women in the novel, left behind, who engage with them most viscerally. These gendered moments of contact with statues and graves – we also find them in Hope Mirrlees's *Paris: A Poem* – trigger 'fresh shock[s]' of memory as well as more critical notions of the glorification of sacrifice.[54] In a second step, the chapter asks how the war informed a way of thinking of books themselves in such tangible terms, as solid objects made not from stone but from paper. This was the case for *Paris* and *Kew Gardens*. Both Hogarth Press editions draw a focus to their physical forms, ranging from typographical experiments (in order to represent a war grave on the page) to a collage aesthetic (in order to negotiate the war's paper shortages). I then illustrate that this material existence of the book – *as an object* with a long shelf life, *as an object* curiously shaped by war – was put to good use in the memorial culture that developed in the war's wake: commemorative books, like statues and gravestones, became tools for memory, standing in the place of the war dead and picked up from the shelf in order to remember. Books such as *Poems by C. N. Sidney Woolf* and *The Collected Poems of Rupert Brooke: With a Memoir* held the capacity to bring back, as Woolf once put it, 'the unknown and the vanished whose only record is, for example, this little book of poems, so fairly printed, so finely engraved, too'.[55]

In Chapter 4, 'Mulk Raj Anand in the Mud', I take embodied engagements with the soil – from tilling the fields to burrowing through No Man's Land – as a point of entry into the subaltern war experience. In *The Village*,

Anand's novel about a farming family in the Punjab, the protagonist's visceral knowledge of the landscape, 'sod clinging to his feet', symbolises his right to this place.[56] Such moments of touch in the novel, I argue, articulate an explicit critique of colonial dispossession. A form of protest underwrites similar encounters with the mud of the trenches in *Across the Black Waters*: a literal erasure of the self, as the sepoy's body becomes stained with mud, figures as a tangible (and racialised) symbol of a more pervasive threat to agency in wartime. At such moments in the mud, the body is at the brink of itself becoming object-like. (An interlude briefly examines the modernist trope of burial, the ultimate merging of body and land, as an indictment of colonial warfare in Thomas Hardy's and T. S. Eliot's poetry.) In a final section, this chapter studies the sepoy's engagement with the soil, from the Punjab grasslands to the French battlefields, in a more abstract sense – as paperwork. Anand's fiction is littered with land debt collection letters and military files, which the characters come upon first and foremost as material objects. Left unread, these functional documents tangibly emblematise how power worked inconspicuously through the written/printed word, without a fault to the detriment of the farmer-sepoy. The epilogue to the chapter briefly hints at expressions of discontent by zeroing in on India's struggle for self-rule in the years following the war. In Anand's *The Sword and the Sickle*, a visceral knowledge of the soil, and a renewed acquaintance with its paperwork, become the basis for a resistance politics, as the novel's Indian protagonist – his political ambitions 'entangled among the roots and stakes of the fields' – develops a sense of ownership over himself and his lands.[57]

Taken together, these four chapters deliberately cast a wide net across the modernist period, medially (novels, poems, shop signs, travel guides, censored letters, trench journals), geographically (India, Britain, France, Egypt) and temporally (extending the war beyond its conventional boundaries into the 'Greater War' period).[58] Reaching as far as the early 1940s, with Mulk Raj Anand, who wrote at a remove from the events studied in this book, enables me to reconstruct the ways in which memories of war – often construed around museum pieces, as explored in my coda – continued to shape modernist writing decades after the cessation of fighting. The five writers who feature in this study cut through divides that have long shaped our cultural histories of the conflict: male/female, combatant/civilian, European/colonial. Furthermore, these writers spoke different languages, and lived, and wrote about, different versions of the war: Apollinaire a gunner at the front, Forster a searcher for the Red Cross, Mirrlees and Woolf civilians in London and Paris, and Anand looking back to a childhood at an outpost in the British Empire. Though this is not a story of influence, many connections may be drawn between these figures: Anand, Forster, Woolf and Mirrlees were all, at different moments, affiliated with the Hogarth Press; Mirrlees read Apollinaire (who himself sought more intimate contact between the British and the French, marvelling, as he did in the *Mercure de France* in 1918, at the idea of a tunnel under the Channel); Anand knew Forster 'for forty years' and 'devoured' his *Passage to India*; Woolf and Forster, too, were close friends.⁵⁹ Briefer glimpses of a diverse cast of minor characters – C. P. Cavafy, T. S. Eliot, Gertrude Stein, Rupert Brooke, Käthe Kollwitz, Rabindranath Tagore, Dora Carrington, Ezra Pound, Socrates Spiro, Toru Dutt, Ford Madox Ford and Stanley Spencer – are meant to move the modernist interest in the things of warfare beyond the confines of these five protagonists and, in doing so, hint at a broader phenomenon.

NOTES

1. Virginia Woolf, 'Modern Novels', in *The Essays of Virginia Woolf*, vol. III: 1919–24, ed. Andrew McNeillie (London: Hogarth Press, 1988), pp. 30–6 (p. 32). 'I liked both of them', Bennett later claimed, 'in spite of their naughty treatment of me in the press.' See Arnold Bennett, 'Mr Bennett and Mrs Woolf', in *Virginia Woolf: Interviews and Recollections*, ed. J. H. Stape (London: Palgrave Macmillan, 1995), pp. 29–30 (p. 29).
2. Barthes would later famously term it the 'reality effect'. Roland Barthes, *The Rustle of Language*, trans. Richard Howard (Berkeley and Los Angeles: University of California Press, 1989), pp. 141–8.
3. Virginia Woolf, *Mr Bennett and Mrs Brown* (London: Hogarth Press, 1924), p. 16.
4. Virginia Woolf, 'Phases of Fiction', in *The Essays of Virginia Woolf*, vol. V: 1929–32, ed. Stuart N. Clarke (London: Hogarth Press, 2009), pp. 40–88 (p. 64).
5. Woolf, 'Modern Novels', p. 35.
6. A first generation of critics, inspired by New Criticism's notion of the text as an entity unto itself, insisted on aesthetic autonomy by reading modernism as a withdrawal from its surroundings into the psyche (against which Marxist scholars, such as György Lukács in 'The Ideology of Modernism', levelled criticism). A second generation grew increasingly attuned to the ways in which the real world entered the spaces of the modernist mind. See, for instance, Fredric Jameson, *The Political Unconscious: Narrative as a Socially Symbolic Act* (Ithaca: Cornell University Press, 1981); Raymond Williams, *The Politics of Modernism: Against the New Conformists* (London: Verso, 1994); Alex Zwerdling, *Virginia Woolf and the Real World* (Berkeley: University of California Press, 1986).
7. Douglas Mao and Rebecca L. Walkowitz, 'The New Modernist Studies', *PMLA* 123.3 (2008), 737–48.
8. Douglas Mao, *Solid Objects: Modernism and the Test of Production* (Princeton: Princeton University Press, 1998), pp. 9, 8–9.
9. George Bornstein, *Material Modernism: The Politics of the Page* (Cambridge: Cambridge University Press, 2001); Elizabeth Outka, *Consuming Traditions: Modernity, Modernism, and the Commodified Authentic* (New York: Oxford University Press, 2009); *The Aesthetics of Matter: Modernism, the Avant-Garde, and Material Exchange*, ed. Sarah Posman et al. (Berlin: De Gruyter, 2013).
10. For some scholars, war gave birth to modern consciousness. See Eric Leed, *No Man's Land: Combat and Identity in World War I* (New York: Cambridge University Press, 2009) and Modris Ekstein, *Rites of Spring: The Great War and the Birth of the Modern Age* (Boston: Houghton Mifflin, 2000). Malcolm Bradbury, too, saw the war as 'lead[ing] the way into Modernism', as 'the source of psychic anxiety'. See 'The Denuded Place: War and Form in *Parade's End* and

USA', in *The First World War in Fiction*, ed. Holger Klein (London: Macmillan, 1976), pp. 193–209 (pp. 193–4).
11. For a critical account of British modernism as 'among the cultural effects of an unprecedentedly traumatic war', see Marina Mackay, *Modernism, War, and Violence* (London: Bloomsbury, 2017), pp. 6–13.
12. 'Introduction', in *War and the Mind: Ford Madox Ford's* Parade's End, *Modernism and Psychology*, ed. Ashley Chantler and Rob Hawkes (Edinburgh: Edinburgh University Press, 2015), pp. 1–16 (p. 6).
13. Ibid., p. 8.
14. Trevor Dodman, *Shell Shock, Memory, and the Novel in the Wake of World War I* (New York: Cambridge University Press, 2015), p. 13. The scholarship is abundant: Wyatt Bonikowski, *Shell Shock and the Modernist Imagination: The Death Drive in Post-World War I British Fiction* (Abingdon: Routledge, 2016); Paul Sheehan, *Modernism and the Aesthetics of Violence* (Cambridge: Cambridge University Press, 2013); Carl Krockel, *War Trauma and English Modernism: T. S. Eliot and D. H. Lawrence* (London: Palgrave, 2011); Annette Becker, 'The Avant-Garde, Madness and the Great War', *Journal of Contemporary History* 35.1 (2000), 71–84; Karen Demeester, 'Trauma and Recovery in Virginia Woolf's *Mrs Dalloway*', *Modern Fiction Studies* 44.3 (1998), 649–73.
15. As Jay Winter has argued, shell shock is not so much a diagnosis as a metaphor, 'the prism through which much of the cultural history of the 1914–18 war has been viewed'. See 'Shell-Shock and the Cultural History of the Great War', *Journal of Contemporary History* 35.1 (2000), 7–11 (p. 7).
16. Wilfred Owen, 'Mental Cases', in *The Complete Poems and Fragments*, vol. I, ed. Jon Stallworthy (London: Chatto & Windus, 2013), p. 169. Siegfried Sassoon, 'Repression of War Experience', in *War Poems of Siegfried Sassoon* (Mineola: Dover, 2004), pp. 80–1 (p. 81). The year 1922, modernism's *annus mirabilis*, also saw the publication of the report of the War Office Committee of Enquiry into 'Shell-Shock'.
17. Richard Aldington, *Death of a Hero* (London: Penguin, 2013), p. 293.
18. The anecdote is recounted in Ernest Hemingway, *A Moveable Feast* (London: Jonathan Cape, 1964), p. 32: '"That's what you all are," Miss Stein said. "All of you young people who served in the war. You are a lost generation."'
19. For these numbers, see Fiona Reid, 'War Psychiatry and Shell Shock', in *1914–1918 Online: International Encyclopedia of the First World War*, ed. Ute Daniel et al., <https://encyclopedia.1914-1918-online.net/article/war_psychiatry_and_shell_shock> (last updated 11 December 2019). Hilary Buxton, 'Imperial Amnesia: Race, Trauma and Indian Troops in the First World War', *Past & Present* 241.1 (2018), 221–58 (p. 246).
20. Allyson Booth, *Postcards from the Trenches: Negotiating the Space between Modernism and the First World War* (New York: Oxford University Press, 1996), p. 4.
21. Woolf, *Mr Bennett and Mrs Brown*, p. 9.
22. Bill Brown also sees war as a moment of transformation in historical engagements with material culture, but points to the American Civil War instead: 'the invention, production, distribution and consumption of things rather suddenly came to define a national culture. [...] This demand for things did not subside after the war, in large measure because the manufacturer had new and no less powerful stimulants on which he could depend.' Bill Brown, *A Sense of Things: The Object Matter of American Literature* (Chicago: University of Chicago Press, 2003), p. 4.
23. Quoted in Richard Cork, *A Bitter Truth: Avant-Garde Art and the Great War* (New Haven and London: Yale University Press in association with Barbican Art Gallery, 1994), p. 9.

24. Mulk Raj Anand, *Morning Face* (Bombay: Kutub Popular, 1968), p. 64. *Egyptian Mail*, 7 January 1918, p. 3.
25. *The Letters of Virginia Woolf*, vol. II: 1912–22, ed. Nigel Nicolson and Joanna Trautmann (London: Chatto & Windus, 1980), p. 325: to Katherine Arnold-Forster, 5 February 1919.
26. Ralph Freedman, *Rainer Maria Rilke: Der Meister* (Frankfurt and Leipzig: Insel Verlag, 2002), p. 238. Some belongings were saved, thanks to André Gide and the concierge.
27. T. S. Eliot, *Collected Poems 1909–35* (London: Faber & Faber, 1936), p. 135.
28. *Modernist Objects: Literature, Art, Culture*, ed. Noëlle Cuny and Xavier Kalck (Clemson: Clemson University Press, 2020); Laura Oulanne, *Materiality in Modernist Short Fiction: Lived Things* (New York: Routledge, 2021); Aimée Gasston, *Modernist Short Fiction and Things* (London: Palgrave Macmillan, 2021).
29. *Objects of War: The Material Culture of Conflict and Displacement*, ed. Leora Auslander and Tara Zahra (Ithaca: Cornell University Press, 2018) and the work of Nicholas J. Saunders, including *Trench Art: Materialities and Memories of War* (London: Routledge, 2003) and the edited volume *Matters of Conflict: Material Culture, Memory and the First World War* (London: Routledge, 2004). See also the publication of trade books such as John Hughes-Wilson, in association with the Imperial War Museum, *A History of the First World War in 100 Objects* (London: Cassell, 2014) and Gary Sheffield, *The First World War in 100 Objects: The Story of the Great War Told Through the Objects That Shaped It* (London: André Deutsch, 2013).
30. Trudi Tate, *Modernism, History and the First World War* (Penrith: Humanities Ebooks, 2013), p. 134.
31. Santanu Das, *Touch and Intimacy in First World War Literature* (Cambridge: Cambridge University Press, 2007).
32. Ford Madox Ford, 'A Day in Battle: Arms and the Mind', in *The Ford Madox Ford Reader*, ed. Sondra J. Stang (London: Paladin, 1987), pp. 456–61 (p. 459).
33. *Selected Letters of E. M. Forster*, vol. I: 1879–1920, ed. Mary Lago and P. N. Furbank (London: Collins, 1983), p. 253: to Goldsworthy Lowes Dickinson, 5 May 1917.
34. Elaine Scarry, *The Body in Pain: The Making and Unmaking of the World* (Oxford: Oxford University Press, 1988); Joanna Bourke, *Dismembering the Male: Men's Bodies, Britain and the Great War* (London: Reaktion, 1996); *Modern Conflict and the Senses*, ed. Nicholas J. Saunders and Paul Cornish (London: Routledge, 2017); and chapters on the body in Booth's *Postcards from the Trenches* and Tate's *Modernism, History and the First World War*. 'War narrative', Santanu Das has claimed, 'is traumatised by the sheer *Thing*-ness of the human body.' See Das, *Touch and Intimacy*, p. 50.
35. See Jane Bennett, *Vibrant Matter: A Political Ecology of Things* (Durham, NC: Duke University Press, 2010).
36. 'The "Palestine News" in Manchester', *Egyptian Mail*, 30 May 1918, p. 2. The note was lifted from the *Manchester Guardian*, 9 May 1918, p. 3.
37. 'Release of Damascus (from a correspondent beyond the Jordan)', *Palestine News*, 10 October 1918, p. 6.
38. See Barbara Green, 'Feminist Things', in *Transatlantic Print Culture, 1880–1940: Emerging Media, Emerging Modernisms*, ed. Ann Ardis and Patrick Collier (Basingstoke: Palgrave Macmillan, 2008), pp. 66–79; Faye Hammill and Mark Hussey, *Modernism's Print Cultures* (London: Bloomsbury, 2016), p. 2.
39. *Selected Letters*, vol. I, p. 260: to Florence Barger, 4 July 1917.
40. 'Lost Mails', *Egyptian Mail*, 22 October 1918, p. 2.

41. On modernism and textual materialism, see Bornstein, *Material Modernism*; Bill Brown, 'Introduction: Textual Materialism', *PMLA* 125.1 (2010), 24–8; Patrick Collier, *Modern Print Artefacts: Textual Materiality and Literary Value in British Print Culture, 1890–1930s* (Edinburgh: Edinburgh University Press, 2016); Mark D. Larabee, *Front Lines of Modernism: Remapping the Great War in British Fiction* (Basingstoke: Palgrave Macmillan, 2011).
42. See Jane Potter, 'For Country, Conscience and Commerce: Publishers and Publishing, 1914–1918', in *Publishing in the First World War: Essays in Book History*, ed. Mary Hammond and Shafquat Towheed (Basingstoke: Palgrave Macmillan, 2007), pp. 11–26; and 'Materiality', in *The Edinburgh Companion to First World War Periodicals*, ed. Marysa Demoor, Cedric Van Dijck and Birgit Van Puymbroeck (Edinburgh: Edinburgh University Press, 2023), pp. 17–31.
43. For the statistic, see Hammond and Towheed, *Publishing in the First World War*, p. 4.
44. Guillaume Apollinaire, 'Vieux Papiers', in *Œuvres en Prose Complètes*, vol. III, ed. Pierre Caizergues and Michel Décaudin (Paris: Gallimard, 1993), p. 1,050. *Egyptian Mail*, 3 February 1918, p. 2.
45. Paul Fussell, *The Great War and Modern Memory* (New York: Oxford University Press, 1977), p. 157.
46. See *Reading and the First World War: Readers, Texts, Archives*, ed. Shafquat Towheed and Edmund King (Basingstoke: Palgrave Macmillan, 2015), p. 11.
47. Laurence Campa, *Guillaume Apollinaire* (Paris: Gallimard, 2013), p. 521.
48. 'Books in combat zones did not necessarily have to be read to have significance for participants in the fighting. They could have meaning simply as objects.' See Towheed and King, *Reading and the First World War*, p. 13.
49. Oulanne, *Materiality in Modernist Short Fiction*, p. 14; John Plotz, *Portable Property: Victorian Culture on the Move* (Princeton: Princeton University Press, 2008), p. 1.
50. Virginia Woolf, *Jacob's Room* (Oxford: Oxford World's Classics, 2008), p. 224.
51. Guillaume Apollinaire, *Correspondance Générale*, vol. II, ed. Victor Martin-Schmets (Paris: Honoré Champion, 2015), pp. 519–20 (p. 519): to Louise Faure-Favier, 24 June 1915.
52. E. M. Forster, 'The Solitary Place', *Egyptian Mail*, 10 March 1918, p. 2.
53. Samuel Hynes, *A War Imagined: The First World War and English Culture* (London: Pimlico, 1992), p. 269.
54. Woolf, *Jacob's Room*, p. 238.
55. Virginia Woolf, 'Street Haunting', in *The Essays of Virginia Woolf*, vol. IV: 1925–28, ed. Andrew McNeillie (London: Hogarth Press, 1994), pp. 480–91 (p. 487).
56. Mulk Raj Anand, *The Village* (Bombay: Kutub Popular, 1960), p. 60.
57. Mulk Raj Anand, *The Sword and the Sickle* (New Delhi: Arnold Heinemann, 1984), pp. 213–14.
58. See for instance *The Greater War: Other Combatants and Other Fronts, 1914–18*, ed. Jonathan Kraus (London: Palgrave Macmillan, 2014) and Paul K. Saint-Amour's concept of the perpetual interwar in *Tense Future: Modernism, Total War, Encyclopaedic Form* (New York: Oxford University Press, 2015).
59. Guillaume Apollinaire, 'Le Tunnel sous la Manche', in *Œuvres en Prose*, vol. III, p. 582; Mulk Raj Anand, 'E. M. Forster: A Personal Recollection', *The Journal of Commonwealth Literature* 18.1 (1983), 80–3 (p. 83); Mulk Raj Anand, *Conversations in Bloomsbury* (London: Wildwood House, 1981), p. 22.

I

GUILLAUME APOLLINAIRE'S CURIOSITIES

'It was on the train that took me back from Nice to Marseille', Madeleine Pagès recalled in 1952, 'that I met, on 1 January 1915, Guillaume Apollinaire.'[1] The young woman had been on her way home to French Algeria after having spent Christmas with her older brother, a second lieutenant in the French forces. On that wartime morning in Nice, she caught the train carrying bags full of souvenirs for her mother and her siblings, including porcelain figurines the size of a finger and a little vase adorned with blue flowers. Seated across from her was a man reading an illustrated magazine, *Le Cri de Paris*, with whom she picked up a conversation. They shared a sandwich and talked Villon and Verlaine. Then, 'very quietly', as Pagès remembered thirty-seven years later, he whispered: 'I, too, am a poet.'[2] They exchanged addresses – one a gunner in training at the barracks in Nîmes, the other a teacher at a girls' school in Lamur, just outside Oran. Apollinaire promised to send Pagès a copy of his first book of poems, *Alcools*, which had appeared in 1913. She could not recall whether they ever said a formal farewell, only that she began running, with a feverish haste, as soon as the train pulled into Marseille, desperate to make it to the docks on time. The poet chased her to the exit of the train station: 'I felt his breath on my neck and his voice whispered: *Au revoir, mademoiselle!*'[3]

While Madeleine Pagès safely made it across the Mediterranean, *Alcools* never did. Apollinaire's editor was in the army, his publishing house closed. The poet wrote to her months later, apologising for this delay and wondering if she recalled their serendipitous encounter between Nice and Marseille.

On the evening of 4 May 1915, Apollinaire, who by then had travelled from the barracks in Nîmes to the front in Champagne, heard a military postman shout: 'A parcel from Algeria for you.'[4] In addition to a letter – 'But of course, dear Sir, I remember you' – it contained cigars from Oran, which he readily shared with the men in his unit.[5] Delighted, the poet sent Pagès not only letters and poems over the months that followed, but mementoes from his life in the army: a kepi, dried flowers from the trenches, a medallion made out of stained glass from the ruined church of Mesnil, inkwells and rings crafted from shells, and a book of poems he had printed at the front, *Case d'Armons*. He would wrap these souvenirs in avant-garde magazines and military newspapers, asking their recipient to keep these documents safe for him. Pagès was pleased with her presents, which were all the more incongruous, in Algeria, for their traces of a far-away conflict. Such intimate traffic of war objects sent home or elsewhere, as Birgit Van Puymbroeck and I have argued, existed on a large scale at the time, forging affective communities between men in the army and women at home.[6] 'Those days when I do not get any letters from you are days without colour,' the poet once admitted to Pagès. '[Y]our letters illuminate my forehead much like shells illuminate the army front.'[7]

This chapter will explore Apollinaire's vanguard embrace of the material culture of the First World War, shedding light on the kinds of curiosities he sent Madeleine Pagès in the mail. By curiosity – a term that entered English via Old French – I mean an object, often small or intricate, that has a certain interest because of its novelty or strangeness.[8] Apollinaire, as will become clear, used the term often in his poetic and journalistic writings. Before the war, his curiosities included both exotic objects, such as an African statuette, and everyday objects, such as a used napkin: the former curious because it was so rare, the latter because it was so unexpected and original a topic for art. Inspired by the cubist aesthetic, Apollinaire in fact did a lot of conceptual thinking about material culture, especially in his *calligrammes*, picture-poems that arranged words on the page to model the object under poetic consideration. However, with the outbreak of war, such experiments became sites of suspicion and contention. 'It was not at all obvious that the arts would flourish, or even survive, in wartime,' Kenneth Silver observes in his landmark *Esprit de Corps: The Art of the Parisian Avant-Garde and the First World War, 1914–1925*. 'Not only were certain styles and modes […] now considered to be tainted with Germanic affiliation, but many would be prepared to dismiss all artistic endeavour as a frivolous luxury at a time of national emergency.'[9] Avant-garde reviews closed down, as artists and poets flooded into the armed forces (or fled abroad, escaping to neutral territories).

Undefeated, Apollinaire turned his poetic attention to the material culture of the army instead. His literary cabinet of curiosities came to include both rare and everyday objects from a life among the troops, such as a Vermorel sprayer and a German bullet, made curious because of their association with the conflict. '[T]he meaning of things to individuals is often magnified or transformed entirely in the context of war and displacement,' write Leora Auslander and Tara Zahra in *Objects of War*.[10] Many artists at the time showed a resourcefulness in incorporating war *matériel* into their aesthetics: Fernand Léger painted on shell-crates and Erich Heckel on army tents; André Derain made mask-like sculptures from discarded shell cases; Paul Klee used linen from the seats of crashed aeroplanes as his canvas.[11] Frisian horses, trench journals, rings made from bullets, gas masks, kepis and helmets, among many other items with which mobilised Frenchmen steadily gained a renewed familiarity, worked their way into Apollinaire's wartime aesthetics. His poems, letters and magazine pieces often appear to take stock of such frontline possessions; they read as inventories of a life in the army. 'It is vital', the poet suggested in the *Mercure de France* in early 1917, 'to put in writing everything that referred to the folklore of the war.'[12] In this chapter, I will probe how these writings reappropriated and reinvented the objects of war, from an impulse to make the everyday strange, which had also informed his pre-war experiments. My argument is that the effect of this repurposing was one of disarmament. Consider the Adrian helmet, which I discuss at greater length in this chapter: a wartime invention, it was envisioned by Apollinaire as a shopping basket to carry groceries in 'Curiosities from the Front', as the barber's basin which Don Quixote wears on his head in a letter to Madeleine Pagès, and as a worthy subject for a funny picture-poem, its military connotations being playfully subverted each time. In the poet's writing from 1915–16, such subversive gestures – transforming an array of military possessions from lethal to harmless, from use as objects to subjects of aesthetic contemplation – figured as a response to the precarious, at times dull, experience of war in the trenches. (From a constant reminder of the precarity of life, the Adrian helmet, for instance, develops into the topic for a joke.) What we see at the back of these experiments, then, is a poet trying to come to terms with what he once described as the everyday tragedies (*tragique quotidien*) at the front: a place where the threat to life was part of the day's work.[13]

At the same time, I seek to illustrate how Apollinaire's texts, much like the objects that feature as the topics of these texts, were themselves transformed into curious war artefacts. This is to say that Apollinaire's impulse to subvert the ordinary informed his engagement with war *matériel*, whether made from steel or paper: like the Adrian helmet, the trench journal and the military postcard were incorporated into his experiments, thus freed from their military connotations. As I will show, this is the case for *Case d'Armons*, Apollinaire's volume of poems made at the front in Champagne in June 1915 and sent to Madeleine Pagès in Oran. Handprinted, the few copies of the volume that circulated during those summer months were unique records of the conflict.

Their poems exuded 'an added attraction', as Apollinaire's war godmother (*marraine de guerre*) understood, 'in that they come from the front'.[14] I am especially intrigued by the poet's aesthetic practices in *Case d'Armons*, which were inspired by pre-war cubist collages. With the insertion of a military postcard into a book of poems, the card shed its associations and was seen anew, in the process rendering both artefacts, postcard and handprinted booklet, as wartime curiosities. Taken together, the poetic and journalistic writings considered in this chapter – 'There's/There are', '1915', 'Postcard', 'Curiosities from the Front', *Tranchman' Echo* and *Case d'Armons* – serve as evidence of the wartime survival of a vanguard aesthetic. As Willard Bohn and Els Jongeneel each point out, Apollinaire's wartime oeuvre has not received much critical commentary, in part because of its often blatantly patriotic stance towards the conflict.[15] However, taking these writings seriously shows just how centrally the material culture of the First World War figured in the modernist aesthetic, shaping its themes and practices.

Cubist Clutter, 1907–14

As his close friend, the French writer André Billy, once remarked, someone should write a booklet about Apollinaire's lodgings.[16] From January 1913 until his enlistment late the next year, the poet lived in a rooftop apartment he named 'The Dovecote', on the fifth floor of a seventeenth-century building at 202 Boulevard Saint-Germain in Paris.[17] He remembered the place very fondly while in uniform. '[M]y apartment is one of the most unique in the world,' he announced, in mid-1915, to his then-girlfriend Louise de Coligny-Châtillon ('Lou'), regretting she had not seen 'this perch in its splendour, with its precious Negro [and] Chinese statues, its beautiful paintings'.[18] The art collection on display had included works by Georges Braque and Le Douanier Rousseau; the poet's most commanding piece was Marie Laurencin's larger-than-life *Réunion à la Campagne*, in which Apollinaire sits among his friends, including Pablo Picasso, Gertrude Stein and Maurice Cremnitz. Avant-garde paintings, hundreds of books, Oceanic sculptures and African masks made up Apollinaire's material world. These objects still appear front and centre in the pictures a French photographer snapped of the poet's apartment in 1952, left unchanged for more than thirty years after his untimely death in the First World War (Figure 1.1).

In the years leading up to the First World War, extraordinary objects cluttered Apollinaire's apartment as they did his imagination. He dwelled in flea markets and ethnographic museums, and wrote about what he encountered there, from 'African and Oceanic Sculptures' in *Les Arts à Paris* to 'Chinese Art' and 'The Sultan's Jewels' in *L'Intransigeant*.[19] In his poetry, 'South Sea and Guinean fetishes' (in 'Zone') feature alongside the Egyptian statuette Cocteau gave Apollinaire as a wedding gift (in 'To Jean Cocteau'); his prose writings

Figure 1.1 Apollinaire's apartment on the Boulevard Saint-Germain in Paris, René Giton, 1952–53. Médiathèque du Patrimoine et de la Photographie and Fondation Foujita (Sabam Belgium 2022).

include short stories about a hydrangea and a poet's napkin.[20] In fact, strange items and familiar objects taken out of context surface in the poet's oeuvre across a range of genres. For the Parisian press, he composed short pieces on 'Items Forgotten in Library Books', 'Children's Drawings', 'Menu of a Chinese

Restaurant in Paris', 'The Pocket Airplane', 'Birds of Oceania', 'Luggage in Train Stations' and 'The Use of Fish in the Wars of Antiquity'.[21] His trademark *anecdotiques* – widely read columns with *faits divers* in such journals as *Festin d'Ésope* (Notes Du Mois), *Excelsior* (Bloc-Notes) and *Mercure de France* (La Vie Anecdotique) – served as suitable receptacles for what Marcel Adéma called Apollinaire's 'encyclopaedic spirit': the genre allowed for short observations and a wide variety of topics.[22] Inadvertently, perhaps, Picasso pointed to Apollinaire's infatuation when he drew the poet as a teapot in the early years of their long friendship.[23]

At the same time, the wide net Apollinaire cast over the object world became the target of his fiercest critics, as is evidenced by a response to the publication of *Alcools*, which collected his poems from 1900 to 1912. In a damning review for the *Mercure de France*, the French author Georges Duhamel observed:

> Nothing makes one think more of a second-hand furniture dealer [*brocanteur*] than this collection of verse published by M. Guillaume Apollinaire under the title, at once simple and mysterious, of *Alcools*. I say second-hand furniture dealer because a litter of incongruous objects have been discarded into this slum, some of which have value but none of which is the product of the merchant's own industry. Precisely there is one of the characteristics of the second-hand trade: it resells but does not manufacture […] In the massing of objects a colourful and dizzy variety takes the place of art.[24]

While Duhamel's review nastily attacks the poet instead of his poems – including, among other things, the wandering life of Apollinaire's mother, who lived out of wedlock with a Jewish man – it is remarkable nonetheless for pointing to *Alcools*'s concern with the material world, with its 'litter of incongruous objects' taking the place of art. What bothered Duhamel intrigued others. For the poet Roger Allard, Apollinaire had 'the soul of an antiques dealer and collector', as exhibited by his 'taste for literary and aesthetic odds and ends [*bric-à-brac*]'.[25] Henri Martineau, writing on the author of *Alcools* for *Le Divan*, praised 'this passionate *brocanteur*' who 'is not afraid to show his taste for the bizarre'.[26] Apollinaire, for one, thought the term *brocanteur* 'very unjust', especially in Duhamel's use, given his implicit accusation of a lack of originality (as one who 'resells but does not manufacture').[27]

In *Alcools* and elsewhere, Apollinaire's tastes, as Peter Read puts it more forgivingly, were 'undogmatic and eclectic', yet also part and parcel of their time.[28] These 'bizarre objects', Apollinaire remarked in 1912 of African and Oceanic sculptures, exerted 'a great influence on the destinies of French art', in part because they taught a way to 'represent the human face without using any element taken from direct vision'.[29] By 'French art' he meant cubism, a loose collective that had begun with Picasso and Braque in 1907 and of which

Apollinaire (though he was never fond of the name) became one of the first theoreticians with the publication of *The Cubist Painters* in 1912. Cubism constituted an assault on impressionism's mimetic project – on 'direct vision' as a ruling principle. As Apollinaire put it in *The Cubist Painters*, 'Only photographers make copies from nature'.[30] Instead, objects were broken up and reassembled on the cubist canvas, a process Peter Read refers to as 'the intellectual perception of an object' that combines visual impressions with memory and imagination.[31] The result may have appeared fragmentary and geometric to the unsuspecting eye but was felt to be truer to life by the cubists: a representation not of visual reality, then, but of conceptual reality.[32] In order to capture the painted object from multiple perspectives, Jean Metzinger explained to readers of *Paris-Journal*, artists like himself also abandoned the notion that the painter 'stand motionless, at a determined distance from the object'.[33] Cubists cared for 'touch', not distance, as they 'move[d] around the object to give a concrete representation of several aspects of it in succession'.[34]

Not everyone in France at the time was as taken by this aesthetic revolution: André Salmon, who himself was all for it, witnessed how 'the hideousness of the faces paralyzed with fright the not-quite-converted'.[35] While the unconverted saw the experimental canvas as too distorted and abstract, it was in fact never entirely divorced from material reality.[36] It aimed to present new perspectives on the everyday material world, to make it unfamiliar, as was the intention of so many of the European avant-gardes, so as to see it anew. As Apollinaire wrote much later of Marcel Duchamp's ready-mades, 'he had taken a common object from life, and removed its usual meaning [...] and, from this point of view, had given a new and purely aesthetic meaning to this object'.[37] One technique by which the cubists withdrew objects from everyday life and subverted their meaning was collage. In 1912, Picasso – whom Apollinaire had first met in a Parisian bar in 1904 – pasted an Italian postage stamp to his now-lost *The Letter*, an oval painting showing a number of everyday items such as a glass, a pipe and an envelope. In his *Still Life with Chair Caning*, he incorporated a piece of printed oilcloth simulating the cane work of a chair, and *Guitar, Sheet Music and Glass* was made of wallpaper and newspaper fragments, the latter dealing with the First Balkan War.[38] Juan Gris even went so far as to feature Apollinaire's poems, cut out from *Soirées de Paris*, in his painting *The Watch*. But to what effect? Displacing everyday objects from their original context and pasting them on to a canvas leaves an unsettling impression. 'It gives us something to think about', as Picasso also knew:

> [The purpose] was to give the idea that different textures can enter into a composition to become the reality of the painting that competes with the reality in nature. We tried to get rid of 'trompe l'oeil' [visual deception] to find a 'trompe l'esprit' [intellectual deception] [...] If a piece of

newspaper can become a bottle, that gives us something to think about in connection with both newspapers and bottles, too. This displaced object has entered a universe for which it was not made and where it retains, in a measure, its strangeness. And this strangeness was what we wanted to make people think about because we were quite aware that our world was becoming very strange and not exactly reassuring.[39]

Collages accentuate the conceptual nature of a certain object (a newspaper as a bottle 'gives us something to think about') as well as the materiality of the work of art (its 'different textures'). 'I have no preconceptions concerning artists' materials,' Apollinaire asserted in *The Cubist Painters*. 'You can paint with whatever you like, with pipes, postage stamps, postcards, playing-cards, candelabras, pieces of oilcloth, shirt-collars, wallpaper or newspapers.'[40]

On the eve of war, Apollinaire came close in verse to the kind of experiment that marked cubist visual art: repurposing objects so as to see their true nature. In a letter to Picasso dated 4 July 1914, the poet announced he had begun writing 'ideograms which borrow their form not from any prosody but from their very subject'.[41] He included, in the correspondence, a few examples of this 'great novelty': two poems about a pipe and a brush with their words on the page taking the shape of a pipe and a brush.[42] With his invention of 'lyrical ideograms' (later termed 'calligrams'), which the poet began publishing in the little magazines in May 1914, poetry developed into an experiment with material culture on a par with cubist collage.[43] The poem gathered bits and pieces from the material world into its fold, drawing attention to the conceptual and material nature of the objects under consideration (and in the process, as I will argue below, to the materiality of the poem itself). On a fundamental level, Willard Bohn has suggested, Apollinaire and Picasso were performing 'analogous experiments with form', each blending verbal and pictorial elements in their art.[44] Before long, *Les Soirées de Paris*, the magazine which Apollinaire co-edited and which folded with the outbreak of war, was littered with his picture-poems on and in the form of such everyday objects as churches, trees and burning cigarettes, here taken out of their usual contexts and transfigured on the page. These were the first of 150 calligrams he would go on to compose in the few years that remained to him.[45] 'If you could find the June and July numbers of *Soirées de Paris*', Apollinaire advised his *marraine de guerre* from the midst of the September 1915 offensive in Champagne, 'you would see the newest thing I have invented in terms of poetic art.'[46]

Like a cubist collage and a ready-made, Apollinaire's picture-poems playfully reflect on the conceptual reality of objects. The gestures at the heart of this aesthetic practice – displacing, recontextualising – bring out the essence of objects, forcing us to see their meanings, uses and material qualities anew. '[I]t is not oddity I like, it is life,' Apollinaire wrote to Henri Martineau, thanking him for his review of *Alcools*, 'and when one knows how to look around oneself, one sees the most curious and endearing things.'[47] By way of brief example: his poem 'The Tie' was composed in 1914 during a conversation at the editorial offices of *Soirées de Paris*, where Apollinaire suddenly took off his tie and threw it on to the table. 'The painful tie which you wear and which adorns you o civilized', the words read as they take the form of a tie on the page, 'take it off if you'd like to breathe better.'[48] By making the object into the focal point of a poem, whose guiding logic is that of spatial arrangement, the reader is newly alerted to the tie as an object that adorns yet strangles its wearer. The move from adornment to containment reads as a subversive gesture, compelling the reader to abandon the tie and, with it, its connotations of formality and bourgeois capitalism ('o civilized'). The poem was published in the pages of the July–August issue of *Soirées de Paris*, alongside a picture-poem on an object with similar meanings in late modernity – the watch. This was to be the final issue of the vanguard magazine, which folded with the outbreak of hostilities a few weeks later. 'Of the sixteen contributors to that last issue', wrote Apollinaire in 1916, looking back, 'two are dead, heroic fighters, 10 fought, were wounded, are still fighting or still mobilized.'[49] Despite these distractions of war making, the poet would continue his experiments, turning his gaze from the objects of Parisian office life to the debris of the military front, and from a conceptual to a more material engagement with objects. 'Like a magician from a tophat', as Walter Benjamin once characterised Apollinaire's aesthetic interests, 'he drew whatever was demanded of him from his own existence: omlets, goldfish, fancy gowns, pocket-watches. He was the Bellachini of Literature.'[50]

Sous le Casque: Souvenirs and Commodities from the Front

Within a few days of the outbreak of war, 3,700,000 Frenchmen had been mobilised, including many avant-garde artists and poets. 'Every hesitation', the writer Blaise Cendrars exclaimed, 'would be a crime.'[51] As a foreigner born in Italy of Polish descent, Apollinaire tried, but failed, to enlist at the editorial office of *Les Marches de l'Est*, near his flat, which had been hastily converted into a recruitment bureau. Travelling south to Nîmes, he ultimately managed to sign up for artillery training at the barracks. Instead of the cubists he associated with in the bars of Montparnasse and the editorial office of *Soirées de Paris*, he now found himself surrounded by men from different walks of life: farmers, students, a planter from Réunion, a professor of philosophy, a mechanic and a banker.[52] Together, these men took courses in military history, mathematics, ballistics and French composition, studying the physical and chemical properties of air and the wars in the reign of Louis XV. They were taught to ride a horse and fire a cannon. Recalling, many years later, how much his letters had enlivened his friends left behind in Paris, Gertrude Stein still saw the French poet 'falling off of horses in the endeavour to become an artillery man'.[53] In the evenings, Apollinaire talked metaphysics in the cafés of Nîmes, submitted pieces about barracks life to the *Mercure de France* and, after lights out, read aloud poems from *Alcools* to the men in his dormitory.[54] He was incredibly popular: a great storyteller and a keen listener, displaying a particular interest to hear from mobilised farmers about their villages and their lives.[55] 'It is amazing to be a soldier,' Apollinaire admitted. 'I think it's the real *métier* for a poet.'[56]

Eager to get to the front, Apollinaire left Nîmes in early April 1915, just a few days ahead of the Germans' first use of chlorine gas around Ypres. He joined the 45th Battery of the 38th Artillery Regiment. Books were too heavy to carry, and he could not bring much else in terms of personal possessions, for a life in the army was, as Apollinaire's contemporary T. E. Hulme also learned, 'nomadic as an animal'.[57] As advised by the French War Ministry, Apollinaire compiled a will on his way to the front, making an inventory of his worldly goods in his apartment on the Boulevard Saint-Germain: paintings and a collection of African statues currently in storage, a library of books, and an annual income of three to four thousand in royalties (*Alcools* alone, he expected, would earn two thousand francs 'in 4 or 5 years').[58] 'It's not much, forgive me for not having more to leave you,' he wrote to his beneficiary, along with careful instructions to inform the editors of *L'Intransigeant* and *Mercure de France* in the event of his death.[59] Once arrived at the front in Champagne, stationed within view of Reims Cathedral, a symbol of France's wartime patriotism, Apollinaire moved into a hut made of straw, reeds and mud, living, by his own admission, like Robinson Crusoe on his island.[60] To make temporary homes for themselves, soldiers had to be 'digger, mason, locksmith, carpenter, everything'.[61] 'It is fun to build a house,' he observed, as he conceived of a plan to buy a plot of land in the countryside after the Germans had been defeated and do it all over again.[62] For his 'villa at the front' he made his own furniture and household goods: a bowl, a four-poster bed constructed from hazelnut branches, a tree-trunk table, an old oil can used as inkwell, a pillow, six coat racks to hang his belongings, a lamp, even a homemade tub installed outside his hut ('a footboard and a canvas bucket next to a wall').[63] He sent a description of his new dwellings, and of his new life, to the *Mercure de France* for readers keen to acquaint themselves with frontline existence.[64] Apollinaire would remain in the area around Reims until mid-June 1915, when he began moving through a series of trench dugouts in the lead-up to the Second Battle of Champagne.

By the time he drafted his letter to Lou dated 20 August 1915, from a forest near La Salle, he had made an inventory of his belongings, assembled in such a way that they were easily packed in case of an evacuation:

> [S]ome papers and three issues of the *Mercure*. On the shelf below, a box with a view of Marseille contains soap and cigarettes from Algeria.

> Above, my artillery lessons taken at dictation, the *Manual for the Artillery* [...] A *Boche* beret, a cavalry mug, hanging up by wires, into which I can empty my pockets. Next to it is a box of Oran cigars with my writing paper in it; above, another box with no lid full of letters I haven't answered. [...] Near the door, a small shelf for reading in bed, my bed cut into the floor (the bottom is made of planks), my quilt, and, on top, my horse blanket and my coat. At the foot of the bed, hanging from logs, are my nickel-plated spurs, my slippers and another pair of infantry shoes. A bench at the table and another against the bed complete this cell: that's the word, it's a cell! In ten minutes all of this can be ready, coat rolled up, horse saddled and your friend booted, spurred and armed.[65]

The poet could have been seeking comfort in looking around and doing a stocktake of his possessions, finding in such gestures an assurance that, despite these extraordinary circumstances, his world continued to exist. Such lists developed into a wartime habit for the poet.[66] His poem 'There's/There are' begins each line with the eponymous stock phrase, *Il y a*, and proceeds to name an object from the world surrounding the poetic 'I':

> There's a ship has sailed off with my love
> There are six sausages in the sky and in the gathering night they look
>   like maggots that turn into stars
> There's an enemy submarine which bore my love a grudge
> There are a thousand little pines felled by shrapnel around me
> There's an infantryman passing blinded by choking gas
> There's the fact we've smashed everything in the Nietzsche Goethe and
>   Cologne trenches
> There's the fact I yearn for a letter which fails to arrive
> There are in my wallet several photos of my love[67]

Much like the inventory in the August letter, Apollinaire's poem takes the form of a fragmentary enumeration of a wartime environment: submarines, zeppelins, infantrymen, trenches, shrapnel, photographs, letters from Oran. The detail, Kate McLoughlin has argued, constitutes 'war's natural representative mode'.[68] Cataloguing individual items does not only give a repetitive rhythm to this poem, but also functions as a way of grasping the war experience. Such is the paradox of war literature, as McLoughlin adds: 'the massive scale of war finds its best communication in localised, focused images recuperated from the generality.'[69] By taking stock of these details – a submarine, six zeppelins, a letter from Oran – the poet frames the conflict for comprehension and makes an implicit point about his world's continued survival amidst destruction (and his place within that world).[70] Apollinaire sent the poem to Madeleine Pagès on 30 September 1915 from the midst of the Second Battle of Champagne, adding the promise of a tally of a different kind – a count of 'the shots I fired during the extraordinary bombardment that surprised the Germans so much'.[71]

For Apollinaire, as for many others at the time, such lists operated as a response to the hostilities. From a vanguard impulse, the poet went on to reinvent the object thus listed ('There's/There are', too, starts out as a war catalogue before it comes into its own as a love poem). One wartime phenomenon Apollinaire became particularly invested in was the creation of trench art out of war debris and whatever could be found near – bark, animal bones, chalk, wood, textile, and especially metal from bullets and discarded shells, of which there were more than a thousand per square metre in the worst affected areas (Figure 1.2).[72] Out of these many materials, metal (from which soldiers made rings, letter openers and matchbox covers) best captured the *Zeitgeist* of this industrial war.[73] In fact, well before 1914, Apollinaire had been attracted to 'iron constructions, machines, bicycles and aeroplanes' in the belief that, as he remarked in *L'Intransigeant*, '[m]odern-style masterpieces are made of cast iron, steel and sheet metal'.[74] A tension between the marvels of the machine age and their capacity for destruction underlay this practice of crafting trinkets from war debris. Still, it was encouraged by army command, for it helped relieve boredom, stimulated cohesion and earned soldiers a bit of pocket money. There was a popular taste for these hand-made mementoes at home – one witness even termed the conflict the first 'war of souvenirs'.[75] As Gertrude Stein recalled in *The Autobiography of Alice B. Toklas*: 'Everybody brought you souvenirs in those days, steel arrows that pierced horses' heads, pieces of shell, ink-wells made out of pieces of shell, helmets, someone even offered us a piece of a Zeppelin.'[76] In *A Farewell to Arms*, a Milan military hospital boasts an errand boy who makes patients cigarette lighters out of empty Austrian rifle cartridges as well as a patient, 'a fine boy', who was wounded when he tried to unscrew the fuse-cap from a shell to keep as a souvenir.[77] So widespread was the phenomenon that even a recluse like Marcel Proust, who thought it in poor taste, did not fail to comment on it.[78] *Le Journal* published a piece about trench art, which Apollinaire read enthusiastically in early May 1915; he followed with his own article on the topic in the *Mercure de France* in August.[79]

Taking war debris as a source material for art, Apollinaire began making rings out of shells for the women in his life – Lou, Madeleine Pagès, Leoncine Havet, Mireille Havet, Georgette Catelain, Chérie Faure-Favier and the latter's mother.[80] 'I listen with pleasure to the bombardments and like everyone else', he wrote to Fernand Divoire, of a process that was technically prohibited under military law, 'I quickly go and look for the burst shell cases to make rings out of them, if they are aluminium.'[81] These rings, including an engagement ring for Madeleine Pagès, were made to specific measurements. The process, as Apollinaire explained it in the spring of 1915, went as follows:

Figure 1.2 Three Belgian soldiers in the 11th Line Infantry Regiment making trench art. Collection P. Vanleene, Ghent.

As for the rings, I think that our battery makes the best ones, it happened like that. We pour the aluminium into a mould dug in a potato and finish it off with a file. For the copper: we make a dovetail in the aluminium, we embed the plate of copper, or bronze, we tighten with a chisel, or with a hammer [...] The embedded copper or bronze plate, as we make it, is a specialty of the 45th battery of the 38th, where, so one says, the most beautiful rings of the front are made, I only needed to learn how to do them. But here are real artists.[82]

Over a period of many months, Apollinaire sent these curiosities across France, in the belief that such objects, coming from the battlefield, carried bits of him and bits of luck: dried flowers, a penholder made from German bullets, a found belt buckle reading *Gott mit uns*, feathers of a barn owl to be pinned on a hat, a shell turned into an inkwell, letter openers, a precious aluminium medallion he made out of fragments of stained glass from the church of Mesnil with butterfly wings pressed between them.[83] He would wrap his trench gifts with pages of the *Bulletin des Armées* and Picabia's *291*, not only adding to the oddity but also hoping these magazines would be preserved for him.

The production of souvenirs out of war debris constituted an effort to humanise the war and its deadly materials, as well as to reassert a sense of artistic agency in a conflict that (as Apollinaire would later note) made men into machines.[84] 'I have seen the first dead man,' he wrote in April 1915 not long after his arrival at the front, where life was 'so precarious'.[85] By July he wondered what would become of him, other than 'death by the instruments of war'.[86] Transforming those instruments into aesthetic artefacts must have provided some mental relief from these stresses, as well as from the boredom that marked the slower days at the front. In a similar gesture, Henri Gaudier-Brzeska, the Vorticist sculptor who had enlisted in the French forces, broke off the butt of a Mauser rifle owned by a German soldier and engraved a design in it in order to, as he put it, 'express a gentler order of feeling'.[87] To be sure, humanising efforts and gentler feelings were at work here. As Birgit Van Puymbroeck and I have shown, these souvenirs travelled intimate routes between the front and the home, constituting what we termed an affective public sphere and closing the gap between both worlds: Apollinaire, for instance, carved, and sent Madeleine in Oran, a ring made from a shell, followed by a poem about how that ring, 'metal of our love', found its rightful place on her finger.[88] The object, literal as well as poetic, overcame the distance between the lovers. For these reasons, Apollinaire was critical of anyone pursuing commercial interests and commodifying what was meant as an authentic gesture.[89] For the *Mercure de France*, he wrote disapprovingly of the sale of charms under the galleries of the Palais Royal in Paris.[90] In Britain, too, the war's informal economy took hold; Evelyn Waugh, collecting war relics as a young boy, recalled a market for them at Victoria Station, 'where soldiers returning on leave could provide themselves with acceptable souvenirs'.[91] '[N]ow that it is said that everyone in the rear zone makes rings', Apollinaire complained to Madeleine Pagès in late October 1915, 'at least this one will look like it came from the front, from where it originates.'[92] The poet's concern with authenticity speaks to a larger worry explored by Walter Adamson in *Embattled Avant-Gardes*: that art would take on the properties of a commodity.[93] From an article in *La Démocratie Sociale*, it is clear that Apollinaire shared in those anxieties; he notes how 'mechanical processes threaten every form of art that involves the physical capacities of the artist'.[94] Part of what must have attracted the poet to trench arts and craft was the fact that it was not reproducible on a mass scale.

Through Apollinaire's affective, uncommercial experiments with war *matériel*, and his writings about the phenomenon, one can observe how productively his vanguard impulse to subvert the ordinary was released on to the material world of the trenches. These experiments, in turn, humanise the debris of an industrial conflict, an impulse this chapter traces through Apollinaire's wartime career. It likewise informed 'Curiosities from the Front', an article by Apollinaire that was first published, in late 1916, in two consecutive issues of *Brise d'Entonnoirs*, the monthly regimental magazine of the 82nd Territorial Infantry Regiment.[95] In what reads like a set of encyclopaedia entries, Apollinaire ironically reinvented the uses of everyday objects from the trenches, such as shells, duckboards, a Vermicelli box and a Vermorel sprayer. The poet's aim, it seems, was both to provide a tongue-in-cheek distraction for the magazine readers stationed at the front and to subtly critique living circumstances in the army.[96] A particular item that sparked Apollinaire's interest was the soldier's characteristically blue uniform, his *tenue bleu horizon*, of which the poet had been 'so proud' (as André Billy remembered) and in which he had looked 'very wonderful' (as Gertrude Stein noted).[97] Part of that uniform was the Adrian helmet. Designed by Louis Adrian and modelled after a fifteenth-century *Bourguignotte*, it replaced the kepi as headgear of choice in the French army in June 1915. Initially, Apollinaire found the new Adrian helmet far from aesthetically pleasing; it reminded him of the barber's brazen basin used as a hood in *Don Quixote*.[98]

In 'Curiosities from the Front', he playfully reinvented the military object:

> The Helmet: Although everyone knows it, we tend to ignore the real purpose of the helmet. The helmet is in reality a seat: placed upside down on the ground, it serves as a comfortable receptacle and lifts you above the too often muddy soil of the trenches. Through their ingenuity, soldiers occasionally transform it into a shopping basket: held by the handle (that is, the strap), it is useful for carrying a dozen eggs from the cooperative. It also serves as a pouch; however, experience has shown that in most cases it is a bit too small. It would not be prudent to entrust it with more than the contents of a soldier's ordinary pocket. The addition of the helmet to the already complicated equipment of the soldier was an embarrassing problem. It was elegantly resolved: we wear the helmet on our heads.[99]

The effect of Apollinaire's play was to disarm the object of its military connotations, thus providing much-needed comic relief for the soldier-readers of *Brise d'Entonnoirs* (as well as *Journal du Soldat* and *Nouvelles de France*, where the excerpt appeared in the following year).[100] Long before the publication of 'Curiosities', Apollinaire had already drawn a calligram, unpublished to this day, in the form of a helmet: 'Hello, but call Napoleon on the tower, Hello, lice with an iron cross.'[101] While the specific references of this poetic phone call may now be lost, the poem's subversive energy remains transparent, turning an object of war, and its political connotations, into a humorous, even absurd thing.[102] Such experiments are the equivalent in words of a gesture that informed avant-garde visual art at the time. The German pacifist Ernst Friedrich displayed a French helmet as a flowerpot in Berlin's Anti-War

Museum in 1925 – to much popular acclaim.[103] Jacob Epstein's 1916 sculpture *The Tin Hat*, too, creates a disjunction between the bust of the soldier and his headgear, which is cast from a real trench helmet. While the helmet merely appears to be clapped on and tilted at a diagonal, rather than being an intrinsic part of the sculpture, such a disjunction must have been intentional: it captured, as Richard Cork has argued, a sense of the soldier's alienation from the violent symbolism of the metal headgear.[104]

Further proof that the poet was so captivated by his equipment abounds: he let himself be photographed in his helmet many times and often drew the object in his Nîmes notebooks and correspondence from the front; he wrote for *Excelsior* about how the helmet was added to the standard uniform of Parisian policemen; and he sent Madeleine Pagès a Bavarian helmet, loot of war, as a souvenir.[105] What, then, was its attraction? As Virginia Woolf argues in *Three Guineas*, uniforms carry 'symbolic meaning', possessing what she termed an advertisement function.[106] Not everyone has the right to don a uniform or wear a helmet: doing so signalled Apollinaire's service to the nation, his participation in the thick of things. The poet's understanding of the symbolic functions of headgear is also clear from a short piece he published in *Excelsior* in September 1918, on the top hat's steady disappearance from view. 'It dies beautifully, but it dies,' he claimed, recalling an early moment in its rich history with Benjamin Franklin's 1790 visit to Paris in a top hat: 'Immediately, the Parisian hatters exhibited it in their shops, and the top hat was adopted by the revolutionaries because it came from America, the land of freedom.'[107] By the time of his piece in *Excelsior*, the helmet had gained a talismanic quality for Apollinaire: it had saved his life. In March 1916, a piece of shrapnel had pierced his right temporal lobe and would have killed him had his helmet not slowed it down (as had been the fate of Henri Gaudier-Brzeska, 'gone out through a little hole in the high forehead', as Ford Madox Ford lamented in disbelief).[108] Days after being wounded, Apollinaire asked his *marraine de guerre*, an aspiring poet herself, to compose 'a little poem on my helmet', which she did: 'On the Helmet that Saved from Death the Lyre Bearer Guillaume Apollinaire'.[109] Apollinaire kept his helmet by his hospital bed (alongside the blood-soaked copy of the *Mercure de France* he was reading while hit) and later hung it in his apartment in Paris, where his war paraphernalia – uniform, helmet, cap, military cross – took pride of place among his avant-garde art (Figure 1.1).[110] At his funeral in November 1918, his helmet made a final appearance as a proud symbol of service. As Blaise Cendrars recalled, 'the casket of Apollinaire left the church of St Thomas of Aquinas, draped in a flag, Guillaume's lieutenant's helmet on the tricolour, among the flowers and wreaths'.[111]

Apollinaire's affinity with the shifting meanings of the Adrian helmet – militaristic, comic, symbolic, talismanic – is symptomatic of his wider engagement with war culture. As with his trench art, he took a distance from, and subverted, its military connotations. Transformative experiments with the world of the trenches crowd Apollinaire's writings from 1914 to 1918, ranging from gas-mask-wearing *poilus* imagined as octopi in 'Ocean of Earth' to calligrams of shells, cigarettes, cannons, artillery horses and Reims Cathedral.[112] In 'Curiosities from the Front', the poet turned the Frisian horse, a barbed-wire defence with wooden spikes meant to impale the approaching enemy, into the actual animal it was named after. This wooden contraption, he observed, 'feeds on brambles, even artificial ones', but 'does not grow fat' – adding, in a pun alluding to the object's spikes, that 'one can already count his ribs'.[113] Earlier, the poet had composed a love poem for Madeleine Pagès under the same title, in which the barbed-wire obstacles come to life and are transformed into a herd of horses galloping off towards Algeria.[114] The object of war was withdrawn from a context of violence and ingeniously reinvented, becoming a symbol for his love. While not a calligram as such, at least one critic draws a connection between the materiality of this curious device and the poem on the material page, wondering 'if the poem's jagged right edge represents spikes waiting to impale the enemy'.[115] This is not far-fetched at all: Apollinaire's fascination with the materiality of war objects often translated itself into a concern with the materiality of the poem – as itself a wartime object. Since the war, he had begun noticing how the army, too, 'ideogrammatised' its typography, with words on military press releases and posters arranged in the form of their subjects. 'I love this new application of my spirit,' Apollinaire admitted.[116] As I go on to show, the poet was attentive to the many ways war prompted an understanding of various writings as curious material objects: pages from the *Bulletin des Armées* used as wrapping paper, letters with passages blacked out by the censor, a postcard cut in the shape of a shell, and a blood-soaked copy of the *Mercure de France*. These writings take their place, as unique products of the conflict, among the war's paraphernalia already discussed, from trench art and steel helmets to Frisian horses.

Bibliographical Curiosities: *Tranchman' Echo* and *Case d'Armons*

One of Apollinaire's initial worries, after the outbreak of hostilities in August 1914, was that he would no longer find an outlet for his projects. Publishing houses closed down, and the publication of his *The Poet Assassinated* and *I Too Am a Painter* was postponed. *Soirées de Paris* and *Mercure de France* both folded. While the latter reappeared as a bi-monthly in 1915, the poet never managed to resuscitate the former, for all his best intentions. 'In France', he complained, 'there are almost no more magazines [and] one cannot publish verse. I have published nothing apart from my "Vie anecdotique" in the June number of the *Mercure de France* which resurfaced, and it was an old anecdote written in Nîmes.'[117] This reality left the poet short of cash, at least until the renewal of a vanguard momentum in the second half of the war, which witnessed the arrival of new little magazines such as *SIC* in 1916 and *Nord/ Sud* in 1917.[118] Yet, creative spirits were far from deadened in those early war months, despite a lack of venues to publish new work. 'My bed was close to that of a brigadier-poet,' Apollinaire noted of his dormitory in Nîmes.[119] In the *Mercure de France*, he showcased the 'numerous' brigadiers and gunners in his battery who all wrote verse: men named Baldy, Alexandre Coulon, Flavien Julian.[120] As these newly minted soldiers quickly discovered, the French army had its own cultural circuits with its own poets, readers and themes – even with its own magazines, published by and for soldiers.

As with trench art, Apollinaire was captivated by the military press. Of the magazines such as *Brise d'Entonnoirs*, in which 'Curiosities from the Front' appeared, an average of 400 different titles circulated in the French forces during the war, ranging from professionally printed to ephemeral, even handwritten productions.[121] Apollinaire was an avid reader of, and contributor to, such publications: *Bulletin des Écrivains*, *Petit Messager des Arts et des Industries d'Art*, *Les Imberbes* and *Le Rire aux Éclats*; his contribution for *Poil … et Plume* was rejected.[122] His many accounts of the phenomenon of trench journalism in the mainstream press – especially his 'History of a Front Gazette' – revisit these and other magazines.[123] He also wrote on the *Gazette Cormon-Collin-Flameng* ('a polycopied little magazine published monthly [at the front] by the students of the School of Fine Arts') and the Italian trench press for *Mercure de France*; on *Looping* for *Europe Nouvelle*; on *Les Imberbes* for both these publications; on *La Ghirba* for *Les Arts à Paris*; and on *Le Petit Messager* for *Excelsior*.[124] Taken together, these short pieces constituted an attempt to familiarise a home readership with a new front culture, the appearance of which, for Apollinaire, symbolised 'a confidence in the life that restores itself so close to death'.[125]

Journalism was second nature to the prolific poet, whom André Billy remembered years later as collaborating 'left and right'.[126] 'He was evidently in his element as the editor of small magazines,' Billy added.[127] The poet had honed his skills as an editor at *Festin d'Ésope* in 1903–4, briefly afterwards at *Tabarin*, while its editor was in prison, and at *Soirées de Paris* in 1912–14. Together with the men in his battery, Apollinaire began his own trench journal, *Tranchman' Echo*, and helped see it to print. Appearing under an odd title, a good-humoured celebration of France's British allies, the periodical was published in only three issues in June 1915 before it folded. Allegedly, the idea came to Apollinaire when he found a copy of a German occupation newspaper, *Gazette des Ardennes*, while riding on horseback near the trenches. The unlikely story, as the poet later recounted it in the *Mercure de France*, was that it was dropped from a German aeroplane chased away by French artillery. 'One would have thought it was a dead leaf,' Apollinaire wrote of the way it swerved, only to realise later it was a newspaper.[128] The first two issues of

Tranchman' Echo, which according to its subtitle 'appear[ed] at each drunken spell of the editor', were handwritten and lost – one by mistake, when a soldier mailed it to his *marraine de guerre*; the other by accident, dropped into a pot of boiling soup.[129] While lost, we know from Apollinaire's piece in the *Mercure de France* that these first two numbers contained the usual topics written in a 'slightly soldierly style', including reflections on the duration of the war, drawings of Germans eating barbed-wire Sauerkraut, and a life of Saint Barbara, the patron saint of artillerymen.[130] As these topics demonstrate, in *Tranchman' Echo* we encounter a military unit talking to itself.

The third issue, however, was preserved. It was printed in eight or twelve copies – Apollinaire's memory was fickle on this point – on a stencil duplicator bought in a neighbouring village.[131] A labour-intensive process, polycopying meant that a handwritten master copy was pressed on to a metal tray filled with copying paste.[132] The imprint left in the gelatine was then transferred to separate sheets of paper, thus producing only a handful of copies often of poor quality. The resulting effect was, according to a contemporary source close to Apollinaire, 'ephemeral', 'sporadic', 'flawed' and 'little agreeable to the eye'.[133] But it was unusual and intriguing, and the DIY-process allowed for the publication of a magazine in the war zone. While the editors failed to finish their final issue in time before their battery was moved along the frontlines, they decided to print *Tranchman' Echo* anyway. Its empty columns, across which the message 'particularly targeted by censorship' was playfully printed, turned an inconspicuous everyday object into what Apollinaire termed a bibliographical curiosity.[134] That the document was to be treasured in such a way is clear from Apollinaire's incentive to forward the magazine not only to Madeleine Pagès, asking her to keep it safe for him, but to Charles de la Roncière, a librarian at the National Library of France who was assembling a collection of war ephemera.[135] He added that the final issue of *Tranchman' Echo* was merely of interest as a curiosity – 'the fact of having been printed at the Front'.[136] Only 'a very small number has escaped destruction', the poet added in an accompanying note folded between the pages of the periodical. 'Of these I send you a copy, the only one I have left.'[137]

Printing a journal on a stencil duplicator in the field was a phenomenon on a par with making souvenirs out of war debris. Like these trinkets, the trench journal is 'an object in itself', as Barbara Green wrote of the periodical form, and an uncanny part of the material culture of the trenches that later found its way into war collections.[138] Even rarer and more incongruous, given its publication context, was *Case d'Armons*, Apollinaire's collection of twenty war poems 'written facing the enemy' and printed as a booklet, on 17 June 1915, on his regiment's stencil duplicator.[139] It is one of the most experimental artefacts to emerge from the conflict. The volume's title is borrowed from the vocabulary of the artillery: a *case d'armons*, a flutchel, is a small box attached to a cannon or artillery carriage in which the gunner typically stored personal effects.[140] The title throws into relief the materiality of the booklet, in the process giving credence to Jeremy Braddock's claim that 'many modernist artworks themselves resemble collections'.[141] Indeed, a collecting aesthetic underwrites *Case d'Armons*, much like the object it was named after. The volume is a repository of sorts: in it, Apollinaire gathered poems on the experiences, impressions and objects of war for safekeeping (much like his protagonist in *The Poet Assassinated*, who tucks away his verses, composed in secret, in an old cigar box). For the cover of the booklet, the poet even drew a few objects which fascinated him so, including a cannon, a Frisian horse and duckboards. *Case d'Armons* was printed with the help of two men in Apollinaire's artillery battery, Lucien Bodard and René Berthier. The latter was his 'best poetic student' who had followed him to the front from the Nîmes barracks – an example of what John Dos Passos once called the war's 'sudden friendships'.[142] Apollinaire, Bodard and Berthier initially meant to print 112 copies of this 'little volume', with the proceeds intended for the wounded.[143] However, the poet was informed that such commercial practices were prohibited in the French army.[144] Instead, he sent twenty-five copies of this 'rarity' – he also called it, like *Tranchman' Echo*, 'a bibliographical curiosity' – to friends scattered across the country, including André Level, Louise Faure-Favier, Marie Laurencin, Jean-Émile Laboureur, Ardengo Soffici and Francis Picabia (André Breton inquired but was too late).[145] '25 copies, one for me, one for you,' the poet wrote to Madeleine Pagès in North Africa; 'that leaves 23 across the universe.'[146]

To the best of my knowledge, this is the most explicit, if not the only, time in Apollinaire's oeuvre that we witness him attaching value to the materiality of the printed book. For, what makes *Case d'Armons* a 'bibliographical curiosity' is not the poems it contains but the fact that it was printed in the way it was. Barely legible, shoddily produced, it came to its reader from the battlefield. In earlier work, the poet appears only to have reflected on the materiality of the single poem, with his experiments in visual poetry begun in May 1914. Calligrams, as Apollinaire once put it in a letter to André Billy, were 'an idealisation of free verse', a typographical freefall 'at a time when typography brilliantly ends its career, at the dawn of the new means of reproduction that are the cinema and the phonograph'.[147] For Apollinaire, the book was dying, if not already dead. 'It is in its decline,' he asserted, not for the first time, in a 1917 interview for *Le Pays*. 'After a century or two, it will die. It will have its successor, its only possible successor in the phonograph disc and the cinematograph film. We will no longer need to learn to read and write.'[148] In *The Poet Assassinated*, the poet launched a similar offensive against the antiquated codex form, imagining other uses the book could be put to: 'A great dressmaker is thinking of launching tailor-made costumes from the backs of old books bound in calf. Charming! All literary women will want to wear it, and one can approach them and whisper into their ears under the guise of reading the titles of the books.'[149] Yet, for a time at the front of the First World War, and in large part because of the unique circumstances of that context, the book mattered as object – a material witness not only in what it said but in what it looked like (which was determined by how and where it was printed). 'If he did not imagine that it would become one of the most prized bibliophilic treasures of the 20th and the beginning of the 21st centuries', writes Laurence Campa, 'then he knew that it would not fail to attract the curious.'[150]

What makes each of the twenty-five copies of *Case d'Armons* 'unique' – the word is Apollinaire's – is at the same time what affords them their modernist credentials: a collage aesthetic.[151] The war's paper shortages were partly responsible. The twenty-five poetry albums were each bound and wrapped for support in pages of a free newspaper edited at the French War Ministry, *Bulletin des Armées de la République* (much like the way the wartime rise in the price of paper forced Virginia Woolf to wrap copies of Hogarth Press publications in wallpaper). The subscription bulletins Apollinaire sent to his acquaintances so that he could print the volume to order were also polygraphed on wrapping paper from parcels his fellow soldiers had received.[152] In the summer of 1915, Apollinaire, it is evident, was acutely aware of the scarce availability and high cost of paper at the front – a shortage that would further increase with the years to come. By 1918, he would complain in *Excelsior* of how his countrymen in Normandy were selling seventeenth-century notarial deeds to paper merchants, to be made into pulp. If it were up to the poet, these documents would be preserved in a national archive for the insight they offered 'in the provincial life of former times and in the small corners of history'.[153] Published in 1918, *Calligrammes* was likewise printed on *papier à chandelles*, a kind of poor-quality paper named for the wrappers candles were covered with at the time. For Apollinaire, proudly, it was 'real war paper'.[154] In any case, the jarring effect Apollinaire's recycling created in *Case d'Armons* – juxtaposing his intimate verse with the official military discourse in the *Bulletin* – was part and parcel of what made the volume so unique, both literally (as a book each one is different) and figuratively (as an experimental, peculiar product of its extraordinary circumstances).

The same jarring effect is achieved within the volume's pages, which are similarly governed by a collage aesthetic: *Case d'Armons* does not only gather poetic images of objects into its flutchel, but includes an actual print object. Two of its poems placed on opposite sides of the same page, '1915' and 'Postcard', incorporate military postcards pasted into the volume, generating the illusion of the poem as a dispatch mailed home (these poems had originally been sent to Lou in a letter on 21 June 1915) (Figure 1.3). Apollinaire had previously played with the postcard form in his poetry, though never included an actual postcard until this time.[155] Since it was impossible to retain the images on the postcard and at the same time to polycopy the text of the poem, '1915' and 'Postcard' had to be copied by hand each time (the only two poems in the volume for which this was the case). The handwriting is Bodard's or Berthier's, not Apollinaire's:[156]

1915
Soldiers
Of porcelain
And gar-
Net
Ô love

Postcard
To Jean Royère

We're doing fine
but the grocery car which they
say is marvelous
doesn't come this far
LUL
We'll get
them yet

please forward
transparent route
France

(Ulysses how many days
To get back to Ithaca)[157]

Like many of the other poems in *Case d'Armons*, and indeed many of Apollinaire's other writings from the period, '1915' and 'Postcard' reflect on the war's peculiar material world, featuring such objects as porcelain figurines, postcards and grocery cars. A wartime invention, the *auto-bazaar* may 'intrigue' by its very name, Apollinaire insinuated, but is in the end only a travelling shop that sold provisions and toiletries to the men in the war zone, including 'tooth brushes, pairs of braces, soap, combs, postcards illustrated with flags of the allies, writing paper ornamented with the portrait of army generals, tobacco pouches, pipes, wallets'.[158]

As Henri Lefebvre argued, war is ruled by mundane dimensions; it quickly becomes part of everyday life.[159] The small objects gathered in 'Postcard' and '1915' imply a sense of domesticity amidst periods of heavy fighting, however

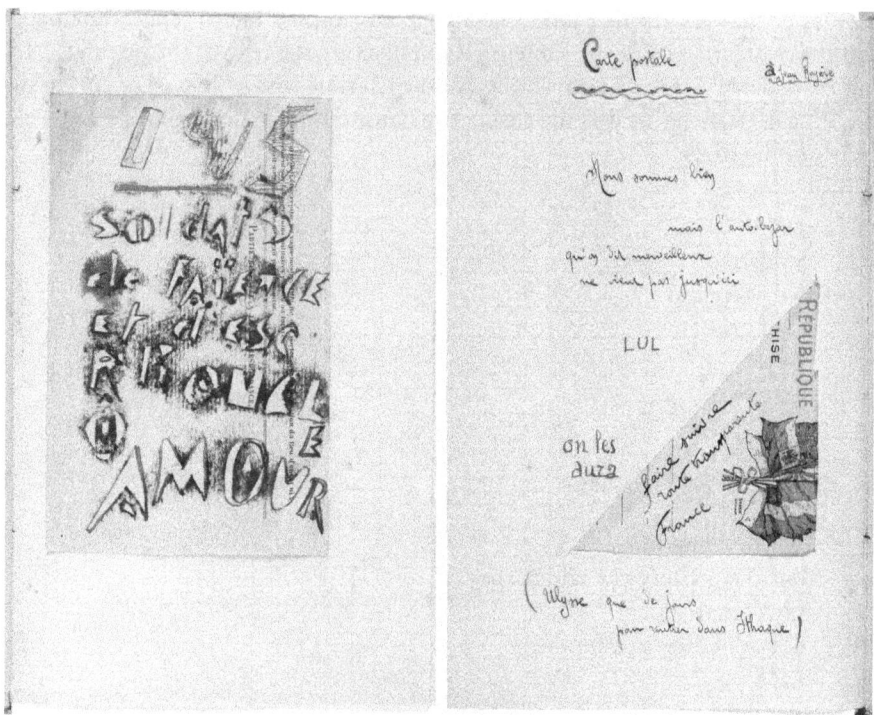

Figure 1.3 '1915' and 'Carte Postale' in *Case d'Armons*. Bibliothèque Nationale de France (RES P-YE-2442).

precarious this respite might have been (as the image of soldiers made from porcelain, in '1915', already suggests). Much like Apollinaire's inventories in 'There's/There are', daily engagement with these objects itself constituted a stubborn refutation of the war's annihilating powers.[160] This sense of the wartime everyday – what David Jones termed 'the intimate, continuing, domestic life of small contingents of men' in the trenches – is reflected in Apollinaire's use of language.[161] The poem's stock phrases, such as 'We're doing fine' and 'We'll get them yet', were used so often in correspondence between the front and the home that they lost something of their referential meaning.[162] In a sense, the poet was known for this informal style, for what he once termed his 'conversation-poems'.[163] His great invention, according to his friend André Billy, was 'to separate the poetry of sensibility from "literature"' by seizing in his writing 'the raw words that men use between them beyond all literary artifice'.[164] Once in the trenches, Apollinaire turned to the lingo of the army, which he found incredibly inventive and playful.[165] If the conversational style of these poems evokes something of the slow everyday at the front, then the use of caesura (elongating the verses) and the choice of title (a year rather than a specific date) enhance this intuition, and so does the reference to Ulysses' long years of travel.[166] The war, like Ulysses' wanderings, slowly eddied on and the poet had nothing much to report home. In a sense, then, 'Postcard' reads like one of those postcards, issued by the military, which prepared answers for the correspondent simply to tick off. An everyday thing for a soldier, but a curiosity for his family at home: 'It was a long time since I had written to the States,' the protagonist in *A Farewell to Arms* declares in a similar vein. 'I sent a couple of army Zona di Guerra post-cards, crossing out everything except, I am well. [...] Those post-cards would be very fine in America; strange and mysterious.'[167]

Yet, alongside the use of pages from the *Bulletin des Armées*, the insertion of a postcard into the volume challenges the poem's (and the war's) tedium. Collage shocks these objects of writing – the newspaper, the postcard, the poetry album – out of their everyday and ephemeral connotations, rendering them 'strange and mysterious'. It was an original move on Apollinaire's part – 'profoundly new', according to Laurence Campa, and 'a unique creation in Apollinaire's oeuvre', according to Claude Debon.[168] Through this insertion, '1915' and 'Postcard' gestured back to cubist experiments with collage, such as in Picasso's use of newspaper articles on the Balkan War in *Guitar, Sheet Music and Glass*. The effect is one and the same: a displaced object, as Picasso put it, enters a new context in which it retains a measure of its strangeness.[169] As a reader, we are made newly aware of the military postcard, whose political connotations are reinvented in the poem. That is to say that the postcard may still hold on to its propagandistic iconography (a *tricolour*) and its censorship guidelines ('This card [...] must not give any indication of the place of dispatch, nor contain any information on military operations past or future'), but these lose some of their power and authority in appearing alongside intimate poetic lines.[170] As an artefact, the military postcard intrigued Apollinaire no end. For the Parisian press, for instance, he wrote of a 'pretty' postcard the Fauvist painter Raoul Dufy had designed, which would become a 'part of the wonderful imagery' spontaneously created by the war.[171] 'I have found a very muddy German military postcard', the poet jotted down in a letter to Madeleine Pagès on 19 November 1915, 'but I'm sending it to you as curiosity.'[172] He also once sent her a poem, 'To Madeleine', written on the verso of a postcard of General Joffre cut in the shape of a shell.[173] Taken together, Apollinaire's gestures raise a simple point: by aligning itself with poetic and aesthetic registers, the military postcard is made to shed its everyday, war-like connotations and becomes a curious artefact, much like the way in which this collage aesthetic calls attention to the materiality of *Case d'Armons* as itself a wartime curiosity.

Time and again, Apollinaire's wartime texts display a productive, vanguard fascination with the material world of the trenches. War objects such as shells, helmets, Frisian horses and military postcards were defamiliarised and reinvented on and off the page, in the process disarmed of their deadly, militaristic affiliations. Instead, war *matériel* became a rarity, valuable only insofar as it acted as odd material witness to, and product of, the 1914–18 war. Such experiments in texts as diverse as 'There's/There are', '1915', 'Postcard' and 'Curiosities from the Front' were a way to come to terms with the war experience – at times precarious, at times dull – and provided an implicit assurance that, despite ongoing hostilities, the poet and his world continued to exist. Intriguingly, Apollinaire was attentive to the way the war in part turned these writings themselves into such curious objects, with the conflict imprinting on their material forms, marking them with a sense of immediacy. The inclusion of military postcards and pages from the *Bulletin des Armées* made *Case d'Armons* a product of its historical circumstances, not only in what it said but in what it looked like. This was not a one-off invention: a similar page from the *Bulletin* served as a frontispiece for *Médaillon Toujours Fermé*, a collection of seven manuscript poems Apollinaire wrote at the front in Champagne and bound together with a purple ribbon. The title for what he termed his 'small poetic war novel' was written across the newspaper page in purple ink, creating a jarring juxtaposition between the intimate registers of poetic language and the official discourses of war, and disarming the newspaper of its military associations in the process.[174] The resulting print artefacts – *Tranchman' Echo*, *Case d'Armons* and *Médaillon Toujours Fermé* – were worth preserving as unusual records of their time and place. Madeleine Pagès, for one, was 'shocked' when *Case d'Armons* arrived on her doorstep in Algeria, and René Berthier admitted the volume conveyed to the reader 'the initial shock felt by the poet'.[175] Remy de Gourmont felt he did not understand the poems in *Case d'Armons* but recognised nonetheless that they were 'full of flashes of a certain beauty'. 'The other day, I received a very singular book from the front,' he wrote. 'It will probably remain one of the curiosities of the war.'[176]

NOTES

1. Madeleine Pagès, 'Préface à l'Édition de 1952', in *Lettres à Madeleine: Tendre comme le Souvenir*, ed. Laurence Campa (Paris: Gallimard, 2005), pp. 27–34 (p. 27). The meeting is also recounted in Laurence Campa, *Guillaume Apollinaire* (Paris: Gallimard, 2013), pp. 523–4. All translations from the French are my own, unless otherwise indicated.
2. Pagès, 'Préface', p. 31.
3. Ibid., p. 33.
4. Guillaume Apollinaire, *Correspondance Générale*, vol. II, ed. Victor Martin-Schmets (Paris: Honoré Champion, 2015), pp. 386–7 (p. 386): to Madeleine Pagès, 5 May 1915.
5. Madeleine's reply is quoted in Campa, *Apollinaire*, p. 552.
6. Birgit Van Puymbroeck and Cedric Van Dijck, 'Apollinaire's Trench Journalism and the Affective Public Sphere', *Texas Studies in Literature and Language* 60.3

(2018), 269–92. I am grateful to Birgit for helping to shape my thinking on Apollinaire's war writings.
7. Apollinaire, *Correspondance*, vol. II, pp. 786–7 (p. 787): to Madeleine Pagès, 26 September 1915.
8. The term has most productively been read in relation to eighteenth- and nineteenth-century literature: Susan Stewart, *On Longing: Narratives of the Miniature, the Gigantic, the Souvenir, the Collection* (Durham, NC: Duke University Press, 1992); *Literary Bric-à-Brac and the Victorians: From Commodities to Oddities*, ed. Jonathon Shears and Jen Harrison (Abingdon: Routledge, 2016); John Mack, *The Art of Small Things* (Cambridge, MA: Harvard University Press, 2009); and Sean Silver, *The Mind Is a Collection: Case Studies in Eighteenth-Century Thought* (Philadelphia: University of Pennsylvania Press, 2015).
9. Kenneth E. Silver, *Esprit de Corps: The Art of the Parisian Avant-Garde and the First World War, 1914–1925* (Princeton: Princeton University Press, 1989), p. 31. Apollinaire felt these tensions in person. In late 1914, he met a Polish painter in a café in Nîmes who was taken there in chains as a spy because they mistook his cubist drawings for military plans. See *Correspondance*, vol. I, p. 711: to André Level, 27 December 1914.
10. *Objects of War: The Material Culture of Conflict and Displacement*, ed. Leora Auslander and Tara Zahra (Ithaca: Cornell University Press, 2018), p. 4.
11. Richard Cork, *A Bitter Truth: Avant-Garde Art and the Great War* (New Haven and London: Yale University Press in association with Barbican Art Gallery, 1994), p. 9.
12. Guillaume Apollinaire, 'Contribution à l'Étude des Superstitions et du Folklore du Front', in *Œuvres en Prose Complètes*, vol. I, ed. Michel Décaudin (Paris: Gallimard, 1977), pp. 1,381–5 (p. 1,382).
13. Guillaume Apollinaire, 'Sur la Mort de René Dalize', in *Œuvres en Prose Complètes*, vol. III, ed. Pierre Caizergues and Michel Décaudin (Paris: Gallimard, 1993), pp. 255–9 (p. 256).
14. From a letter dated 2 September 1915, which the poet received from his *marraine de guerre*: <http://www.brissonneau.net/html/fiche.jsp?id=2489588&np=2&lng=fr&npp=20&ordre=1&aff=1&r=>.
15. Willard Bohn, *Reading Apollinaire's* Calligrammes (London: Bloomsbury, 2019), p. 123; Els Jongeneel, 'Les Combats d'Orphée: La Poésie de Guerre de Guillaume Apollinaire', *RELIEF: Revue Électronique de Littérature Française* 8.2 (2014), 1–14 (p. 1).
16. André Billy, *Apollinaire Vivant* (Paris: Éditions de la Sirène, 1923), p. 28.
17. See, for instance, *Correspondance*, vol. III, p. 534: to Max Jacob, June 1918.
18. *Correspondance*, vol. II, pp. 259–61 (p. 260): to Lou, 2 April 1915. Ibid., pp. 342–3 (p. 342): to Lou, 24 April 1915.
19. Guillaume Apollinaire, *Œuvres en Prose Complètes*, vol. II, ed. Pierre Caizergues and Michel Décaudin (Paris: Gallimard, 1991), pp. 1,415–16, 347–8, 384.
20. Guillaume Apollinaire, *Œuvres Poétiques*, ed. André Billy, Marcel Adéma and Michel Décaudin (Paris: Gallimard, 1959), pp. 39–44, 834. Apollinaire, *Œuvres en Prose*, vol. I, pp. 519–22, 191–4.
21. Apollinaire, *Œuvres en Prose*, vol. II, pp. 1,377–8, 755–6; vol. III, pp. 137, 489, 563, 1,108, 539.
22. Marcel Adéma, *Guillaume Apollinaire le mal-aimé* (Paris: Plon, 1952), p. 82. For Willard Bohn, the form was 'the perfect outlet for his ready wit and endless curiosity'. See 'Apollinaire and the New Spirit: *Le Festin d'Ésope* (1903), *Les Soirées de Paris* (1912–14), and *L'Élan* (1915–16)', in *The Oxford Critical and Cultural*

History of Modernist Magazines, vol. III, ed. Peter Brooker et al. (Oxford: Oxford University Press, 2013), pp. 120–42 (p. 123).
23. Picasso's watercolour is included in *Album Apollinaire*, ed. Marcel Adéma and Michel Décaudin (Paris: Gallimard, 1971), p. 97.
24. Quoted in Walter L. Adamson, *Embattled Avant-Gardes: Modernism's Resistance to Commodity Culture in Europe* (Berkeley: University of California Press, 2007), p. 121. Duhamel's review evoked responses from Max Jacob, André Billy and André Salmon in *Mercure de France*, *Paris-Midi* and *Gil Blas* respectively.
25. Roger Allard, 'Untitled', *SIC*, January–February 1919, pp. 281–2 (p. 281).
26. Quoted in Apollinaire, *Œuvres Poétiques*, p. 1,041.
27. *Correspondance*, vol. I, pp. 534–5 (p. 535): to Henri Martineau, 19 July 1913: 'mais brocanteur me paraît un qualificatif très injuste pour un poète qui a écrit un si petit nombre de pièces dans le long espace de quinze ans.'
28. Peter Read, *Apollinaire and Cubism* (Midsomer Norton: Artists Bookworks, 2002), p. 13.
29. Guillaume Apollinaire, 'Art et Curiosité: Les Commencements du Cubisme', in *Œuvres en Prose*, vol. II, pp. 1,514–16 (p. 1,514). The poet makes a similar claim in *The Cubist Painters*, trans. Peter Read (Midsomer Norton: Artists Bookworks, 2002), p. 19. He event went on to publish an illustrated book on African art, *Sculptures nègres*, with Paul Guillaume.
30. Apollinaire, *Cubist Painters*, p. 11. 'The difference between Cubism and earlier painting', he adds, 'is that it is not an imitative art, but a conceptual art' (p. 27).
31. Read, *Apollinaire and Cubism*, p. 53.
32. On cubism as 'the art of painting new compositions with formal elements that are derived not from visual reality but from the reality of concepts', see Guillaume Apollinaire, 'Die Moderne Malerei', in *A Cubism Reader: Documents and Criticism, 1906–14*, ed. Mark Antliff and Patricia Leighten, trans. Jane Marie Todd (Chicago: University of Chicago Press, 2008), pp. 471–6 (p. 472).
33. Jean Metzinger, 'Cubisme et Tradition', in *Cubism Reader*, pp. 123–37 (p. 123).
34. For 'touch', see Metzinger quoted in André Salmon, 'Histoire Anecdotique du Cubism', in *Cubism Reader*, pp. 357–69 (p. 362). For 'move around', see Metzinger, 'Cubisme et Tradition', in *Cubism Reader*, p. 123. The influence of Bergson is evident here: 'several aspects of it *in succession*' reads *durée* in the original. On Bergson and cubism, see *Cubism Reader*, pp. 172–7.
35. Salmon, 'Histoire anecdotique du cubisme', in *Cubism Reader*, p. 361.
36. Read, *Apollinaire and Cubism*, p. 46.
37. Guillaume Apollinaire, 'Le Cas de Richard Mutt', in *Œuvres en Prose*, vol. II, pp. 1,378–80 (p. 1,379).
38. See Cork, *A Bitter Truth*, pp. 21–2. For a discussion of Apollinaire's take on Picasso's collages, see Read, *Apollinaire and Cubism*, p. 68, as well as 'La Peinture Moderne' and 'Lacerba', in *Œuvres en Prose*, vol. II, pp. 501–5, 822.
39. Quoted in Willard Bohn, 'Picasso, Gertrude Stein, and Guillaume Apollinaire', in *The Cambridge History of Modernism*, ed. Vincent Sherry (Cambridge: Cambridge University Press, 2017), pp. 626–45 (p. 632).
40. Apollinaire, *Cubist Painters*, p. 41.
41. *Correspondance*, vol. I, p. 631: to Pablo Picasso, 4 July 1914.
42. Ibid., p. 631.
43. For the link between picture-poems and collage, see *Cubism Reader*, p. 656, and Marjorie Perloff, *The Futurist Moment: Avant-Garde, Avant Guerre, and the Language of Rupture* (Chicago: University of Chicago Press, 1986).
44. Bohn, *Reading Apollinaire's* Calligrammes, p. 98. Elsewhere, he adds: 'As numerous critics have noted, Apollinaire was essentially a collage poet. Long before

cubism was invented, he had developed a patchwork method of constructing poetry. Bits and pieces of other poems, rough drafts of earlier projects, notes scribbled down in haste – everything was grist for his poetic mill. When he encountered cubism, his method simply accelerated.' Bohn, 'Picasso, Stein, Apollinaire', p. 639. The poet had also meant to publish his picture-poems as *Et moi aussi je suis peintre*, the title of which underlines the visual character of the poetry. The volume's appearance was initially interrupted by the outbreak of war, and it never materialised. See *The Cubist Poets in Paris: An Anthology*, ed. Leroy C. Breunig (Lincoln: University of Nebraska Press, 1995), p. 77.
45. For the statistic, see Willard Bohn, *Reading Apollinaire's* Calligrammes, p. 93.
46. *Correspondance*, vol. II, pp. 788–9 (p. 789): to Jeanne-Yves Blanc, 28 September 1915.
47. Ibid., vol. I, pp. 534–5 (p. 534): to Henri Martineau, 19 July 1913. He would go on to make the same claim in his 1917 essay 'The New Spirit and the Poets': 'One can begin with an everyday event: a dropped handkerchief can be for the poet the lever with which to move an entire universe.' See *Selected Writings of Guillaume Apollinaire*, trans. Roger Shattuck (New York: New Directions, 1971), pp. 227–37 (p. 234).
48. Guillaume Apollinaire, 'La Cravate et la Montre', in *Œuvres Poétiques*, p. 192.
49. Guillaume Apollinaire, 'Alan Seeger', *Bulletin des Écrivains*, September 1916, p. 3. Among the dead were Seeger himself and Gabriel Arbouin, who published the first theoretical statement of ideograms in the final issue of *Soirées*: 'the connection between these fragments is no longer that of grammatical logic, but that of an ideographical logic culminating in an order of spatial arrangement diametrically opposed to that of discursive juxtaposition. It is a revolution in the strongest sense of the word.' Gabriel Arbouin, 'Devant l'Idéogramme d'Apollinaire', in *Cubism Reader*, pp. 652–7 (p. 652).
50. Quoted, from Walter Benjamin's 'Bücher, die übersetzt werden sollten', in Willard Bohn, *Apollinaire and the International Avant-Garde* (Albany: State University of New York Press, 1997), p. 127.
51. Quoted in Campa, *Apollinaire*, p. 504.
52. See Jean René-Maurel, 'Guillaume Apollinaire à la Caserne', *Mercure de France*, December 1918, pp. 560–2.
53. Gertrude Stein, *The Autobiography of Alice B. Toklas* (London: Penguin, 2001), p. 172.
54. See René-Maurel, 'Apollinaire à la Caserne', p. 561. 'Tous les types de la chambrée, la chambrée 33,' Apollinaire wrote to Lou, 'veulent que je fasse un livre dont ils ont trouvé le titre: *Les Poilus de la 33*. Ce n'est pas mal pour des charretiers, chacun me racontait son histoire.' *Correspondance*, vol. I, pp. 716–17 (p. 717): to Lou, 29 December 1914.
55. René-Maurel, 'Apollinaire à la Caserne', p. 561.
56. *Correspondance*, vol. II, pp. 25–6 (p. 25): to Mireille Havet, 3 January 1915. See also ibid., p. 35: to Lou, 7 January 1915: 'Ce matin il a fallu que j'explique au tableau les différentes mesures angulaires, puis que je parle des trajectoires, puis du problème du défilement. Tu vois si je deviens calé. D'ailleurs c'est intéressant. Le projectile est un petit astre dont il s'agit de connaître la vie, les propriétés afin de le diriger au but. C'est évidemment très poétique et tu le comprends sans faire d'artillerie.'
57. From T. E. Hulme's war diary entry for 2 March 1915, included in *Further Speculations by T. E. Hulme*, ed. Sam Hynes (Minneapolis: University of Minnesota Press, 1955), p. 16.
58. *Correspondance*, vol. II, pp. 298–300 (p. 299): to Lou, 9 April 1915.

59. Ibid., p. 299.
60. Ibid., pp. 291–3 (p. 291): to Lou, 8 April 1915. He includes a drawing of the hut. See also *Les Dessins de Guillaume Apollinaire*, ed. Claude Debon and Peter Read (Paris: Buchet-Chastel, 2008), p. 113.
61. *Correspondance*, vol. II, pp. 288–91 (p. 289): to Lou, 8 April 1915.
62. Ibid., pp. 351–2 (p. 352): to Lou, 26 April 1915.
63. Ibid., pp. 351–2 (p. 352): to Lou, 26 April 1915; ibid., pp. 333–5 (p. 334): to Lou, 21 April 1915.
64. Guillaume Apollinaire, 'Agréments de la Guerre en Avril', in *Œuvres en Prose*, vol. III, pp. 223–7.
65. *Correspondance*, vol. II, pp. 668–9 (p. 669): to Lou, 20 August 1915. In late October, he drew a floorplan of yet another dugout, and sent it to his fiancée Madeleine Pagès, together with a request that she return the favour by sending him a description of her room and her bed – a question with more than a little flirtation to it. See ibid., pp. 892–6 (p. 893): to Madeleine Pagès, 27 October 1915, and *Dessins de Guillaume Apollinaire*, p. 119.
66. For another example of an inventory poem, see *Correspondance*, vol. II, pp. 271–2: to Lou, 5 April 1915.
67. Guillaume Apollinaire, 'Il y a', in *Œuvres Poétiques*, pp. 280–1. For the translation, see Guillaume Apollinaire, *Selected Poems*, trans. Martin Sorrell (Oxford: Oxford University Press, 2015), p. 183.
68. Kate McLoughlin, *Authoring War: The Literary Representation of War from the Iliad to Iraq* (Cambridge: Cambridge University Press, 2011), p. 82.
69. Ibid., p. 72.
70. For Timothy Mathews, 'There's/There are' reads as 'a series of affirmative statements about the world'. See *Reading Apollinaire: Theories of Poetic Language* (Manchester: Manchester University Press, 1987), p. 217. For Willard Bohn, who sees Rimbaud's 'Enfance III' as a potential source, such lists present 'a way of fighting back, of resisting warfare's corrosive effects on the human psyche'. *Reading Apollinaire's* Calligrammes, p. 155.
71. *Correspondance*, vol. II, pp. 795–7 (p. 796): to Madeleine Pagès, 30 September 1915.
72. For a discussion of trench art, see Nicholas J. Saunders, *Trench Art: Materialities and Memories of War* (London: Routledge, 2003). The statistic is Saunders's, too, in 'Material Culture and Conflict: The Great War, 1914–2003', in *Matters of Conflict: Material Culture, Memory and the First World War*, ed. Nicholas J. Saunders (London: Routledge, 2004), pp. 5–25 (p. 9).
73. Saunders, *Trench Art*, p. 105.
74. Quoted in Read, *Apollinaire and Cubism*, p. 88.
75. Saunders, *Trench Art*, p. 129.
76. Stein, *Autobiography of Alice B. Toklas*, p. 172.
77. Ernest Hemingway, *A Farewell to Arms* (London: Arrow Books, 2004), p. 97.
78. Quoted in Annette Becker, 'Art, Material Life and Disaster: Civilian and Military Prisoners of War', in *Matters of Conflict*, pp. 26–34 (p. 32).
79. *Correspondance*, vol. II, pp. 388–9 (p. 389): to Lou, 6 May 1915. Apollinaire, 'Agréments', p. 223. The phenomenon features across a wide range of Apollinaire's war poems, including 'Oracles', 'Lock of Hair Found' and 'Photography'. See *Œuvres Poétiques*, pp. 230, 248, 257. He even made a drawing of his friend Debaer polishing an aluminium ring. See *Dessins de Guillaume Apollinaire*, p. 114.
80. *Correspondance*, vol. II, pp. 374, 552, 568, 635, 699. Catelain asked for a trench jewel after reading Apollinaire's piece on the phenomenon in the *Mercure*. See

Annette Becker, *La Grande Guerre d'Apollinaire: Un Poète Combattant* (Paris: Texto, 2014), pp. 119–20.
81. *Correspondance*, vol. II, pp. 348–9 (p. 348): to Fernand Divoire, 25 April 1915. On the prohibition, see Saunders, *Trench Art*, p. 59.
82. *Correspondance*, vol. II, pp. 529 and 543: two separate letters to Madeleine Pagès, dated 27 June 1915 and 1 July 1915.
83. For 'carried luck', see ibid., pp. 590–1 (p. 590): to Lou, 26 July 1915. For these objects, see ibid., pp. 590, 560, 812, 854, 738, 742, 622–3.
84. See Becker, *Guerre d'Apollinaire*, p. 99.
85. *Correspondance*, vol. II, p. 252–3 (p. 253): to André Dupont, April 1915; ibid., pp. 607–11 (p. 608): to Madeleine Pagès, 3 August 1915.
86. Quoted in Campa, *Apollinaire*, p. 573.
87. Henri Gaudier-Brzeska, 'Vortex (Written from the Trenches)', *Blast*, 1915, pp. 33–4 (p. 34).
88. Van Puymbroeck and Van Dijck, 'Apollinaire's Trench Journalism', pp. 269–92. Apollinaire, *Œuvres Poétiques*, pp. 614–15 (p. 615).
89. On the 'commodified authentic', see Elizabeth Outka, *Consuming Traditions: Modernity, Modernism, and the Commodified Authentic* (New York: Oxford University Press, 2009).
90. Guillaume Apollinaire, 'Superstitions de Guerre', in *Œuvres en Prose*, vol. III, p. 492. See also Saunders, *Trench Art*, p. 107, and *Correspondance*, vol. II, pp. 607–11 (p. 610): to Madeleine Pagès, 3 August 1915.
91. Evelyn Waugh, *A Little Learning: An Autobiography* (London: Penguin, 2019), p. 135.
92. *Correspondance*, vol. II, pp. 871–4 (p. 872): to Madeleine Pagès, 20 October 1915.
93. Adamson, *Embattled Avant-Gardes*, p. 111.
94. Quoted ibid., p. 127.
95. Guillaume Apollinaire, 'Curiosities from the Front', intr. and trans. Cedric Van Dijck, *PMLA* 134.3 (2019), 555–61, and 'Curiosités du Front', *Brise d'Entonnoirs*, November–December 1916, pp. 1–2. Some parts of the article were reproduced elsewhere, including on the popular quotation pages of the official magazine of the French army, *Bulletin des Armées de la République*.
96. For instance, the Vermorel sprayer, normally used against gas, is now a water pump to dry out dugouts that are constantly flooded. See *Correspondance*, vol. II, pp. 986–8 (p. 987): to Madeleine Pagès, 30 November 1915.
97. André Billy, 'Guillaume Apollinaire', *SIC*, January 1919, pp. 284–6 (p. 285). Stein, *Autobiography of Alice B. Toklas*, p. 67. On the poet's pride, see also Campa, *Apollinaire*, pp. 596–7. Picasso often drew Apollinaire in his uniform; see for instance Cork, *A Bitter Truth*, pp. 59–60, 147–8.
98. *Correspondance*, vol. II, pp. 786–7: to Madeleine Pagès, 26 September 1915.
99. Apollinaire, 'Curiosities', pp. 558–9.
100. It appeared in the *Journal du Soldat* in December 1916 and *Nouvelles de France* on 22 February 1917.
101. The calligram is kept in the Collection Adéma at the Bibliothèque Historique de la Ville de Paris. Becker, *Guerre d'Apollinaire*, pp. 124–5. An image is included in *Album Apollinaire*, p. 236.
102. In doing so, Apollinaire's 'Helmet' finds its place in a tradition of vanguard poems which align headgear with bourgeois traditions. Decked out in their Sunday best for a local agriculture show, villagers in Flaubert's *Madame Bovary* try to avoid smudging their hats, as symbols of their aspirational status: 'menfolk were concerned rather with their hats, covering them with their pocket-handkerchiefs, one

103. corner of which they held between their teeth' (Harmondsworth: Penguin, 1971), p. 145. In Jakob van Hoddis's 1910 expressionist poem 'Weltende', for instance, the wind carrying a hat off a civilian's pointy head comes to symbolise the end of the bourgeois world.
103. See Christine Beil, *Der Ausgestellte Krieg: Präsentationen des Ersten Weltkriegs 1914–39* (Tübingen: Tübinger Vereinigung für Volkskunde, 2005). Two further helmets decorated with a painted view of Péronne are kept today in the collection of the Historial de la Grande Guerre. See Saunders, *Trench Art*, p. 136.
104. Cork, *A Bitter Truth*, pp. 133–4. Indeed, a fascination with the helmet was shared across the European avant-gardes, as in Otto Dix's 1914 *Self-Portrait with Artillery Helmet* and Isaac Rosenberg's 1916 *Self-Portrait in a Steel Helmet*.
105. For the drawings, see *Dessins de Guillaume Apollinaire*, p. 108, and *Correspondance*, vol. II, pp. 418 and 945: both to Lou, 17 May and 12 November 1915. Guillaume Apollinaire, 'Le Casque des Agents', in *Œuvres en Prose*, vol. III, p. 1,095.
106. Virginia Woolf, *A Room of One's Own* and *Three Guineas* (London: Penguin, 2000), pp. 134, 137. 'Clothing and its part in the psychology of war', notes Wyndham Lewis, 'is a neglected subject.' See *Blasting and Bombardiering* (Berkeley and Los Angeles: University of California Press, 1967), p. 121.
107. Guillaume Apollinaire, 'Le Chapeau Haut-de-Forme', in *Œuvres en Prose*, vol. III, p. 1,063.
108. Quoted in Cork, *A Bitter Truth*, p. 79.
109. *Correspondance*, vol. III, pp. 150–1 (p. 151): to Jeanne-Yves Blanc, 26 March 1916. For Blanc's response – 'Certainly, I will write a poem for your helmet which has immolated its beautiful blue Joffre surface to save a precious head in many ways, to protect a beautiful defender of France' – see ibid., vol. II, p. 661. Pleased, Apollinaire urged her to send the poem to *La Grande Revue*.
110. When André Billy saw Apollinaire in Val-de-Grâce, he noticed that '[a]t the head of his bed hung his helmet, and this helmet had a hole; a number of *Mercure* showed its pages stiffened with almost-black blood on the night table'. Billy, *Apollinaire Vivant*, p. 86. Today, Apollinaire's helmet is kept in the Collection Adéma at the Bibliothèque Historique de la Ville de Paris.
111. Blaise Cendrars, *Œuvres Complètes*, vol. VIII (Paris: Denoël, 1964), p. 662. The translation is Jay Winter's.
112. See Billy, *Apollinaire Vivant*, p. 81, and Apollinaire, *Œuvres Poétiques*, pp. 210, 214, 268, 771.
113. Apollinaire, 'Curiosities', p. 559. The Frisian horse is named after the Dutch War of Independence, when it was invented. See Guillaume Apollinaire, *Calligrammes: Poems of Peace and War, 1913–16*, trans. A. H. Greet (Berkeley: University of California Press, 1980), pp. 347–508 (p. 492).
114. The poem was sent to Pagès on 18 November 1915 and later published in the November 1917 issue of *La Grande Revue*.
115. Bohn, *Reading Apollinaire's* Calligrammes, p. 162.
116. *Correspondance*, vol. II, pp. 900–2 (p. 900): to Jeanne-Yves Blanc, 30 October 1915.
117. Ibid., pp. 571–4 (p. 573): to Madeleine Pagès, 18 July 1915.
118. See Becker, *Guerre d'Apollinaire*, p. 45. Apollinaire addresses this renewal of a vanguard momentum in an interview on 'The New Tendencies' in *SIC*. See *Œuvres en Prose*, vol. II, pp. 985–7.
119. Ibid., vol. III, p. 21.
120. Guillaume Apollinaire, 'Les Poètes de ma Batterie', in *Œuvres en Prose*, vol. III, pp. 228–31. See 'Littérateurs-Soldats' and 'Le Caporal Larguier', ibid., p. 221.

121. Robert Nelson, 'Soldier Newspapers: A Useful Source in the Social and Cultural History of the First World War', *War in History* 17.2 (2010), 167–91 (p. 175).
122. For references to these trench journals, see *Correspondance*, vol. II, pp. 638, 78, 82; vol. III, pp. 26, 170, 203. In addition to the magazines already named, his library contained copies of *Le Crocodile*, *Tactacteufteuf*, *La Ghirba*, *Echo des Gourbis*, *Gazette Cormon-Collin-Flameng*, *Les Imberbes* and *Seau à Charbon*. See *La Bibliothèque de Guillaume Apollinaire*, vol. II, ed. Gilbert Boudar and Pierre Caizergues (Paris: Éditions du Centre Nationale de la Recherche Scientifique, 1987), pp. 30, 75, 32, 166, 42, 45, 73.
123. Guillaume Apollinaire, 'Histoire d'une Gazette du Front', in *Œuvres en Prose*, vol. III, pp. 247–50.
124. For his journalism on the phenomenon, see *Œuvres en Prose*, vol. II, pp. 1,383–4, 1,413, 1,456, and vol. III, pp. 247–50, 255–9, 260–2. For the quote, see Guillaume Apollinaire, 'Gazette Cormon-Collin-Flameng', in *Œuvres en Prose*, vol. III, pp. 260–4 (p. 261).
125. In his review of Duhamel's *La Vie des Martyrs* for the *Mercure de France*. Guillaume Apollinaire, 'Ouvrages sur la Guerre Actuelle', in *Œuvres en Prose*, vol. II, pp. 1,182–3 (p. 1,183).
126. André Billy, *Avec Apollinaire: Souvenirs Inédits* (Paris: La Palatine, 1966), p. 29. Pierre Caizergues estimates that Apollinaire contributed to more than 140 periodicals and newspapers in his relatively short career. 'Apollinaire Journaliste: Textes Retrouvés et Textes Inédits avec Présentation et Notes', II (doctoral thesis, University of Paris III, 1977), Service de Reproduction des Thèses, University of Lille III, 1979, p. 37.
127. Billy, *Apollinaire Vivant*, p. 17.
128. Apollinaire, 'Histoire d'une Gazette du Front', p. 247.
129. *Tranchman' Echo: Journal Mondain Paraissant à Chaque Cuite du Rédacteur* 3, June 1915, p. 1.
130. Apollinaire, 'Histoire d'une Gazette du Front', p. 248.
131. For eight, see *Correspondance*, vol. II, pp. 932–3 (p. 933): to Georgette Catelain, 7 November 1915. For twelve, see 'Histoire d'une Gazette du Front', p. 249. The number was most likely twelve: eight for subscribers, three for the editors and one for the legal depot at the Bibliothèque Nationale de France. In any case, the number is much smaller than the sixty counted by Roger Shattuck in *The Banquet Years: The Origins of the Avant-Garde in France 1885 to World War I* (New York: Anchor Books, 1958), p. 290.
132. For the procedure, see Stéphane Audoin-Rouzeau, *Men at War, 1914–18: National Sentiment and Trench Journalism in France during the First World War* (Oxford: Berg, 1995), pp. 24–5, and anon., 'Grande Importance de Pâte à Copier', *Mercure de France*, 1 October 1915, pp. 397–8.
133. Ibid., pp. 397–8.
134. Apollinaire, 'Histoire d'une Gazette du Front', p. 249; *Correspondance*, vol. II, pp. 677–9 (p. 679): to Madeleine Pagès, 23 August 1915 ('une aimable plaisanterie et une rareté Hémérographique, c'est-à-dire Presque bibliographique').
135. *Correspondance*, vol. II, pp. 765–6: to Charles de la Roncière, 20 September 1915; ibid., pp. 677–9 (p. 678): to Madeleine Pagès, 23 August 1915.
136. Ibid., p. 765.
137. Ibid., p. 765.
138. Barbara Green, 'Feminist Things', in *Transatlantic Print Culture, 1880–1940: Emerging Media, Emerging Modernisms*, ed. Ann Ardis and Patrick Collier (Basingstoke: Palgrave Macmillan, 2008), pp. 66–79 (p. 77).
139. See manuscript copy at the Bibliothèque Nationale de France; it was later included

in *Calligrammes*. *Case d'Armons* was a rare, though not a singular, phenomenon. In the summer of 1916, Paul Éluard handprinted *Le Devoir* while working in a field hospital in the Somme valley. Paul Éluard, *Lettres de Jeunesse* (Paris: Seghers, 1962), pp. 120–1.
140. Becker, *Guerre d'Apollinaire*, p. 76. The metaphor returns in Apollinaire's 'SP', in *Œuvres Poétiques*, p. 223.
141. Jeremy Braddock, *Collecting as Modernist Practice* (Baltimore: Johns Hopkins University Press, 2012), p. 1.
142. *Correspondance*, vol. II, pp. 749–50 (p. 749): to Madeleine Pagès, 17 September 1915. John Dos Passos, *The Best Times: An Informal Memoir* (London: André Deutsch, 1968), p. 57.
143. *Correspondance*, vol. II, p. 1,008: to Marie Laurencin, 6 December 1915. For Apollinaire's division of the proceeds, see ibid., pp. 467–8: to André Level, June 1915.
144. 'I just learned that we are not allowed to trade and I could get into trouble', ibid., pp. 568–9 (p. 569): to Chérie Faure-Favier, 16 July 1915.
145. Ibid., pp. 467–8 (p. 467): to André Level, June 1915 ('rarity'). Ibid., pp. 519–20 (p. 519): to Louise Faure-Favier, 24 June 1915 ('curiosity').
146. Ibid., pp. 665–6 (p. 665): to Madeleine Pagès, 18 August 1915.
147. Quoted in Billy, *Apollinaire Vivant*, p. 104.
148. Gaston Picard's interview, 'M Guillaume Apollinaire et la Nouvelle École Littéraire', appeared in *Le Pays* on 24 June 1917, *Œuvres en Prose*, vol. II, pp. 988–91 (p. 989).
149. Guillaume Apollinaire, *The Poet Assassinated*, trans. Matthew Josephson (New York: Broom, 1923), n.p.
150. Campa, *Apollinaire*, p. 582.
151. *Correspondance*, vol. II, pp. 470–1: to Lou, 1 June 1915.
152. *Œuvres Poétiques*, p. 1,076. His name is misspelled on the subscription notice: *Appolinaire*.
153. Guillaume Apollinaire, 'Vieux Papiers', in *Œuvres en Prose*, vol. III, p. 1,050; 'Le Papier', ibid., p. 516. On paper shortages at the French front, see Campa, *Apollinaire*, p. 562.
154. *Correspondance*, vol. III, p. 540: to André Breton, 20 June 1918. Billy disagreed. See Campa, *Apollinaire*, p. 738.
155. See for instance Apollinaire, *Œuvres Poétiques*, p. 200 ('Tour') and p. 297 ('Carte Postale').
156. Claude Debon, *Calligrammes dans Tous ses États – Édition Critique du Receuil de Guillaume Apollinaire* (Paris: Éditions Calliopées, 2008), p. 184.
157. Apollinaire, *Calligrammes: Poems of Peace and War*, pp. 152–5.
158. *Correspondance*, vol. II, pp. 635–6 (p. 635): to Chérie Faure-Favier, 11 August 1915. The list of objects comes from an article in *Le Cri de Paris*, 4 July 1915, p. 6.
159. Henri Lefebvre, *Critique de la Vie Quotidienne*, vol. II (Paris: L'Arche, 1961), p. 61. See also Mary A. Favret, 'Everyday War', *ELH* 72.3 (2005), 605–33.
160. Silver, *Esprit de Corps*, p. 78: 'among the most popular subjects depicted by artists at the front are what we may call genre scenes, the everyday life of the poilu.'
161. David Jones, *In Parenthesis* (London: Faber & Faber, 2010), p. ix.
162. The message *We'll get them yet*, for instance, was found everywhere at the front. Written on to trench walls or shells fired across No Man's Land, it even becomes the title of a poem Apollinaire published in another trench journal, *Le Rire d'Éclat*. For a discussion of this poem, see Van Puymbroeck and Van Dijck, 'Apollinaire's Trench Journalism', pp. 273–4.

163. Billy, *Apollinaire Vivant*, pp. 55–6.
164. Ibid., p. 56. For Walter Benjamin, too, 'Apollinaire's verses are the product of social interaction, contain bits of conversations, immerse themselves in everyday experience like the poet himself. They are so unceremonious that they make prose ashamed.' Quoted in Bohn, *Apollinaire and the International Avant-Garde*, pp. 127–8.
165. Guillaume Apollinaire, 'Aphorismes Touchant le Fantassin du Front', in *Œuvres en Prose*, vol. III, p. 240. In a letter to Paul Léautaud dated 1 September 1915, the poet asks his 'dear friend' for 'a book by an author with an Italian name on the various slangs'. *Correspondance*, vol. II, p. 701. See also Becker, *Guerre d'Apollinaire*, pp. 64–5.
166. For Henri Lefebvre, too, the everyday is 'undated'. See *Everyday Life in the Modern World*, trans. Sacha Rabinovitch (London: Penguin, 1971), p. 24. See *Correspondance*, vol. II, pp. 463–4 (p. 463): to Madeleine Pagès, 28 May 1915: 'Je vous ai envoyé une petite bague que j'ai faite pour vous, anneau tout à fait simple, j'y ai gravé (mal gravé même) 1915 – ne trouvant rien d'autre à y mettre qui fût plus éloquent ...'
167. Hemingway, *Farewell to Arms*, p. 35.
168. Campa, *Apollinaire*, p. 571; Debon, *Calligrammes dans tous ses états*, p. 184.
169. For Apollinaire's take on wartime collages, see for instance 'Les Journaux de Tranchée Italiens' and 'La Ghirba' in *Œuvres en Prose*, vol. II, pp. 1,383–4 and 1,413, where he discusses Ardengo Soffici's caricatures made from newspaper pages (*papiers collés*). Soffici was a Futurist in the Italian army whom Apollinaire knew well enough to send one of the few copies of *Case d'Armons*. The collages were published in Soffici's trench journal. For the poet, the effect of Soffici's *papiers collés* is 'powerful [and] very singular in appearance'; he finds it 'unexpected' (p. 1,413).
170. For Apollinaire's take on censorship, see 'L'Hellespontienne' and 'Petites Annonces' in *Œuvres en Prose*, vol. III, pp. 221 and 281–4; 'La Littérature Tchèque et la Censure Autrichienne' in *Œuvres en Prose*, vol. II, pp. 1,353–4. The military censor targeted Apollinaire himself, cutting out parts of his journalism from the *Mercure*. See *Correspondance*, vol. II, pp. 934–5 (p. 935): to Madeleine Pagès, 7 November 1915. Ironically, the poet would himself become a censor: 'Et voilà notre Apollinaire censeur! La guerre a suscité d'étranges choses [...] On l'affecta au bureau des périodiques, et il eut pour mission spéciale de lire les petites revues. J'ai vu, de mes yeux vu, le censeur Guillaume Apollinaire, un crayon bleu à la main, scruter d'un oeil sévère les épreuves de *SIC*.' See Billy, *Apollinaire Vivant*, pp. 91–2.
171. Guillaume Apollinaire, 'L'Art Vivant et la Guerre', in *Œuvres en Prose*, vol. II, pp. 857–8. See also 'La Pochette de la Marraine' (p. 1,373) and Laboureur's 'pretty Christmas card for 1917' sent from the front in 'Le Burin' (p. 1,317). Mark Wollaeger has a chapter on the history of postcards in relation to modernism in *Modernism, Media, and Propaganda: British Narrative from 1900 to 1945* (Princeton: Princeton University Press, 2006), chapter 2.
172. *Correspondance*, vol. II, pp. 966–7 (p. 967): to Madeleine Pagès, 19 November 1915.
173. *Œuvres Poétiques*, pp. 614–15.
174. *Correspondance*, vol. II, pp. 710–13 (p. 711): to Madeleine Pagès, 3 September 1915.
175. Ibid., pp. 665–6 (p. 665): to Madeleine Pagès, 18 August 1915. René Berthier, 'Espoir en Guillaume Apollinaire', *SIC*, August 1916, p. 10.
176. Quoted in Marcel Adéma, *Guillaume Apollinaire* (Paris: La Table Ronde, 1968), p. 276.

2

E. M. FORSTER IN THE STREETS

By the time hostilities broke out across Europe, E. M. Forster had stopped writing. In the preceding decade, four novels had appeared under his name in almost as many years. However, by the summer of 1914, Forster had just finished a novel that proved unpublishable, *Maurice*, and had been stuck for some time on another, his last, which would only see the light of day ten years later as *A Passage to India*. 'Civilisation as it topples carries my brain with it,' the novelist jotted down in his diary on 1 August 1914.[1] A few months later: 'I find it even less possible to finish novels since the war than before it.'[2] By the end of the conflict, Forster would quietly admit to Siegfried Sassoon that he still suffered from writer's block. His unfinished 'Inferior', a short story about two officers handing out cigarettes in a military hospital, was itself 'an inferior story', the novelist confessed to the poet. 'It's not that I'm off writing, but I can't any more put words between inverted commas and join them together with "said" and an imaginary proper name.'[3] Instead, Forster dedicated his first war year to work of a more practical nature, cataloguing paintings two days each week at the National Gallery in London and serving as one of its night-time watchmen on the look-out for air raid fires.[4]

Just like E. M. Forster, many other modernists recorded a struggle to write during, and about, the First World War. Ford Madox Ford felt himself unable to 'evoke pictures of the Somme [...] as for putting them – into words! No: the mind stops dead.'[5] In 1917, Margaret Anderson left a page of the *Little Review* blank to represent the conflict; Henry James had likewise admitted two years earlier, in an interview with the *New York Times*, that he found it 'as hard to apply one's words as to endure one's thoughts', famously adding that 'the war has used up words'.[6] Taken together, the doubts Forster, Ford, Anderson and James articulated are consistent with a larger moment of epistemological crisis prompted by the conflict. Across divides of class, gender and nationality, from the trenches in No Man's Land to the home front, contemporaries grappled with the question of how to put the war into words.[7] Some – the 'men grown silent', as Walter Benjamin famously put it – found that their unprecedentedly difficult experiences eluded description, which was already much restricted because of the introduction of censorship under the Defence of the Realm Act.[8] Others came up with an inventive army language to get around these censored and self-censored silences – a phenomenon that became the focal point for much scholarly interest in the immediate post-war period, as evidenced by Albert Dauzat's *Argot de la Guerre*, Lorenzo Smith's *Lingo of No Man's Land*, Gaston Esnault's *Le Poilu Tel Qu'Il Se Parle*, Edward Fraser and John Gibbons's *Soldier and Sailor Words and Phrases*, and John Brophy and Eric Partridge's *Songs and Slang of the British Soldier*. As Julian Walker has argued in *Words and the First World War: Language, Memory, Vocabulary*, much of this slang – from 'Old Man Fritz' (German) to 'going over the top' (attack) to 'narpoo' (from *il n'y a plus*, gone, dead) – ironically existed to avoid naming the war and its realities as such.[9] In spite of these linguistic inventions, then, the First World War continued to evade accurate description.

What happens to this sense of crisis once we move our focus beyond the familiar terrain of the Western Front?[10] Rarely considered as part of the wartime pressures on communication, but perhaps equally disorienting, was the fact that military personnel abroad found themselves surrounded by non-European languages and scripts, as many of them travelled for the first time in their lives. This lacuna is all the more surprising, considering that the First World War was a global conflict and that military slang had been shaped by colonial expansion long before 1914. Some of the conflict's most characteristic idioms and expressions, such as *blighty* and *khaki*, had entered the English language through the Anglo-Indian forces (deriving from the Urdu for 'foreigner' and 'soil-coloured'). E. M. Forster's life and work allows us to give a global turn to this discussion of the war's effects on language. For, in late 1915, as the author struggled with his craft and attempted to avoid conscription, Forster moved to Alexandria as a searcher for the Red Cross, from where he had meant to return after three months, but where he stayed for more than three years. '[I]t's an odd backwater the war has scooped out for me,' the novelist wrote from the Middle East.[11] As a searcher, he visited convalescing soldiers in local hospitals to question them for news of their missing comrades, filing the information into reports with the War Office in London.[12] '[I]f one does get news about the missing', he admitted to his friend Syed Ross Masood, 'it is generally bad news.'[13] Still, the practical work – filing reports, talking to soldiers, reading them Dickens and Tolstoy, writing their letters, running their errands – gave Forster a sense of purpose at a time when he felt unable to write fiction. '[W]e must be materialists,' ran his wartime belief. 'Let us look after bodies that there may be a next generation which may have the right to look after the soul.'[14]

As Vincent Sherry maintains in *The Great War and the Language of Modernism*, 'the most expressive record of the meaning of this war lies in the failure of language'.[15] This chapter argues that these failures were perhaps nowhere as revealing as on the colonial front in Egypt, a place Forster found 'difficult to describe' and 'hard to observe unobserved'.[16] In Alexandria, the novelist learned of all the reasons that made writing and communicating so difficult in wartime. 'We live among rumours and gossip, as I suppose does everyone,' he wrote to his aunt late in the summer of 1916.[17] He had witnessed military authorities lecture convalescing soldiers on atrocities committed by the Turks and would later come across similar falsehoods in accounts of the First Battle of Gaza in the English papers (in which a retreat was described as an advance, leaving readers in England, so Forster felt, 'amazingly and genuinely in the dark').[18] Added to these familiar concerns about the widespread uses of propaganda and censorship was a set of encounters with the material world of wartime Egypt that have not received as much consideration: Forster came across, and began writing about, shop signs and monument inscriptions. Found scattered across colonial fronts, these objects similarly diagnosed a language in crisis: difficult to decipher, no longer intelligible, no longer depicting reality in a transparent way. If scholars such as Randall Stevenson and Juliette Taylor-Batty have shown that the modernist literature of the 1920s was marked by forms of 'linguistic eclecticism' and 'linguistic plurality' that highlight a language in crisis (both point to T. S. Eliot's 'The Waste Land' by way of example), then the case of Forster in Egypt suggests just how clearly this sense of crisis was grounded in the experience of the First World War.[19]

This chapter will follow E. M. Forster through wartime Egypt and will explore his engagement with dictionaries, shop signs, monument engravings and inscriptions. I will argue that Forster's local journalism and travel guide staged such encounters with the material objects of writing to show that the war obfuscated language's signifying relationship to reality. As words lost their opacity, they began to take on the qualities of a material object: Forster, I contend, became newly interested in words as 'dead' and 'mute' things (words the war had rendered into motor-car tyres, as Henry James famously proposed).[20] In making this claim, the chapter takes its cue from the work of Edgar Garcia, Jessie Schotter and Christopher Bush on the modernist fascination with pictographs, hieroglyphs and ideographs, but accords the First World War a key role in the development of this contemporary interest in the visual qualities of writing over its referential meaning.[21] In the first section, zeroing in on Forster's *Alexandria: A History and a Guide* and his pieces for the *Egyptian Mail*, I examine how local English newspapers, dictionaries and travel guides helped soldiers newly arrived in Egypt to find their bearings. These print artefacts, I argue, were objects to be used: carried into the streets and read in such a way that already drew the focus to their material forms. The shop sign, an object Forster was captivated by, had a similar effect on the novelist. As I show in the next section, its uncanny uses of typography and diction – erroneous or unnecessarily convoluted phrases printed in large capital letters – brought language newly into view, especially by calling attention to its artificial qualities. By Forster's account, the object figured as a symbol of how the war weighed on words; his anxieties about the war's effects on language crystallise around moments of looking at, and feeling his way around, these shop signs. The final section explores inscriptions on the monuments of Ancient Egypt, which spoke mostly 'dead words' (as Forster once put it).[22] Rendered unintelligible over time, these symbols had been pushed towards the status of visual objects – once more pointing to the arbitrary nature of language and thus turning into symbols for the war's linguistic and representational crisis.

Going Abroad: Newspapers, Dictionaries, Travel Guides

Languages must have floated around E. M. Forster from the moment he docked in Egypt. Arabic, Turkish, Armenian, Hebrew, French, Italian, Greek and English were all spoken in wartime Alexandria. Unlike soldiers in barracks and nurses in hospitals, where English was the lingua franca, the novelist lived in what he once described as 'a room in the house of the Italian-speaking Greek maid of the Norwegian Judge's American widow'.[23] For £4 per month, he taught English (using the poetry of Thomas Hardy) to Pericles Anastassiades, a Greek who worked in the colonial administration under a friend from Forster's time at Cambridge, Robert Furness. Slowly, the author later wrote, 'I had inserted myself a little into Levantine life'.[24] His cosmopolitan set came to include a Syrian Orientalist, an Italian museum director, a Syrian police officer, a French director of the ports, a British-German official in the post office, a Swiss director of the trams, and an Italian composer, to whom he sang *Leitmotiven* under water.[25] Best known among this group of friends was C. P. Cavafy, the Greek-Alexandrian poet whom Forster met through Furness in 1916. In a 1951 piece for the *Listener*, Forster recalled an occasion in Cavafy's flat at 10 Rue Lepsius, where the poet challenged the novelist to translate one of his Greek poems into English. To Cavafy's surprise, Forster 'detected some coincidences between its Greek and public school Greek', and his resulting effort was not half bad.[26] Even all these years later, he still remembered how much had been gained through 'personal stumblings'.[27]

It is difficult to grasp in retrospect just how well or how poorly Forster stumbled through Arabic, but the few words scattered across his correspondence suggest he was never very skilful. The fact that these words are transcribed means it is likely he never learned to read the language. The author initially claimed an instinctive dislike of Arabic, though he soon regretted that statement, especially after meeting Mohammed El Adl, an Egyptian tram conductor with whom he fell in love in 1917.[28] Proficient in English, El Adl was a lover of languages, 'a lively talker'.[29] As Forster later remembered, he was full of 'entertaining proverbs and anecdotes'.[30] The novelist jotted down some of these phrases in a notebook during their courtship, including El Adl's belief that 'All is exceptions in men as in English grammar'.[31] There must have been many such notebooks over the years, for it was a lifelong habit: Virginia Woolf once glanced in his diary and noticed that 'Morgan writes conversation – word for word, when the humour takes him'.[32] The interest in languages, in individual cadences and figures of speech, was certainly there, though any evidence of proficiency in Arabic is missing from the historical record. Forster once wrote he wished El Adl had given him lessons so that he could read *The Arabian Nights*, but the latter never did.[33]

If Forster failed to pick up Arabic during his time in Egypt – 'I live in a haze,' he had similarly admitted of the 'unknown tongue[s]' surrounding him in India – it is because there was no need to.[34] In Alexandria, he was part and parcel of the colonial establishment.[35] Print artefacts existed in great supply to help new arrivals find their bearings in this multilingual setting: local newspapers in English, Arabic-English dictionaries, grammars, maps and travel guides. Many of these documents, which were particularly useful for foreigners new to this place, had arrived with the coloniser over time. The first Greek grammar, Forster enjoyed pointing out, was developed, around 100 BC, not in Greece but at the Mouseion, the famous library complex in Alexandria.[36] The first book ever printed in Egypt was an Arabic-Italian dictionary.[37] The first newspaper, too, came to the country as a colonial import. When the French *Armée d'Orient* invaded the gateway to the East in 1798, it brought a printing press. On that press, one of Napoleon's interpreters printed a 'Proclamation to the Egyptians' in Arabic, which messengers carried into the villages of the Nile Delta ahead of the French troops. A few months into the occupation, the French started their own newspapers, printed at their newly founded Institut d'Égypte. Counting mainly military men among their readers, *Courrier de l'Égypte* and *La Décade Égyptienne* were nonetheless the first newspapers printed and circulated in the country. They were followed, in 1828, by *Al-Waqa'I' al-Misriyya*, the first Egyptian newspaper composed in Ottoman Turkish and Arabic.[38] Upon retreating in 1801, Napoleon took his moveable types with him. *Al-Waqa'I' al-Misriyya* was printed, instead, on the government presses Mehmed Ali Pasha had bought from Europe. With the establishment of Ali's Bulaq Press, Cairo became the first Ottoman city with a lasting urban print culture, which thrived throughout the mid-century and collapsed with the invasion of the British in the late 1870s.[39]

During the years between 1914 and 1918, these colonial newspapers received a new lease of life. Because of the country's position on the Mediterranean and Suez Canal, the media landscape in cities such as Alexandria, Port Said and Cairo was incredibly rich. An average newsstand carried periodicals in Arabic, from the nationalist *al-Ahram* to the overwhelmingly pro-British *al-Mokattam*, and in English, from a seasonal society magazine, *Sphinx*, to the 'semi-official journal of the Occupation', the *Egyptian Gazette*.[40] In addition, papers in French, Italian and Greek were widely available, as well as multilingual publications, such as the *Egyptian Herald/al-Mubashshir al-Misri*, composed, as its masthead suggests, in English and Arabic. In the bars and streets of Alexandria, more copies of *The Times*, the *Daily Mail* and the major French newspapers were on sale than before the war, as the French avant-garde poet Guillaume Apollinaire also pointed out, though he never set foot in the Middle East.[41] Even in a place as remote as Ismailia, on the Suez Canal, the officers' mess club sported copies of a 'Canal Zone Edition' of a local English paper, the Italian *L'Illustrazione* and *La Guerra Illustrata*, and the French *La Vie Parisienne* (alongside 'a useful *Larousse*', a French dictionary).[42]

The Eastern Mediterranean counted more reading materials than Forster ever knew existed: 'little magazines', he wrote of this corner of the world, 'spring up and die without ceasing.'[43] That so many periodicals were available, and in so many languages, is explained, in large part, through the new readership the First World War had brought to this far end of the Mediterranean, which became the base for campaigns in the Dardanelles, Sinai, Palestine and Mesopotamia. 'They have stuffed Egypt full of soldiers,' Forster complained to Leonard Woolf of the 250,000 British, Imperial and Commonwealth troops stationed in the country over the war.[44] As was the case on all fronts, these soldiers, in turn, started their own weekly and monthly publications – small-scale, short-lived ventures such as the *Cacolet* (Australian Camel Field Ambulance), *Barrak* (Camel Corps), *The Gnome* (Royal Flying Corps), *Te Korero 'Aotea* (Aotea Convalescent Home, Cairo), *Citadel* (Cairo Citadel Garrison), *Kia Ora Coo-Ee* (Australian and New Zealand Expeditionary Forces) and the *Egyptian Labour Corps News* (Egyptian Labour Corps). Among these, the most widely circulated was the *Palestine News*, the official newspaper of the Egyptian Expeditionary Force, published at GHQ in Cairo. Founded rather late in the war, it featured editions in English, Arabic and Hebrew, and quickly became a household name in the region, counting T. E. Lawrence among its readers and one-time contributors.[45]

Soldiers, it is clear, were voracious readers – especially of the documents, such as a local newspaper in English, that helped them find their bearings in this (to them) unfamiliar setting.⁴⁶ In a photograph from early 1916 that survives today in the collection of the Australian War Memorial, the men of the 5th Battalion pose for the camera as they travel in an open rail wagon to the Suez Canal (Figure 2.1). If they look ragged, it is because they have just returned from Gallipoli. Sitting at the core and centre of the composition, a man proudly displays a copy of the *Egyptian Mail*. The *Mail*, a daily four-page broadsheet founded in 1912, was one of those papers that saw its readership increase dramatically with the arrival of the troops – as the photograph indicates. Owned by a French advertising concern and edited from 30 Sharia Kasr-el-Nil in Cairo, the *Mail* served as the morning paper for the English community in Egypt (its rival, the *Gazette*, appeared in the evenings). For four years, the war completely took over the pages of the paper, with stories copied out of the London *Times* or compiled from Reuters cables. Only a handful of columns were reserved for news of a more local interest, including steamer departure times for Europe, wheat prices, daily weather reports and news about Nile floods. It is not easy now to summon the paper's anonymous cast of contributors. Its wartime editor, appointed by the colonial government, was Hugh Evelyn Wortham.⁴⁷ Its writing staff, in these early years, included Sydney

Figure 2.1 Men in the 5th Battalion travelling to the Suez Canal, Egypt, 1916. Australian War Memorial (A00089).

Moseley (later official correspondent to the Mediterranean Expeditionary Force), Frank Reid (a prolific Australian journalist-turned-soldier and editor of *Kia Ora Coo-Ee*), Evelyn Byng (a novelist and wife of the General Officer Commanding in the British Army of Occupation) and 'Miss N. Griffiths' (editor of *Sphinx* and the paper's social correspondent). For two years, from 1917 to 1919, E. M. Forster joined their ranks, walking in and out of the *Mail*'s Alexandria offices across from the Gare de Ramleh and contributing at least twenty-three pieces under his chosen pseudonym, 'Pharos'. Upon his arrival in Egypt, the well-known novelist had begun writing for the *Gazette*, but quickly left it for its rival, the better-paying *Mail*.[48]

Forster's pieces for the *Mail* remain little-known today.[49] They deal with a great variety of topics, from a royal visit to Alexandria, the countryside around the city and concerts in military venues to episodes out of the city's famed history, and visits to a hashish den, a local cinema and the cotton bourse. From these subjects it is clear that the *Mail* aimed to open a window for the Englishman abroad to glimpse into Egypt. It not only carried advertisements for the services of English-speaking doctors and nannies, and schedules for ships from and to England, but also sported daily translations from the Arabic newspapers in a column entitled 'The Native Press'. While unsigned, these translations were probably drawn up with the help of the *Mail*'s Egyptian sub-editor, Socrates Spiro, a former government official, translator of Dante and lecturer in Arabic at the University of Geneva.[50] Spiro was the author of the standard dictionary and grammar foreign soldiers in Egypt consulted, at a time when few such books were around. His first best-seller was *An Arabic-English Dictionary of the Colloquial Arabic of Egypt*. Published in 1895 with the support of Lord Cromer, it was quickly followed by *A New Practical Grammar of the Modern Arabic of Egypt* and *A Pocket Grammar and Vocabulary of the Modern Arabic of Egypt*. These dictionaries and grammars were advertised in the *Egyptian Mail* and were for sale in its offices.[51] In the pages of the newspaper, too, Spiro wrote about 'Foreign Words in Arabic' and 'Street Cries', a series of pieces which offered translations of the cries of hawkers overheard in Cairo and which thus introduced English readers to the poetic soundscape of a place where literacy levels were still, in 1917, at a prevalence of 6.8 per cent.[52] 'I think that the total number of articles contributed by me to the Egyptian press, English and Arabic, amounts to many hundreds,' Spiro once admitted, as he leafed through 'two huge volumes' of his press cuttings. 'My pen is never idle.'[53]

If Spiro's pen was never idle, and if his writing about the Arabic language for an English readership gave him 'world-wide fame' (at least according to the Cairo-based society magazine *Sphinx*), then it was simply because the war created a new need for dictionaries, glossaries and English newspapers.[54] From 1914 to 1919, waves of British, Australian and New Zealand troops flooded into Egypt. As Julian Walker puts it, writing of a context on the Western Front where language barriers were much less insurmountable, such documents provided 'a fundamental tool for understanding the war'.[55] That these documents enabled such quick understanding was a result of the way they require a different reading experience. A novel is read cover to cover, in private and mostly seated, often indoors. Newspapers and pocket dictionaries, on the other hand, can be carried around and consulted on the spot. They are scanned, dipped into or browsed, rather than read consecutively and chronologically. Their layout and typographical uniformity – columns and headlines in newspapers, lemmas and indices in dictionaries – allow for such forms of non-reading. With this in mind, Spiro's glossaries for the press were composed as easily navigable lists: *aiwa* (yes), *la* (no), *sa'îda* (happy), *khalâs* (finish; that's all), *izzayak* (how are you).[56] So was 'Arabic Made Easy', a regular series of articles in an Alexandrian military magazine, *Alpha/Omega*, which were penned by Mohammed Dulab, an Egyptian interpreter to the British army. Printed in three neat columns – English original ('boy'), Arabic transcription ('walad'), mnemonic device ('what a lad!') – Dulab's glossaries were easily consulted, ripped out of the magazine and carried into the streets of Alexandria.[57]

Spiro's phonetic transcriptions and Dulab's mnemonic devices already give an initial sense – explored further below – of how language could be dismantled and played with. This notion was made explicit on the cover of *Alpha/Omega*, the magazine for which Dulab wrote: it sported a clown taking apart and juggling the letters of the masthead. If a soldier-reader might have been encouraged to draw conclusions about the material and artificial nature of language from this cover image, then the manner in which he read the magazine on whose cover the image appeared (or Dulab's glossaries in it) must have inspired similar insights about the materiality of print. Scanning, browsing and searching are ways of reading that underline the material form of what is read. Dictionaries and periodicals are not only print artefacts that are dipped into and put down rather than read privately and sustainably; they are often carried into the streets. Military dictionaries came in pocket-size editions so that they could be consulted while on the move. Newspapers, too, had 'a palpable, material presence in the streets', as one scholar notes: they were sold by hawkers, advertised on newsstands and newspaper bulletin boards, and read on café terraces and public transport.[58]

Alongside Spiro's dictionaries, Dulab's glossaries and Forster's *Egyptian Mail*, soldiers would resort to a travel guide, which required being read in a similarly fragmented, interrupted way (thus throwing into relief its own materiality). Guides to destinations such as Palestine, Syria, Lebanon, Judea and the Dead Sea were published by the British military in Cairo.[59] The standard guide to Alexandria, Evaristo Breccia's *Alexandria ad Aegyptum*, was translated from the original French into English during the war. Known as the chronicler of the modern tourist in his fiction (from 'The Story of a Panic' and *Where Angels Fear to Tread* to *A Room with a View*), Forster also tried his hand at the genre of the guidebook.[60] '[A]s I went to and fro to my work in Alexandria, and joggled over the waste spaces where the ancient city had once stood,' he reminisced in 1956, 'I began to think I should like to write a Guide Book to the complex city.'[61] *Alexandria: A History and a Guide*, which grew out of a lecture Forster delivered to convalescing troops, was written with English-speaking soldiers in mind. The novelist had envisioned these soldiers 'walking about singly or in groups with the convenient little volume in their hands'.[62] The volume offered a sense of direction in the disorienting landscape – often quite literally in the form of forceful, precise instructions and hand-drawn maps. 'The Rue Rosette now passes the Native Courts (left) and reaches the Municipal Buildings,' we read. 'Behind the latter, a few yards up the Rue du Musée, is the Municipal Library; go up the steps opposite the entrance gate; push the door.'[63] Though a travel guide was an unlikely source, such instructions must have felt familiar to the soldier, whose wartime everyday, regimented and scripted, was marked by a much more comprehensive loss of agency.

'Convenient little volume' in hand, the soldier was made to move and made to see. Like the dictionary and the colonial newspaper, the manner in which the travel guide provided a sense of orientation in foreign terrain was fostered through the way in which the book was laid out and conceived. Forster was drawn to the genre because it constitutes, he felt, 'a branch of literature which follows its own laws'.[64] *Alexandria: A History and a Guide* is based on routes in and around the city rather than on chapters – 'the ~~sense~~ spirit of a procession is to inform it,' its author wrote in 1919.[65] Additionally, the book contains cross references between its introductory history section and the actual guide to encourage ease of movement between past and present. As the novelist explained:

> The 'History' is written in short sections, and at the end of each section are references to the second part – the 'Guide'. *On these references the chief utility of the book depends*, so the reader is begged to take special note of them: they may help him to link the present and the past. Suppose, for instance, he has read in the History about the Pharos: at the end of the section he will find references to Fort Kait Bey where the Pharos stood, to Abousir where there is a miniature replica of it, and to the Coin Room in the Museum, where it appears on the moneys of Domitian and Hadrian.[66]

For Forster, the guide was meant as an object to be used on the spot, and with this in mind it was printed in a light and small edition.[67] To turn the guide clockwise, so as to read a map, was to recognise the book as an object in space.

Or: to move through the guide in the way the novelist intended – picking it up and leafing through its pages, tracing references and in the process feeling the pages pass through one's hands – was to be made aware of its materiality (Forster initially insisted on lavish illustrations, for 'the casual purchaser opens a book of this sort to see if it is full of pictures').[68] One leapt through the book as the book itself leapt through time. 'Reading one must not ignore the writer's instructions – to go to-and-fro between Parts I and II,' an early reader, Elizabeth Bowen, observed. 'Good: so I did.'[69]

This much is evident: for a soldier or nurse in wartime Cairo and Alexandria, navigating these foreign cities on their own invariably meant carrying around colonial newspapers, glossaries, dictionaries or travel guides. To dip into these documents, taken up and put down rather than read consecutively, was to be constantly reminded of their status as print artefacts. For some readers, it must have called attention to the materiality of language itself – a point, as I go on to show, that becomes especially pertinent in Forster's encounters with other material objects of writing, such as shop signs and monument inscriptions. From these examples, however, it is clear that the war was a key moment in the modernist history of the book: in many ways, it helped motivate an interest in thinking about writing in more material terms. While the conflict did not bring dictionaries, newspapers and glossaries into existence per se, its colonial front did provide a context in which their use became much more commonplace. It created a need to which E. M. Forster, as the author of *Alexandria: A History and a Guide* and contributor to the *Egyptian Mail*, shrewdly responded.

Egypt's Streetscape I: Shop Signs

Spiro's dictionaries and Forster's *Alexandria: A History and a Guide* occupied a central place in the colonial enterprise. Coming in the tradition of *Description de l'Égypte*, a monumental survey commissioned by Napoleon after he invaded the country in 1798, but published many years later, these volumes constituted attempts at rendering the colonised state legible for a foreign audience and thus facilitated colonial rule and repression.[70] Put simply, such books functioned as veiled means of control, turning their authors, Forster included, into the empire's accomplices – a role the novelist was conscious of and felt uncomfortable about, and which ultimately led him to grow into a vocal proponent of Egyptian independence.[71] As Timothy Mitchell has argued in his landmark history, *Colonising Egypt*:

> the colonial project would try and re-order Egypt to appear as a world enframed. Egypt was to be ordered up as something object-like. In other words, it was to be made picture-like and legible, rendered available to political and economic calculation. Colonial power required the country to become readable, like a book, in our own sense of such a term.[72]

Scanning a dictionary for clues (or a guidebook, or a map, or an English newspaper) is much like scanning the street for signs.[73] If the war had newly shown the relevance of such print artefacts, driven by the massive influx of foreigners in Egypt, then the conflict also brought an avalanche of English signs to the built environments of places like Alexandria and Cairo. These signs, too, had been erected in great numbers in response to the arrival of the troops, helping to make Egypt 'readable, like a book'.

'Everything has meaning,' declared Virginia Woolf in passing in 1920, 'placards leaning against doorways – names above shop-windows'.[74] Forster grasped the truth behind this claim, as his fascination with the words on public display in Egyptian streets, from military notices forbidding entry to commercial signs advertising restaurants, took hold. For the novelist, encounters with these objects – emblematic of much vaguer, less immediately visible phenomena such as propaganda and failing political discourses – drew the wartime epistemological crisis into sharper focus. As Yair Wallach shows, in his history of urban text in the Middle East, signs and other public forms of writing were ubiquitous in the streetscapes of the region: ceramic street nameplates, stone inscriptions in mosques, bank notes, advertisement posters, labels, house numbers, banners, slogans and graffiti. Little-noticed, half-erased, fragmentary, made from many materials and composed in as many scripts, these artefacts marked a clear-cut break with what Walter Benjamin termed the 'pretentious gestures of the book'.[75] Indeed, as scholars have begun to point out, street signs are far from trivial; they challenge, David Henkin argued, 'the disproportionate weight [attached] to the novel as the paradigmatic object of literate consumption'.[76] Signs, as I will illustrate, emphasise a reading experience that turns around looking as much as reading, underscoring the visual and material qualities of the text on display and hence betraying the artificial, arbitrary nature of language. Engaging with these objects, instead of reading papers for less immediately visible traces of propaganda, was a way for Forster to grapple with this sense of crisis.

In 'Gippo English', one of his contributions to the *Egyptian Mail*, Forster reflected on these issues. Commercial signs had been erected across Cairo and Alexandria from the moment the troops had been stationed nearby – as a gesture both of goodwill and of good marketing. Looking back, Forster remembered these signs fondly:

> In the early years of the war there was in Heliopolis a certain street that offered a rich harvest to the philologist. It ran from the centre of the city to the Aerodrome – indeed it still runs, but its richness has departed. For in those days the Aerodrome was full of Colonial troops, and the street thither was lined with shops and booths and lean-tos, all decorated with hospitable inscriptions.[77]

Many of these inscriptions had disappeared, or been replaced, by the time of Forster's writing, late in 1917. In fact, the novelist regretted never copying them before they had vanished, but he remembered a few phrases: 'Here is Alexandre's garden where Australian heroes eat and shoot,' read one sign at a Heliopolis restaurant; a nearby barber's shop was advertised as 'Antiseptic Red Cross civility and cleanliness', alongside a shop named, simply, 'Ten Thousand Things'.[78] On the tram from downtown Cairo to Abassia, another contemporary witness thought the signs he spotted through the carriage window would not have been out of place in an issue of *Punch*: 'COFFEE CHOP OF EUROP' and 'HIGH T LIF TAILOR'.[79] There are clear racist undertones at work in Forster's 'Gippo English', whose satirical sharpness comes at the expense of a colonised people.[80] At the same time, this collage of signs instilled in the novelist a sense of appreciation for the inventive, inadvertent ways in which Egyptians bent and stretched the English language. For, these public words 'feared nothing' and 'attempted all things both in prose and rhyme'.[81] In this sense, Forster's little-known commercial signs resemble, but also give an important global turn to, the much-studied puns and wordplay of army slang ('the overwhelming impression', Julian Walker noted in his study of the languages of the First World War, 'is of people using language as play, a deadly game in cases of propaganda, but creative nevertheless').[82] Such play was not always intentional; it was also, Forster recognised, not only the prerogative of the European soldier. Another notice board (on display at a fruit stall in Alexandria, 'The Garden of the Hesperides', which its owner had freely translated as 'Le Jardin des Soirées') reminded the novelist, coming out of the local cinema, that 'life can be more beautiful and amusing than art – an agreable reminder [sic]'.[83] The film he had just seen had been disappointing: 'A fruit shop beats it as poetry,' he observed.[84]

That many of these placards had faded from view by the time 'Gippo English' appeared in the *Egyptian Mail*, in December 1917, was proof, so Forster believed, of the way in which the war eradicated a sense of individuality. Over the years, the English of the Egyptians (and, with it, their signs) grew less original, more uniform, more stereotyped: every Englishman became 'Johnny', while 'finish' simply denoted a closed bar, a departing train, a refusal to sell and a wish for sleep.[85] '[O]ne's summer walks are no longer brightened by the wish of A Happy New Year,' Forster noted by way of example. 'And, saddest of all,' he added:

> the inscription has gone that once guarded the western entrance to Montazah. It dated from Khedivial times, and stood not far from the sea, among a wilderness of broken palings and sand. And it announced, in faded and tremulous capitals: 'No admission this way even if the Fence has Fallen Down'. In Arabic such inscriptions may be common

but in English they produce a poignant effect. This crazy notice board symbolised to me the attempt of the East to resist the Western methods – an attempt that must always fail. The notice board has gone, and the Khedive from behind it, and Montazah is now a Red Cross Hospital – not 'antiseptic Red Cross' like the barber's shop but plain Red Cross – within whose enclosure the native orderlies cry 'Hullo Johnny!' to the patients, and the patients reply 'Hullo Johnny!'[86]

Loosely and oddly translated, but with a certain poetic effect as a result, the phrase on the sign had meant to keep colonial tourists out of the grounds of the Khedive's summer palace at Montazah (a place Forster once likened to paradise).[87] Its capital letters and forceful language indicate that the sign dated from a time when the Khedive held some authority; its literal translation from the Arabic (to 'poignant effect') might even be read as betraying a wider refusal to conform to the rules of English grammar and conduct. However, that the sign stood 'faded and tremulous', and 'among a wilderness of broken palings', when Forster first happened upon it, suggests that the Khedive's authority may have waned over the years.[88] Not long after December 1914, when Egypt was proclaimed a British Protectorate, the summer palace was turned into a Red Cross hospital. The loss Forster mourns here is complex: not just of a sign, but of the Khedive behind it (a time when the Egyptians still held a semblance of self-determination) and of the creativity with language that marked this pre- and early war period (before the arrival, en masse, of British and Anzac troops made English a lingua franca on the streets of Alexandria and Cairo).

The point Forster raised in the *Egyptian Mail* is that shop signs showed the war's impact on language. Encountered affectively and tangibly, they were visual markers of a moment of linguistic crisis. The novelist made a similar observation in 'Army English', a vignette that appeared in the same colonial newspaper, on 12 January 1919:

> There is a certain notice past which I occasionally hurry on awestruck feet. At first sight it has nothing intimidating about it, being modestly painted in black capitals upon a board of wood. But it runs as follows: 'No person will loiter within the vicinity of these steps', and I know from the diction that it has been put up, or as they would say 'erected', by the Military Authorities, and that if I did not hurry, my bright young life might come to an end. It is an example of Army English.[89]

Composed in 'Army English' and carrying more authority than the Khedive's notice board at Montazah, the sign was difficult to decipher. Pulling out the Oxford Dictionary, 'a shallow pre-war compilation', would prove of little help.[90] What the notice meant to convey, Forster clarified for his readers, was simply 'Don't loiter', but the military had rendered English much too convoluted and stale, choking the writer, as George Orwell noted of a similar tendency after World War II, 'like tea leaves blocking a sink'.[91] As he was drafting 'Army English', Forster admitted in a letter to Robert Trevelyan: 'Life here goes on as usual, though I grow increasingly irritable and increasingly unable to communicate that fact to others.'[92] The reason he identified as the source of this inability to communicate was official language, which 'weigh[s] one down like masses of decaying flesh'.[93]

War made Forster a philologist. In more ways than one, the context in which he published his investigations of the written words imprinted on the built environments of Cairo and Alexandria – tangible reminders of how the war had rendered language more standardised ('Johnny') and formal ('No person will loiter within the vicinity') – brings these exact issues unequivocally into view. The 12 January 1919 issue of the *Mail*, in which 'Army English' appeared, opens with a propaganda piece, 'Britain's Fighting Aeroplanes: Why Germany Failed in the Air', featured alongside ads for a language school across from the Shepherd's Hotel in Cairo ('Special Terms for Military') and an article on 'the tongue' and 'its abuse' in the Bible.[94] Such abuses were condoned by the British military in Egypt, which placed propaganda pieces in the local papers and put on 'lectures on Armenian atrocities' in Alexandria's hospitals, as Forster witnessed, in order to re-educate its convalescing soldiers.[95] Reporting for the *Mail*, the novelist attended one such lecture, wondering about the loud man 'shouting and waving his arms' and choosing words 'not because he understands them but in the hope that they will stick'.[96] 'When a man makes a statement now', complained Forster, 'it seldom has any relation to the ~~truth~~ facts.'[97] These and similar remarks – of 'the decent young men' convalescing in Alexandria's hospitals over whose heads hung 'solemn edifying bloody lies' – may explain why Forster was never recruited by Britain's propaganda machine, famously started with a secret meeting of twenty-five men of letters convened by C. F. G. Masterman in September 1914 (when the novelist was still in England).[98] Masterman and Forster had been Cambridge acquaintants after all. The former served on the editorial board of the *Independent Review*, to which the latter contributed his earliest pieces, and also laudingly reviewed three of Forster's novels for the *Daily News* and *Nation*. If Forster was ever invited to the propaganda meeting at Wellington House (and there is, to the best of my knowledge, no evidence that he was), then he chose not to attend.[99]

As Mark Wollaeger has argued, this timely curiosity about 'the subtle ways in which facts are already and always mediated' registered across a wide range of modernist texts, including, as I show here, Forster's letters and journalism.[100] However, a more poignant trace of the military's hold over language in that copy of the *Egyptian Mail* in which 'Army English' was published – and a more directly visible marker than what Wollaeger calls the 'epistemological decline of the fact' – is the blank column on its front page, which must have been created when part of an article was cut out at the last moment.[101] Traces of censorship litter the paper. Egypt had found itself in what Forster termed 'an anomalous position' at the outbreak of hostilities in 1914.[102] While technically under Ottoman sovereignty, the country had been effectively ruled by the British after they had purchased its national debts and had taken control of the Suez Canal. As soon as the Ottomans entered the First World War in November, on the side of the Central Powers, Britain declared martial law in Egypt, further strengthening censorship measures already in place (such as the obligation to acquire a printing licence for the publication of a newspaper).[103] A British-run censorship office was established at the Egyptian Ministry of the Interior in Cairo; its Alexandria branch was under the direction of E. M. Forster's close friend Robert Furness. These efforts led to an eradication of local print culture: a staggering decline of 70 per cent in the appearance of new Arabic magazines and newspapers, from 278 in the 1900s to just 80 in the 1910s.[104] War, it is evident, only strengthened the intimate link Christopher Bayly discerns between the tracking of local information networks and the survival of a colonial regime.[105]

While indirectly owned by colonial and military governments, local publications in European languages, including the *Egyptian Mail*, suffered under these imperatives – rules, as Forster acknowledged, 'of more than average stupidity'.[106] Not only the columns of the *Mail*, but also those of its rival, the *Gazette*, were regularly printed blank. Robert Snelling, the *Gazette*'s wartime editor, at times had to resort to 'scissors and paste' in taking liberally from the London *Times* to fill his daily copy.[107] Even these passages were blacked out by an over-zealous military censor, while *The Times*, taking two weeks to arrive from England yet not falling under the auspices of the local censor, was for sale unabridged. The Cairo society paper *Sphinx* in turn feared, a day after Egypt was declared a British Protectorate at the end of 1914, that the 'roaring lion, the Press Censor, suddenly fall upon us with gnashings of teeth and rending of moist proof sheets at inopportune moments'.[108] Such references to the work of the censor would soon disappear from *Sphinx*'s pages in a move Forster termed a 'crowning absurdity': in wartime Egypt, censorship itself became a prohibited subject in print.[109]

Indirectly, censorship put an emphasis on the material qualities of a document: the gap on the front page of the issue of the *Egyptian Mail* in which Forster's 'Army English' appeared drew the reader's attention not to any words, but to the look of the page, much as was the case for print artefacts such as the dictionaries and travel guides discussed above. (In fact, the many typos in the *Egyptian Mail*, which Forster often complained about, had the same fortuitous effect, emphasising the curious, affective materiality of the document.)[110] Such a shift in focus, from the message to the medium, ultimately underlies Forster's wartime investment in shop signs, examined in the pages of the censored newspaper. By their nature, these signs were displayed to be seen; they begged to be looked at. From the 'crazy notice board' at Montazah, in 'Gippo English', to the one erected by the military authorities near a flight of steps in Alexandria, in 'Army English', these placards were prominently placed and painted in capital letters, which, perhaps, may have 'faded' over time, but certainly once aimed to foster quick comprehension. At some point in the war, an Egyptian owner renamed his Cairo eatery 'NEW BELGIUM ARMENIAN RESTAURANT CO', alluding to the occupation of Belgium and Armenia by the Central Powers (Figure 2.2). Forster probably never ate here, but he made mention of a similar place in Heliopolis, 'Heroic Belgium's Restaurant', whose name change he understood as responding to the 'larger issues of the war'.[111] For both restaurants, the new name was clearly meant to target the troops, an untapped source of customers. With this in mind, a large sign in capital letters was put up alongside an English menu on the wall in order to advertise the establishment. The reference to the war in the restaurant's name, and the Aussie slogan 'This joint is dinkum', must have appealed to the Anzac soldiers camping nearby.[112] But the sign must also have captured their attention simply because of its typography, erected in capitals and large print, and hence visible from afar and laying claim to an aura of authority.[113]

Still, despite its confidence, the sign for 'NEW BELGIUM ARMENIAN RESTAURANT CO' would have evoked a sense of estrangement in the reader. It is a clear example of how a sign, as a material object, was a visible reminder of a language in crisis. An alienating combination of political references to the

Figure 2.2 Restaurant sign, Egypt. Australian War Memorial (PS1275).

war ('Belgium', 'Armenian'), Australian dialect ('dinkum'), spelling mistakes ('Belgium' instead of 'Belgian') and capitalist lingo ('co') did not make for easy reading, given the restaurant's location in larger Cairo, where English was supposed to be out of place.[114] My point is that a collage of such discourses and errors, displayed in large, capital letters, brought language newly into view; its unintelligibility drew attention to the artificial qualities of these words. If Egypt's signs – from 'No person will loiter within the vicinity of these steps' to 'COFFEE CHOP OF EUROP' – were difficult to decipher, then the war had a role to play in this, for it gave rise to a drastic increase of English speakers in Egypt who suddenly had to be catered for, and it introduced its own convoluted, standardised and stale military diction. While 'hurry[ing] on awestruck feet', E. M. Forster was forced to stop and *look* at these signs, rather than *read* them in passing, because their words no longer held a natural, immediate, imperceptible connection to reality – a language, then, which in wartime had become newly disassociated from the world it purported to represent. With the partial loss of that signifying relationship, war had rendered words into arbitrary, material objects.

The defamiliarising effect of words *as matter* is a common modernist preoccupation. The theoretical works of Ferdinand de Saussure, Hugo von Hofmannsthal and Viktor Shklovsky, among others, were founded on precisely such a premise, which also underpins experiments with typography in much avant-garde poetry.[115] However, that the war evoked similar views, that a novelist like E. M. Forster was met with a feeling of alienation as he encountered the crisis of language in the streets of wartime Alexandria, has never been fully explored. Engagements with the material objects of writing took centre stage on the colonial front, where the war inspired Forster's peers to examine language's material qualities anew. As Allyson Booth has argued, the conflict encouraged modernist writers 'not to see through language but to see language'.[116] For Forster, then, who does not feature in Booth's argument, Alexandria's streetscape provided a palpable context – much more so than the often-studied 'epistemological decline of the fact' in the papers – for grappling with the ways the war revealed language's artificial nature. Tensions between the meaning and materiality of words convened not only around the street sign or the censored newspaper page, but also, and much more explicitly, around the illegible and unintelligible inscriptions on the monuments of Ancient Egypt. At the time, these monuments, too, came into their own as symbols of the epistemological crisis brought on by the war.

Egypt's Streetscape II: Ancient Inscriptions

If there are many Egypts, as E. M. Forster once claimed, then the 'Egypt of the Pharaohs' most moves tourists and popular novelists.[117] Servicemen and women in the First World War were no exception. In a rare photograph from

Figure 2.3 Billet room in Egypt, 1914–15. Imperial War Museum (Q 102963).

the first year of fighting that survives today in the collection of the Imperial War Museum, we catch a glimpse of the billet room of two lieutenants in the Manchester Regiment, Frederick Hardman and Jim Clegg (Figure 2.3). The room these two men shared contains the usual clutter: uniforms, books, photographs, two camp beds, two chamber pots, an oil lamp for reading. The photograph could have been taken anywhere, were it not for the designs that decorate the walls, which Hardman and Clegg probably bought as souvenirs. In showing us images from the times of the pharaohs, especially images of Egyptian gods, these wall hangings suggest that this was a billet room in Egypt, most likely in Heliopolis, just outside of Cairo, where the Manchester Regiment was stationed. Wilfred Owen, a better-known lieutenant in that regiment than either Hardman or Clegg, once wished he could have been billeted there; Rupert Brooke, too, spent three days' leave happily riding camels around the pyramids and buying souvenirs in the Cairo bazaars.[118] 'Instead of being sent to the Ypres Salient', one of Forster's acquaintances in the Royal Army Medical Corps wrote, 'we had been detailed for service in a place [...] where most of us, at any rate, were actually looking forward to enjoying new sights and scenes.'[119] Hundreds of other photographs from the period now serve as proof of such long-lost enjoyment: British nurses standing in front of the pyramids at Giza and Sakkara; Anzac soldiers posing for the camera among the ruins at the Siwa Oasis; Lt. Col. Byrne sitting next to the enormous statue of Rameses II, at the Temple of Karnak, in Luxor, and vanishing by comparison. The First World War marked what Jay Winter has called the 'Kodak revolution'.[120]

Some knowledge and much ingenuity were needed to make sense of these remnants. In the Alexandria of the 1910s, much of what was left was, in Forster's words, 'sea or stones [and] nothing else'.[121] His writing, especially his travel guide and the occasional piece for the *Mail*, existed to help the imagination reconstruct these half-buried remains: 'the past has to do full-time work if the present is to work at all,' he wrote elsewhere.[122] The city's famous Ptolemaic lighthouse is a case in point: all that still stood at the time of the First World War was a battered fort and mosque, damaged during the British bombardment of Alexandria in 1882. 'Again and again, looking at the mosque, have I tried to multiply its height by five, and thus build up its predecessor,' Forster admitted to readers of the *Athenaeum*. 'The effort always failed.'[123] Such an archaeology of the mind, the work of building up and multiplying in height, became a particular fondness of the novelist, who in Alexandria began 'touring in time, since space is a military zone'.[124] The same hermeneutic movement was turned into the topic of a short, decidedly modernist poem by C. P. Cavafy.[125] 'In the Month of Athyr' was one of Forster's favourites: he quoted it, in full, in his assessment of Cavafy's poetry for the *Athenaeum*, where it appeared for the first time in English translation in the company of Woolf, Mansfield, Eliot and Russell. In the 1917 poem, a speaker tries to interpret an ancient tombstone and find out something about its dedicatee, like a latter-day Pip from the opening lines to *Great Expectations*:

> It is hard to read ... on the ancient stone.
> 'Lord Jesus Christ' ... I make out the word 'Soul'.
> 'In the month of Athyr ... Lucius fell asleep'.
> His age is mentioned ... 'He lived years ...' –
> The letters KZ show ... that he fell asleep young.
> In the damaged part I see the words ... 'Him ... Alexandrian'.
> Then come three lines ... much mutilated.
> But I can read a few words ... perhaps 'our tears' and 'sorrows'.
> And again: 'Tears' ... and: 'for us his friends mourning'.
> I think Lucius ... was much beloved.
> In the month of Athyr ... Lucius fell asleep.[126]

All of this must have sounded incredibly familiar – 'poignant' is the word Forster used – to the *Athenaeum*'s readers, who first encountered the poem in May 1919: the tears, the sorrow, the gravestone, the uncertainty ('perhaps'), the young life now lost (Lucius was twenty-seven, 'KZ', when he died).[127] With its many ellipses, the poem takes on the look of a censored text, suggesting an intimate connection between the kind of deductive reading in which an amateur-archaeologist and a wartime reader engaged.[128] The way in which the poetic 'I' attempts to unlock the 'ancient stone' is much like the way in which E. M. Forster tried to decipher the signs put up in Alexandria's streets in the years between 1915 and 1919. Both wartime confrontations with the material world of Egypt – ancient and modern – left behind an uncanny feeling that language itself might be material-like.

Like Cavafy's, Forster's Egyptian work depicts many such encounters with ancient stones that were 'hard to read'.[129] His *Guide*, for instance, directed visitors to Alexandria's Graeco-Roman Museum, where among Roman coins and mummies 'not good enough for Cairo' soldiers would have come across a cast of the Rosetta Stone (the original of which, though discovered nearby, was kept in the British Museum in London).[130] Its trilingual inscriptions in hieroglyphs, Demotic and Ancient Greek would have been unintelligible to most of these soldiers, but not the reputation of this famed stone, which had enabled Jean-François Champollion to decipher the hieroglyphic writing system. Forster, too, could make little out of the carved engravings, even though his grandfather authored a study on the languages and scripts of Ancient Egypt.[131] In the *Egyptian Gazette*, in one of his earliest pieces of local journalism, the novelist wrote up an account of a similar moment: Eliza Fay, travelling through the country in the late eighteenth century, failed to decode the hieroglyphs on Cleopatra's Needle, an obelisk for Thotmes III which then still stood in Alexandria.[132] Equally clueless must have been the visitor to Pompey's Pillar, who would resort to *Alexandria: A History and a Guide* for information on a 'subordinate monument' preserved by 'the accident of time':

> 84 feet high and about 7 thick; made of red granite from Assouan. An imposing but ungraceful object. [...] On the eastern face (nearest turnstile) is a block of green granite with an inscription in Greek in honour of Arsinoe, the sister and wife of Ptolemy Philadelphus (p. 22). On the opposite face (upside down in a recess) is the figure and hieroglyph of Seti I (B.C. 1350), suggesting the great age of the settlement on Rhakotis. Why and when was the pillar put up? Probably to the Emperor Diocletian, about A.D. 297. There is a four line Greek inscription to him on the granite base on the western side, about 10 feet up. It is illegible and indeed invisible from the ground. Generations of scholars have worked at it with the following result: – 'To the most just Emperor, the tutelary God of Alexandria, Diocletian the invincible: Postumus, prefect of Egypt'.[133]

It is easy to imagine the contemporary reader arriving at Pompey's Pillar, taking out Forster's *Guide* and jumping through the text – '(p. 22)' – in pursuit of references to the figure of Ptolemy Philadelphus. As I argued above, this global war brought on a new familiarity with dictionaries and travel guides as objects: the interrupted and fragmented way in which we read them directs our initial attention to the materiality of the text. That sense of print as material and artificial is further reinforced here through the object of encounter: 'an inscription in Greek', a 'hieroglyph of Seti I (B.C. 1350)', 'a four line Greek inscription [...] illegible and indeed invisible'. Staring at the ancient stone, the soldier may not have made much of these engravings, and the guidebook's claims likewise are mostly a matter of informed speculation ('probably', 'illegible', 'invisible'). Over time, the gap between sign and signified had widened such that these ancient writing systems had become visual and material in the first instance, and only later (if at all) were they understood. The public words on display in wartime Alexandria – not only signs but also engravings on local monuments such as the Rosetta Stone, Cleopatra's Needle and Pompey's Pillar – were looked *at* rather than looked *through*. These stones only spoke, as Forster tellingly put it, 'dead words'.[134] The increasingly unbridgeable divide between the modernist and the ancient past developed into the topic of a handful of modernist texts, such as Ezra Pound's 'The Tomb at Akr Çaar', in which a soul addresses the lifeless body of a mummified Egyptian with which it had been entombed for five millennia: 'I have read out the gold upon the wall / And wearied out my thought upon the signs / [...] you say / No word, day after day.'[135]

As the casual reader turned over the page of his *Guide* – composed as a series of routes, that is, informed by what Forster termed the 'spirit of procession' – he or she would have come across the catacombs of Kom es Chogafa, which were a few hundred metres down the road from where the Pillar stood and which had only recently been laid bare when a donkey had fallen through the earth.[136] The tombs were littered with the iconography of Egypt's Pharaonic and Hellenic pasts: columns with capitals and pilasters with square papyrus, limestone statues, reliefs – 'Left, a king before a god (Chons?)', we read in the *Guide*, 'right, two "Canopic" deities, one ape headed, one a mummy'.[137] The confusion was complete upon reaching the tomb chamber containing three sarcophagi:

> They are classical in style – decorated with festoons of fruit or flowers, Medusa heads, Ox skulls, &c. The lids do not take off; the mummies would have been pushed in from the passage behind (*See* below). But as a matter of fact none of the three sarcophagi have ever been occupied; it is part of the queerness of Kom-es-Chogafa that its vast and elaborate apparatus for mourning should culminate in a void. In the niche over each sarcophagus are bas reliefs, Egyptian in style but executed with imperfect understanding.[138]

Once more, the author, and with him the reader of the *Guide*, arrived at the far limits of understanding. Forster had no explanation for the queer void at the heart of the catacombs, suggesting that 'one must not read too much into them or into anything here'.[139] However, facing the unintelligibility of a place of mourning, as is also clear from Cavafy's 'In the Month of Athyr', was an experience familiar and legible in new ways in the years around Forster's 1917 visit to the tomb. '[H]istory repeats herself, just as she has done in the Cemeteries,' the former wrote of the toll the war exerted elsewhere in his *Guide*.[140]

Implicitly, Forster appears to ask his reader to draw a connection between the unintelligible iconography of these ancient places – 'Left, a god before a king (Chons?)', 'a four line Greek inscription [...] illegible and indeed invisible' – and the unintelligibility of the war itself. Much like shop signs, ancient inscriptions became symbols for the wartime crisis of language. Encounter after encounter with objects in Forster's Egyptian writing, this chapter aims to illustrate, circle around such failures to read and decipher, hence underscoring the artificial qualities of language. Turned into matter in this way, words themselves became part of the material world of war. As such, Forster's wartime interest in the look of language begins to fit squarely within a modernist tradition that joins together (among many others) Hart Crane, Sergei Eisenstein, Charles Olson, Gertrude Stein, William Faulkner and Guillaume Apollinaire, whose experiments with picture-poems discussed in Chapter 1 stem from an early fascination with ideographic writings, especially Chinese and cuneiform characters.[141] At the time of the First World War, the Chinese character loomed large in the modernist imagination (in Forster's *Howards End*, too, Tibby Schlegel is found reading a Chinese grammar, in his room at Oxford, as his landlady walks in with cutlets).[142] Like hieroglyphs, Chinese characters were thought to be visual and immediate: 'you can *see* it's a horse,' Henri Gaudier-Brzeska famously remarked of 馬.[143] For Ernest Fenollosa, whose *The Chinese Written Character as a Medium for Poetry* Ezra Pound edited during the war years, Chinese showed us language at its very beginning, when signs represent the visible world before they evolve to a level of abstraction.[144] Visual immediacy is key to the modernist's concern with these ancient scripts: the ideogram was a call to see rather than to read, in the understanding that its meaning could be deduced by looking. Indeed, Ezra Pound insisted one 'LOOKED, really looked at an ideogram', in words whose typography – typical of the poet – appears to insist on the same point.[145] In the Chinese character, the wartime modernists found 'a whole basis of aesthetic', as Pound once asserted: it inspired a poetry, Imagism, the language of which was meant to be visual and immediate in comparable ways.[146]

Much of this is a familiar story. Less known, however, is the extent to which the First World War prompted a renewed interest in this modernist tradition of looking at rather than through language. In *Signs of the Americas: A Poetics of Pictography, Hieroglyphs and Khipu*, Edgar Garcia recently asked how an apparently defunct sign can remain 'historically interactive', given its 'archival silencings, colonial interdicts, and transcultural corrosions'.[147] Can we think of Forster's 'dead words', of which he began to take note around the time Pound turned Chinese characters into 'a whole basis of aesthetic', as interactive in precisely these terms? As Christopher Bush argues in *Ideographic Modernism: China, Writing, Media*, the question of the material forms of language was precisely about the connection between linguistic form and social-historical consciousness.[148] For him, the modernists started reading about Chinese characters at a moment when new forms of writing, such as the photograph and the phonograph, encouraged awareness of the medium rather than the message.[149] Jesse Schotter's *Hieroglyphic Modernisms: Writing and New Media in the Twentieth Century*, in turn, provides another explanation of this historical use of hieroglyphs, making a compelling case for modernism's place in a tradition that connected visual languages with aspirations for a more perfect communication.[150] What one does with and reads into ideograms, then, depends on one's historical moment. For Forster and his contemporaries in wartime Egypt, that moment was the First World War. In their writing, ancient scripts came to symbolise not so much a project for more perfect communication, but rather its opposite. The illegibility of these 'dead words', reducing them to material objects, was paradoxically what made them newly relevant, as they began to figure as symbols for the war's representational crisis. Forster's contemporaries in Egypt, I want to suggest, looked at hieroglyphs much in the same way they initially looked at the censored pages of the *Mail* or at signs displaying 'COFFEE CHOP OF EUROP', 'Antiseptic Red Cross civility and cleanliness' and 'No person will loiter within the vicinity of these steps': as words that are material and artificial, in the first instance, rather than referential and intelligible.

These tensions come together in 'The Register of Um-Nefer: A Remarkable M.S.', a spoof article published in the first issue of *The Gnome*, the organ of the Middle East Brigade in the Royal Flying Corps (Figure 2.4).[151] It was for sale only briefly, in November 1916, at hut no. 21 on the RFC base in Abu-Qir, just outside of Alexandria, from where Forster would take off on his first-ever flight a year later.[152] The article in *The Gnome* details the discovery of an Ancient Egyptian manuscript on the grounds of the aerodrome. The facts, apparently, were as follows: a flying officer was delving 'among the ruins of ancient Canopus' to construct another landing strip and in doing so discovered a papyrus roll dating back to the time of Thutmosis III, around 1400 BC, which had ended up in Cleopatra's library in Alexandria.[153] Like Cavafy's 'In the Month of Athyr', the piece in *The Gnome* presents the officer as an accidental amateur-archaeologist, a role increasingly common in attrition warfare (it is only natural, as Paul Saint-Amour put it, that 'a war that excavates will awaken the geological, paleontological, and archaeological imaginations of its participants').[154] The four panels of the newly discovered papyrus, most likely drawn by Stuart Reid, a painter in the RFC, were published alongside a corresponding article:[155]

Figure 2.4 A page from *The Gnome*, 1916. The British Library (P.P.4039.wes).

The first panel illustrated represents the Highest Aviation Authorities, probably resident at Memphis, at sunrise. Below is a busy scene at Abu-Qir at the same hour. It may reasonably be inferred that Abu-Qir had been accused of lack of energy. We discover the Highest Authorities symbolised by the sleeper; over him are the emblems of authority. At the bedhead a slave carries his morning tea: below are other slaves preparing the food for the day. The text runs: – 'Salatis found land very proper for his purpose and which lay upon the Bubastite Channel. This he levelled, and made very great sheds thereon and very strong by a most numerous garrison.'[156]

The article progresses in the same manner: a second panel illustrates cadets on the flying ground; a third shows the authorities feasting at sundown and being attended to by slaves; a final image, set during the Technical Training course, displays 'a Squad Commander reporting a member of the class – for not being properly dressed'.¹⁵⁷ Some motifs in these panels – the enthroned king, the figure with the upraised arms, the Nubians among the trees – borrow from the battle scenes carved into the forecourt of a temple of Rameses II at Beit el-Wali, which were well known at the time from plaster casts on display in the British Museum.¹⁵⁸ Still, even without any knowledge of Ancient Egyptian iconography, and without the corresponding article offering translations of the hieroglyphs in the margins, the contemporary reader of *The Gnome* would have been able to make sense of these images, which speak for themselves. The papyrus read like a comic strip about their own lives on the military base. On multiple occasions, Forster, too, wrote of the visually attractive character of Ancient Egyptian sources, of the 'exquisite deformities who haunted Egyptian art in the reign of Akhnaton' and of 'the beauty and freshness of the colours of the human figures and animals' on the famous Papyrus of Ani.¹⁵⁹

When faced with the material remains of Ancient Egypt, the soldier's imperative was to look rather than to read. In fact, 'The Register of Um-Nefer: A Remarkable M.S.' turned the way in which the scripts of Ancient Egypt defied easy decipherment into its focal point (much like the 'tablets bearing sacred inscriptions', in *To the Lighthouse*, which stand in the chambers of a woman's mind and heart – 'like the treasures in the tombs of kings' – never to be revealed).¹⁶⁰ Such was the fate, for the time being, of the hieroglyphs in the last panel, as the author of 'The Register of Um-Nefer' explains:

> The text is too involved to allow of a translation at the time of going to press, but among the hieroglyphics are pictured aerial bombs as well as diagrams of the clock code and method of squaring maps. The whole of the papyrus illustrated we may term the first chapter, and is a dignified and gentle assurance to the High Authorities that even during normal periods of rest the 'land on the Bubastite Channel' is a scene of unceasing toil. International differences unfortunately prevent us from submitting the papyrus for the criticism of Dr. F. W. von Bissing, the learned author of 'Geschichte Aegyptens in Umriss'.¹⁶¹

Certain aspects of the war were 'too involved' in similar ways to allow of a description or translation – 'unspeakable' and 'surpass[ing] my power', as Forster himself admitted.¹⁶² My point, then, is not simply that these stunning images on the papyrus draw our initial attention, but that we are prompted to consider the hieroglyphs printed alongside them in the same light; we approach them in terms of the visual and material, not the textual (a perspective implicit in the many censored passages that turned *The Gnome* itself into a curiously material artefact).¹⁶³ These symbols recall Hegel's famous description of hieroglyphs as mere 'mute works of art', and, like the engravings Forster detected on Alexandria's monuments, were looked *at* rather than looked *through*.¹⁶⁴ In this way, hieroglyphs in 'The Register of Um-Nefer' provided a vocabulary to frame the war experience – it is, after all, a thinly veiled depiction of the Abu-Qir base in 1916 – around questions of illegibility and unintelligibility. The current war, too, turned words hieroglyphic, such that they became 'too involved to allow of a translation'.

Epilogue: On to India

In 'On Not Knowing French', Virginia Woolf articulated a feeling with which E. M. Forster had grown intimately acquainted in the years between 1915 and 1919:

> In reading a language that is not one's own, consciousness is awake and keeps us aware of the surface glitter of the words; but it never suffers them to sink into that region of the mind where old habits and instincts roll them round and shape them a body rather different from their faces. [...] And if it is a delight to have a change of scene, it is also a delight to have a change of tongue. Habit has made English – the ordinary daily English of which most books are made – as colourless, as tasteless as water. French, even the French of daily use, has wine in it; it sparkles; it tingles; it has its savour. Here and there, in Saint Simon, for instance, a curious word unknown and therefore uncoloured by habit, emerges, so that we can feel it and see it apart from the text, and wonder for a moment what sort of meaning we shall fill it with when we have looked it up in the dictionary.[165]

Contending with a foreign language, or a familiar language made foreign, meant relying on the 'surface glitter of the words'. French did to Woolf what Egypt's scripts did to Forster: it made them both consider the material forms of language, to 'feel it and see it apart from the text'. For Forster, this experience was associated with a sense of loss, of crisis. His writing in the *Egyptian Mail* and *Alexandria: A History and a Guide* – print artefacts, as I have shown, which called attention to their own materiality in the way they were used – staged encounters with signs and monument inscriptions as a way of grappling with the war's linguistic crisis. Erroneous, unnecessarily formal, unintelligible, displayed in large capitals and engraved in illegible scripts, these objects threw into relief the material, visual, arbitrary nature of language. Wartime words moved away from immediacy and transparency, and towards the status of mere material objects: 'we can feel it and see it apart from the text'.

In illustrating how the war on the colonial front made language newly visible, this chapter has made two related interventions in the study of the modernist war. First, if the conflict created a widening disjunction between language and the reality it was supposed to represent, then Forster examined this crisis through an engagement with the material world of war. Not merely minds as they started to unravel, political discourses as they became corrupted, or veiled propaganda statements as they began to appear in the papers, but much more concrete encounters with shop signs and monument inscriptions provided a context to explore historical attempts at making sense of this particular aspect of the war experience. In ways still little understood, material culture was at the core of modernist responses to the conflict. Second, Forster's fascination with these shop signs and monument inscriptions, alongside the censored newspaper page or the travel guide that 'follows its own laws', demonstrates that the First World War helped revive the modernist interest in the materiality of print itself – as objects of writing were so uniquely and curiously moulded by the conflict. The war was a watershed moment in the modernist history of the book. While newspapers, dictionaries, travel guides and signboards were not wartime inventions, the conflict in the colonies made these documents newly relevant and created a renewed familiarity with them *as objects*.

E. M. Forster ultimately got through the war unscathed. In late January 1919, a few weeks before the Egyptian Revolution, he returned to London and began to direct his attention elsewhere. He sailed for Bombay two years later – '& I think for ever,' Virginia Woolf noted in her diary.[166] Marginalised in scholarship, Forster's time in Egypt has been read mainly for its implications for *A Passage to India*, which the novelist had begun in 1912 but heavily revised after his years in the Middle East. Some of his Egyptian pieces were collected in a 1923 Hogarth Press volume, *Pharos and Pharillon*, for which the Woolfs even had to buy Greek type in order to print it.[167] But they remain for the most part, as Rose Macaulay remarked in 1938, 'in the faint grey print and shaggy grey paper of the *Egyptian Mail*'.[168] Yet, in wartime Alexandria, we find the roots of a question that resurfaces at the heart of *A Passage to India*. The novel's plot is driven by an impulse to sightsee and decipher: 'I want to see the *real* India,' Miss Quested, freshly arrived from England, exclaims early on.[169] Forster's indictment of colonialism pivots around the observation that such a 'pose of "seeing India" [...] was only a form of ruling India'.[170] In its final conclusion, the novel marvels at an India that escapes from the British gaze, a refusal to conform that can be read on (and into) an inscription at a Hindu shrine. Much like the poorly translated notice at the gate to Montazah Forster examined in the *Egyptian Mail* – the odd translation and uncanny typography 'produce[d] a poignant effect', as the sign attempted 'to resist the Western methods' – the shrine in the palace at Mau, in *A Passage to India*, offers another accidental image of resistance to the coloniser's attempt to read:

> The inscriptions which the poets of the state had composed were hung where they could not be read, or had twitched their drawing-pins out of the stucco, and one of them (composed in English to indicate His

universality) consisted, by an unfortunate slip of the draughtsman, of the words, 'God si Love'.

God si Love. Is this the final message of India?[171]

There is a long history to that 'unfortunate slip', which runs through Forster's war years.

NOTES

1. Quoted in P. N. Furbank, *E. M. Forster: A Life*, vol. I (London: Secker & Warburg, 1978), p. 260.
2. In a letter dated 7 November 1914. Quoted ibid., p. 259.
3. *Selected Letters of E. M. Forster*, vol. I: 1879–1920, ed. Mary Lago and P. N. Furbank (London: Collins, 1983), p. 289: to Siegfried Sassoon, 2 May 1918.
4. In a letter to *The Times* of 14 July 1959, he described his wartime work as that of an 'amateur watchman and amateur catalogue-compiler' (p. 9).
5. Ford Madox Ford, 'A Day in Battle: Arms and the Mind', in *The Ford Madox Ford Reader*, ed. Sondra J. Stang (London: Paladin, 1987), pp. 456–61 (p. 456).
6. 'Henry James's First Interview', in *Henry James on Culture: Collected Essays on Politics and the American Social Scene*, ed. Pierre A. Walker (Lincoln: University of Nebraska Press, 1999), pp. 138–45 (p. 144).
7. See, for instance, Paul Fussell, *The Great War and Modern Memory* (New York: Oxford University Press, 1977) and Randall Stevenson, *Literature and the Great War: 1914–18* (Oxford: Oxford University Press, 2014), chapter 1. The latter points to 'a need to wrestle with the written word, on a scale new in history' (p. 13).
8. Walter Benjamin, 'The Storyteller: Observations on the Works of Nikolai Leskov', in *Selected Writings*, vol. III: 1935–38, trans. Edmund Jephcott et al., ed. Howard Eiland and Michael W. Jennings (Cambridge, MA: Harvard University Press, 2002), pp. 143–66 (pp. 143–4).
9. Julian Walker, *Words and the First World War: Language, Memory, Vocabulary* (London: Bloomsbury, 2017), p. 81.
10. Julian Walker deals exclusively with the Western Front, where speakers of French, English, Dutch and German encountered each other. Army slang, he argues, 'shrugged off the foreign'. See ibid., p. 262.
11. *Letters*, vol. I, pp. 236–8 (p. 237): to Goldsworthy Lowes Dickinson, 28 July 1916. On the Red Cross information bureau, see also Jay Winter, *Sites of Memory, Sites of Mourning: The Great War in European Cultural History* (Cambridge: Cambridge University Press, 1995), pp. 36–44.
12. Lord Northcliff included one of Forster's reports in *At the War* (London: Hodder & Stoughton, 1916), pp. 146–7.
13. *Letters*, vol. I, pp. 232–3 (p. 232): to Syed Ross Masood, 29 December 1915.
14. Ibid., pp. 250–4 (p. 253): to Goldsworthy Lowes Dickinson, 5 May 1917. Forster found most of his patients 'pleasant and grateful and quite charming'. Ibid., p. 232: to Syed Ross Masood, 29 December 1915.
15. Vincent Sherry, *The Great War and the Language of Modernism* (New York: Oxford University Press, 2003), p. 274.
16. E. M. Forster, 'The Solitary Place', *Egyptian Mail*, 10 March 1918, p. 2, and 'Photographic Egypt', *Egyptian Mail*, 13 January 1918, p. 2.
17. *Letters*, vol. I, pp. 240–1 (p. 240): to Laura Mary Forster, 25 August 1916.
18. Ibid., pp. 254–6 (p. 254): to George Barger, 16 May 1917.

19. See Stevenson, *Literature and the Great War*, p. 17, and Juliette Taylor-Batty, *Multilingualism in Modernist Fiction* (London: Palgrave Macmillan, 2013), p. 4. For Raymond Williams, too, writing of modernism at large, 'endless border-crossing [...] worked to naturalize the thesis of the *non*-natural status of language'. See 'When Was Modernism?', in *The Politics of Modernism: Against the New Conformists* (London: Verso, 1994), pp. 31–6 (p. 34).
20. E. M. Forster, 'The Objects', *Athenaeum*, 7 May 1920, p. 600. 'Henry James's First Interview', p. 144.
21. See Edgar Garcia, *Signs of the Americas: A Poetics of Pictography, Hieroglyphs and Khipu* (Chicago: University of Chicago Press, 2020); Jessie Schotter, *Hieroglyphic Modernisms: Writing and New Media in the Twentieth Century* (Edinburgh: Edinburgh University Press, 2017); Christopher Bush, *Ideographic Modernism: China, Writing, Media* (New York: Oxford University Press, 2010).
22. Forster, 'Objects', p. 600.
23. E. M. Forster, 'The Lost Guide', in *Alexandria: A History and a Guide* and *Pharos and Pharillon*, ed. Miriam Allott (Cairo: American University of Cairo Press, 2004), pp. 351–9 (p. 355).
24. In Forster's introduction to the 1961 preface to his guidebook. See Forster, *Alexandria*, p. 5. For the author, the city had always been 'a civilisation of eclecticism and of exiles'. See 'A Musician in Egypt', *Egyptian Mail*, 21 October 1917, p. 2.
25. Furbank, *Forster: A Life*, vol. II, pp. 44–5.
26. E. M. Forster, 'In the Rue Lepsius', *Listener* 46, 5 July 1951, pp. 28–9 (p. 28).
27. Ibid., p. 28.
28. *Letters*, vol. I, pp. 238–40 (pp. 238–9): to Malcolm Darling, 6 August 1916. 'It's damnable and disgraceful', he admitted, 'and it's in me.'
29. *Selected Letters of E. M. Forster*, vol. II, 1921–70, ed. Mary Lago and P. N. Furbank (London: Collins, 1985), p. 23: to Florence Barger, 25 February 1922.
30. Ibid., p. 23.
31. Forster, 'Memoir to Mohammed El Adl', in *Alexandria*, pp. 329–46 (p. 335).
32. *The Diary of Virginia Woolf*, vol. II: 1920–24, ed. Anne Olivier Bell and Andrew McNeillie (London: Penguin, 1981), p. 27.
33. 'He ought from the first to have given me Arabic lessons in my room.' *Letters*, vol. I, pp. 290–2 (p. 292): to Florence Barger, 16 July 1918. 'I wish I could talk Arabic [...] to read the elf Lela wah Lela [*The Arabian Nights*],' he explained to El Adl in their first proper conversation (a book he finally finished for his 1927 Clark Lectures at Cambridge). Forster, 'Memoir', p. 330.
34. E. M. Forster, *The Hill of Devi* (London: Penguin, 1965), pp. 59–60.
35. Critics such as Hala Halim and Khaled Fahmy have faulted Forster for his concern with cosmopolitan rather than Egyptian/Arab Alexandria. See Hala Halim, *Alexandrian Cosmopolitanism: An Archive* (New York: Fordham University Press, 2013), pp. 120–78. Forster was aware of his Eurocentric bias. In a recently discovered theatrical sketch, he satirises his community of exiles, whom he would later describe as 'aliens in Egypt [...] come to exploit it'. See, respectively, E. M. Forster, 'Pericles in Paradise', *PMLA* 134.2 (2019), 359–65, and *The Government of Egypt: Recommendations by a Committee of the International Section of the Labour Research Department, with Notes on Egypt by E. M. Forster* (London: Labour Research Department, 1920), p. 9.
36. Forster, *Alexandria*, p. 39.
37. Ibid., p. 39.

38. For these early newspapers, see 'A Chronology of Nineteenth-Century Periodicals in Arabic (1800–1900)' at Leibniz-Zentrum Moderner Orient: <https://archiv.zmo.de/jaraid/index.html>.
39. Kathryn Schwartz, 'A New History of Print in Ottoman Cairo', Ottoman History Podcast, hosted by Nir Shafir, 15 July 2016, <http://www.ottomanhistorypodcast.com/2016/07/print-cairo.html>. The same printing press was reused, over thirty years later, to publish *Le Moniteur algérien* (1832).
40. H. F. Wood, *Egypt under the British* (London: Chapman & Hall, 1896), p. 118.
41. Guillaume Apollinaire, *Œuvres en Prose Complètes*, vol. II, ed. Pierre Caizergues and Michel Décaudin (Paris: Gallimard, 1991), p. 1,461.
42. Martin Briggs, *Through Egypt in War-Time* (London: Fisher Unwin, 1918), pp. 90–1.
43. *Letters*, vol. I, p. 266: to Robert Trevelyan, 6 August 1917.
44. Unpublished letter to Leonard Woolf dated 12 December 1916 (E. M. Forster Papers, Berg Collection, New York Public Library). As Martin Briggs noted in *Through Egypt in War-Time*: 'The streets and shops in the centre of town were crowded with khaki' (p. 12).
45. [T. E. Lawrence], 'Release of Damascus (from a correspondent beyond the Jordan)', *Palestine News*, 10 October 1918, p. 6. The same letter appeared in *The Times* a week later. Lawrence also wrote for the *Arab Bulletin*, a secret weekly publication issued by the Arab Bureau in Cairo.
46. *Reading and the First World War: Readers, Texts, Archives*, ed. Shafquat Towheed and Edmund King (Basingstoke: Palgrave Macmillan, 2015).
47. A post 'he retained through the war at the request of the British Government'. See 'Week in Books', *Newsweek*, 22 April 1933, p. 32. Wortham was also at King's College, Cambridge, a few years behind Forster.
48. *Letters*, vol. I, pp. 278–80 (p. 279): to Alice Clara Forster, 26 November 1917: 'I wish the Egyptian Mail didn't print so badly: it pays properly and is businesslike and civil, so I have left the Gazette for it. I must try to write another article now.'
49. They have been republished once, in a throwaway edition, as *The Uncollected Egyptian Essays of E. M. Forster*, ed. Hilda D. Spear and Aly Abdel-Moneim (Dundee: Blackness Press, 1988).
50. Horatio S. White, *Willard Fiske, Life and Correspondence: A Biographical Study* (New York: Oxford University Press, 1925), p. 159. Spiro was also private secretary to Alfred Milner, a colonial administrator and the author of *England in Egypt*.
51. On phrasebooks in World War I, see Walker, *Words and the First World War*, pp. 34–5, 54–61. Similar publications include *Lockwood's Egyptian and Syrian Arabic Self-Taught* (advertised as 'vest pocket size') and *A List of Useful Arabic and French Words and Phrases, Published at the Sailors and Soldiers Institute in Alexandria*. See, for instance, *Palestine News*, 22 August 1918, p. 15. Such books were not available to Forster while he travelled in India: 'I think I could have got on with Urdu if I had had a decent grammar, but there seems none. I have to learn by asking people the words.' *Letters*, vol. I, pp. 162–7 (p. 167): to Alice Clara Forster, 1 December 1912.
52. For the statistic, see Ziad Fahmy, *Ordinary Egyptians: Creating the Modern Nation through Popular Culture* (Palo Alto: Stanford University Press, 2011), p. 6. Spiro's 'Street Cries' was later abbreviated and reprinted in a soldiers' magazine: S. S. [Socrates Spiro], 'Cairo Street Cries', *Kia Ora Coo-Ee*, 15 July 1918, p. 17. Forster shared the Egyptian scholar's interest. See 'Gippo English', *Egyptian Mail*, 16 December 1917, p. 2.
53. Quoted from a letter to the author in White, *Willard Fiske*, p. 167.

54. 'Mainly about People', *Sphinx*, 16 June 1923, p. 14.
55. Walker, *Words and the First World War*, p. 54.
56. S. S. [Socrates Spiro], 'Arabic Made Easy', *Kia Ora Coo-Ee*, 15 October 1918, p. 13.
57. Mohammed Dulab, 'Arabic Made Easy', *Alpha/Omega*, May 1917, pp. 11–13.
58. See David M. Henkin, *City Reading: Written Words and Public Spaces in Antebellum New York* (New York: Columbia University Press, 1998), pp. 104, 111–13.
59. For a discussion of guidebooks in wartime, see Mark D. Larabee, *Front Lines of Modernism: Remapping the Great War in British Fiction* (Basingstoke: Palgrave Macmillan, 2011). He argues that the war called into question the positivist methodology of Baedeker guides.
60. Forster's guide has received little scholarly attention so far. Larabee, who discusses *A Room with a View* in his chapter on guidebooks and war, fails to mention it.
61. Forster, 'Lost Guide', p. 356.
62. Ibid., p. 357. For Hala Halim, in *Alexandrian Cosmopolitanism*, the implied reader and addressee of the guide is exclusively male and British (p. 162). Because of circumstance, Forster's guidebook only appeared after the war. The publisher had been enthusiastic at first to bring out 'their own small Baedeker', but had little idea of what was at stake. As delays persisted, Forster was forced to finish the volume from England and finished correcting the proofs in India. The guide finally appeared in December 1922; it was only for sale in Alexandria and 246 copies were lost in a fire. On the publication history, see Forster, 'Lost Guide', p. 357, and *Letters*, vol. I, pp. 306–9 (p. 307): to G. H. Ludolf, 10 October 1919. On the story of the fire – how Forster's guide perished 'in personal flames' – see Michael Haag, *Alexandria: City of Memory* (New Haven: Yale University Press, 2004), p. 81.
63. Forster, *Alexandria*, p. 89.
64. Forster, 'Lost Guide', p. 356.
65. *Letters*, vol. I, pp. 298–9 (p. 298): to Forrest Reid, 10 January 1919. In his 1922 preface, Forster writes of how the book was modelled 'after the fashion of a pageant'. Forster, *Alexandria*, p. 7.
66. Forster, *Alexandria*, p. 8.
67. The guide, according to Forster, was 'written from the practical standpoint, and is intended to be used on the spot'. Ibid., p. 8.
68. *Letters*, vol. I, pp. 306–9 (p. 307): to G. H. Ludolf, 10 October 1919. Virginia Woolf made a similar point in 'Craftsmanship': 'Baedeker carries the sign language still further into the sublime realms of art. When he wishes to say that a picture is good, he uses one star; if very good, two stars; when, in his opinion, it is a work of transcendent genius, three black stars shine on the page, and that is all. So with a handful of stars and daggers the whole of art criticism, the whole of literary criticism could be reduced to the size of a sixpenny bit – there are moments when one could wish it.' See *The Essays of Virginia Woolf*, vol. VI: 1933–41, ed. Andrew McNeillie (London: Hogarth Press, 1987), pp. 91–102 (p. 93).
69. Forster, *Alexandria*, p. 383. Other early readers included Evelyn Waugh, D. H. Lawrence, T. E. Lawrence, Lawrence Durrell and Rose Macaulay. Woolf once suggested Forster write 'a comic guide to Bloomsbury'. See J. H. Stape, *An E. M. Forster Chronology* (London: Macmillan, 1993), p. 118.
70. Guides became suspect in wartime because their topographical details could facilitate invasion. See Larabee, *Front Lines of Modernism*, p. 86.
71. See Forster, *Notes on Egypt*; 'The Trouble in Egypt: Treatment of the Fellahin', *Manchester Guardian*, 29 March 1919, p. 8; 'The Egyptian Labour Corps', *The*

Times, 8 November 1919, p. 8. The novelist was offered a permanent job in the Foreign Office, which he nearly accepted. See *Letters*, vol. I, pp. 315–16: to Florence Barger, 18 March 1920.
72. Timothy Mitchell, *Colonising Egypt* (Berkeley: University of California Press, 1991), p. 33. See also Yair Wallach, *A City in Fragments: Urban Text in Modern Jerusalem* (Palo Alto: Stanford University Press, 2020), p. 8: 'Textuality, in its modern sense, was a machinery at the service of capital and colonialism. The logic of capitalism (accumulation) and colonialism (appropriation) reduced people and their environment to a readable text.'
73. On the analogy between reading a paper and scanning the street for public words, see Henkin, *City Reading*, pp. 51, 104.
74. Virginia Woolf, 'An Unwritten Novel', in *The Mark on the Wall and Other Short Fiction* (Oxford: Oxford World's Classics, 2001), pp. 18–29 (p. 23).
75. Walter Benjamin, *Selected Writings*, vol. I, ed. Marcus Paul Bullock et al. (Cambridge, MA: Belknap Press, 1996), p. 456.
76. Henkin, *City Reading*, p. 6.
77. Forster, 'Gippo English', p. 2.
78. Ibid., p. 2.
79. Briggs, *Through Egypt*, p. 180.
80. Irony was his trademark: 'I do some journalism now – it is appreciated locally being over-facetious.' *Letters*, vol. I, p. 283: to Robert Trevelyan, 29 January 1918.
81. Forster, 'Gippo English', p. 2.
82. Walker, *Words and the First World War*, p. 299.
83. E. M. Forster, 'Diana's Dilemma', *Egyptian Mail*, 26 August 1917, p. 2.
84. Ibid., p. 2. To revel in such mistakes and loose translations was perhaps a particular modernist occupation. See Rebecca Beasley, 'Modernism's Translations', in *The Oxford Handbook of Global Modernisms*, ed. Mark Wollaeger (Oxford: Oxford University Press, 2012), pp. 551–70, and *Modernism and Non-Translation*, ed. Jason Harding and John Nash (Oxford: Oxford University Press, 2019).
85. Forster, 'Gippo English', p. 2.
86. Ibid., p. 2.
87. *Letters*, vol. I, pp. 232–3 (p. 232): to Syed Ross Masood, 29 December 1915.
88. Forster's faded inscription at the entrance to Montazah is an example of how a sign always remains 'unstable' and 'threatened by itself': it exists, as Yair Wallach argues, at the threshold of being rewritten. See *City in Fragments*, p. 9, and Henkin, *City Reading*, p. 60.
89. E. M. Forster, 'Army English', *Egyptian Mail*, 12 January 1919, p. 2.
90. Ibid., p. 2.
91. See 'Politics and the English Language', in *The Collected Essays, Journalism and Letters of George Orwell: In Front of Your Nose, 1945–50*, ed. Sonia Orwell and Ian Angus (New York: Harcourt, Brace & World, 1968), pp. 127–40 (p. 135). Orwell argues there exists 'a special connection between politics and the debasement of language' (p. 136).
92. *Letters*, vol. I, pp. 294–6 (p. 295): to Robert Trevelyan, 23 August 1918.
93. Ibid., p. 295.
94. 'The Wholesome Tongue', *Egyptian Mail*, 12 January 1919, p. 2. The ad appears on page 4.
95. *Letters*, vol. I, pp. 240–1: to Laura Mary Forster, 25 August 1916.
96. E. M. Forster, 'John McNeill Has Come', *Egyptian Mail*, 10 February 1918, p. 2.
97. *Letters*, vol. I, pp. 250–4 (pp. 250–1): to Goldsworthy Lowes Dickinson, 5 May 1917.

98. Ibid., pp. 254–6 (p. 256): to George Barger, 16 May 1917. For an account of the meeting, see Peter Buitenhuis, *The Great War of Words: Literature as Propaganda 1914–18 and After* (London: B. T. Batsford, 1989), pp. 14–20, and Mark Wollaeger, *Modernism, Media, and Propaganda: British Narrative from 1900 to 1945* (Princeton: Princeton University Press, 2006), pp. 13–26.
99. According to Wollaeger, Forster (as a member of a younger generation and an associate of the Bloomsbury Group) was not invited to the Wellington House meeting. *Modernism, Media, and Propaganda*, p. 16.
100. Ibid., p. 15. Modernism and propaganda, for Wollaeger, are 'like conjoined twins' (p. 1).
101. Ibid., p. 21.
102. Forster, *Notes on Egypt*, p. 5. On Egypt's 'uniquely awkward position', see also Khaled Fahmy, 'The Egyptian Revolution of 1919: The Birth of a Nation', unpublished keynote lecture, 'The Great Theft of History: World War One and the Prelude to Revolution', London, 27 March 2019.
103. Fahmy, *Ordinary Egyptians*, pp. 103–4.
104. Ibid., p. 118.
105. Christopher Bayly, *Empire and Information: Intelligence Gathering and Social Communication in India, 1780–1870* (Cambridge: Cambridge University Press, 1996).
106. Forster, *Notes on Egypt*, p. 5. 'There is so little Art in the Army that it is narrowly watched.' E. M. Forster, 'The Scallies', *Egyptian Mail*, 18 November 1917, p. 2.
107. J. E. Marshall, *The Egyptian Enigma 1890–1928* (London: John Murray, 1928), p. 25.
108. N. Griffiths, 'Editorial', *Sphinx*, 19 December 1914, p. 2.
109. Forster, *Notes on Egypt*, p. 5.
110. In a book review of Faivre's *Canopus, Menouthis, Aboukir*, Forster wrote the book sported 'a crop of obvious typographical errors. But perhaps it is not for the EGYPTIAN MAIL to call attention to them.' See 'Canopus, Menouthis, Aboukir. By the Rev. Father J. Faivre, S. J.', *Egyptian Mail*, 29 December 1918, p. 2.
111. Forster, 'Gippo English', p. 2.
112. The photograph was taken by Philip Frederick Schuler, sometime before the summer of 1917 when he died in action. Schuler wrote *Australia in Arms*, the first history of the Gallipoli campaign, which he covered as a correspondent for the Melbourne *Age*.
113. Henkin, *City Reading*, p. 57.
114. Less likely is that the sign referred to 'New Belgium', the region ceded by Germany to Belgium following the First World War. It would still read as odd in conjunction with 'Armenian'.
115. See Taylor-Batty, *Multilingualism in Modernist Fiction*, chapter 1. Stevenson quotes from de Saussure's *Cours de linguistique générale*: 'there is no internal connexion, for example, between the idea "sister" and the French sequence of sounds s-ö-r [...] The same idea might as well be represented by any other sequence of sounds. This is demonstrated by differences between languages, and even by the existence of different languages.' *Literature and the Great War*, p. 18.
116. Allyson Booth, *Postcards from the Trenches: Negotiating the Space between Modernism and the First World War* (New York: Oxford University Press, 1996), p. 156.
117. Forster, 'Musician in Egypt', p. 2. On the contemporary fascination with Ancient Egypt, see Eleanor Dobson, *Writing the Sphinx: Literature, Culture and Egyptology* (Edinburgh: Edinburgh University Press, 2020) and Richard B.

Parkinson, 'The Use of Old Objects: Ancient Egypt and English Writers around 1920', in *Ancient Egypt in the Modern Imagination*, ed. Eleanor Dobson and Nichola Tonks (London: Bloomsbury, 2020), pp. 199–211.
118. *Wilfred Owen: Collected Letters*, ed. Harold Owen and John Bell (London: Oxford University Press, 1967), p. 553. *The Collected Poems of Rupert Brooke: With a Memoir* (London: Sidgwick & Jackson, 1918), p. cxiv.
119. Briggs, *Through Egypt*, p. 9. Forster reviewed the book for the *Athenaeum* and Briggs helped Forster with a section of his guide. See Halim, *Alexandrian Cosmopolitanism*, p. 162.
120. Jay Winter, *War Beyond Words: Languages of Remembrance from the Great War to the Present* (Cambridge: Cambridge University Press, 2017), p. 36. As Briggs noted, 'The number of Kodaks in the E. E. F. is phenomenal.' See *Through Egypt*, p. 182. Forster also wrote about photography in the country in 'Photographic Egypt'.
121. Quoted in Furbank, *A Life*, vol. II, p. 22.
122. Forster, 'Lost Guide', p. 356. 'I'm constructing by archaeological and other reading an immense ghost city.' *Letters*, vol. I, pp. 292–4 (p. 293): to Siegfried Sassoon, 3 August 1918.
123. E. M. Forster, 'Pharos (Part III)', *Athenaeum*, 12 December 1919, pp. 1,030–1 (p. 1,031).
124. In a letter to Florence Barger quoted in Furbank, *A Life*, vol. II, p. 44. 'There is not much to see here, but there is very much to think about.' Quoted from a letter to his mother dated 28 October 1918 in Stape, *An E. M. Forster Chronology*, p. 65.
125. The poem dramatises what Gregory Jusanis calls 'the praxis of archaeology'. See 'Farewell to the Classical: Excavations in Modernism', *Modernism/modernity* 11.1 (2004), 37–53 (p. 42).
126. E. M. Forster and George Valassopoulos, 'The Poetry of C. P. Cavafy', *Athenaeum*, 9 May 1919, pp. 247–8 (p. 248). Valassopoulos, who provided the translations, was a fellow Kingsman and acquaintance of Forster in Alexandria.
127. For Forster, the poem is about 'the obscurity, the poignancy, that sometimes arise together out of the past, entwined into a single ghost'. Forster and Valassopoulos, 'Poetry of Cavafy', p. 248.
128. It is unclear who added the ellipses – Cavafy, Valassopoulos, Forster or an editor at the *Athenaeum*. They feature in *Pharos and Pharillon* but not in *C. P. Cavafy: Selected Poems*, ed. and trans. Avi Sharon (London: Penguin, 2008). On 'newly sceptical or deductive forms of reading', see Stevenson, *Literature and the Great War*, p. 45.
129. Forster often turns to tombstones and war graves, from a poignant entry in his guide on the recent French and British military cemeteries around Alexandria to 'Our Graves in Gallipoli: A Dialogue', which appeared in the *New Leader* in October 1922.
130. Forster, *Alexandria*, p. 92. Of the city of Rosetta, Briggs writes in *Through Egypt in War-Time*: 'The famous "Rosetta Stone" was discovered here, but that fact does not justify a certain guide-book in devoting a whole page to the stone and not a word to the Arab city. A traveller who visits Rosetta does not wish to read a whole page about something he can only see in the British Museum' (p. 108).
131. For Charles Forster's discussion of the Rosetta Stone, see *The Monuments of Egypt and their Vestiges of Patriarchal Traditions* (London: Richard Bentley, 1853). At the Greifswald Festival in Nassenheide in July 1905, Forster sat next to a professor who, on hearing his name, said, 'There is an Englishman named

Forster, an excellent scholar, who wrote about the Rosetta Stone!!' 'He regarded me as a repository of knowledge in consequence,' the novelist wrote to his mother. *Letters*, vol. I, pp. 79–81 (p. 79): to Alice Clara Forster, 8 July 1905.
132. E. M. Forster, 'Eliza in Egypt: Alexandria in 1799', *Egyptian Gazette*, 5 April 1917, p. 5. Forster would go on to edit Eliza Fay's letters for the Hogarth Press in 1925.
133. Forster, *Alexandria*, p. 121.
134. Forster, 'Objects', p. 600.
135. *Ripostes of Ezra Pound* (London: Stephen Swift, 1912), pp. 14–16. For Angus Fletcher, Pound's interest in Ancient Egyptian tombs is decidedly modern in that it challenges the Victorian fascination with classical Greek sculpture. See 'Ezra Pound's Egypt and the Origin of the "Cantos"', *Twentieth-Century Literature* 48.1 (2002), 1–21.
136. Forster first visited the catacombs on a date with Mohammed El Adl in the summer of 1917. *Letters*, vol. I, pp. 270–1 (p. 270): to Florence Barger, 13 September 1917.
137. Forster, *Alexandria*, p. 127.
138. Ibid., p. 126.
139. Ibid., p. 127.
140. Ibid., p. 136.
141. Many examples could be given here: Mina Loy wrote that 'Gertrude Stein has given us the Word, in and for itself' (*The Last Lunar Baedeker* (Manchester: Carcanet, 1985), p. 19). William Faulkner's Addie Bundren admits, 'I would think about [Anse's] name until after a while I could see the word as a shape, a vessel' (*As I Lay Dying* (London: Vintage, 2004), p. 157). Charles Olson was the author of 'The Art of the Language of Mayan Glyphs' (1951). Sergei Eisenstein constructed a theory of cinema and montage around Egyptian hieroglyphs, which also feature in Hart Crane's poetry, including his elegy 'At Melville's Tomb'. On Apollinaire's interest in Chinese characters, see *Œuvres Poétiques*, ed. André Billy, Marcel Adéma and Michel Décaudin (Paris: Gallimard, 1959), p. 1,074.
142. E. M. Forster, *Howards End* (Harmondsworth: Penguin, 1971), p. 234.
143. Quoted in Schotter, *Hieroglyphic Modernisms*, p. 37. It was long thought, even into the twentieth century, that hieroglyphs denoted a single object or thought – that they were visual rather than phonetic.
144. Bush, *Ideographic Modernism*, p. 34. Fenollosa claimed that the Chinese themselves had forgotten how to read – that is, look at – their own writing. Ibid., p. 56.
145. From Ezra Pound's *Machine Art and Other Writings*, quoted ibid., p. 38.
146. See Pound's June 1915 letter to Felix E. Schelling, quoted in Michael Levenson, *A Genealogy of Modernism: A Study of English Literary Doctrine, 1908–22* (New York: Cambridge University Press, 1986), p. 128.
147. Garcia, *Signs of the Americas*, p. 9.
148. Bush, *Ideographic Modernism*, pp. 3–4.
149. Bush argues that 'the ideograph and its accompanying imaginary [became] available for use in modernism's struggle to write of the simultaneously semiotic and cultural transformations of language in the age of technological media' (ibid. p. 21).
150. Schotter, *Hieroglyphic Modernisms*, p. 37.
151. *The Gnome*, edited by J. E. Dixon Spain, a camp instructor, was conceived as 'a current scrap book, a collection of momentary things'. The editor added: 'Our achievement is complete if, in years to come, an officer [...] turns up a copy and finds pleasure in a quickened memory of the time when he sojourned with the

Royal Flying Corps in the Land of the Pharaohs.' Editorial, *The Gnome*, March 1917, p. 2.
152. See E. M. Forster, 'Higher Aspects', *Egyptian Mail*, 5 May 1918, p. 2.
153. 'The Register of Um-Nefer: A Remarkable M.S.', *The Gnome*, November 1916, p. 6.
154. Paul Saint-Amour, 'Afterword: Deep War Time', *Modernism/modernity* Print Plus 5.2 (2020), <https://modernismmodernity.org/forums/posts/stamour-deep-war-time>. Leo Mellor makes a similar point about World War II in *Reading the Ruins: Modernism, Bombsites and British Culture* (Cambridge: Cambridge University Press, 2011). On Forster and the archaeological imagination, see 'The Solitary Place', p. 2.
155. Other drawings in the same issue are signed by Stuart Reid. The Imperial War Museum holds a small collection of Reid's drawings and paintings from his time flying in Egypt and Palestine.
156. 'Register of Um-Nefer', p. 6.
157. Ibid., p. 6.
158. Richard Bruce Parkinson, of Oxford University, drew my attention to these references. British Museum guides were in all likelihood the artist's source. On the left, the famous battle scenes depict Pharaoh Rameses II, alongside his sons Amunherkhepsef and Khaemwaset, as they charge into battle against the Nubians, who camped in a palm grove; on the right, we see Rameses II in kiosk receiving two registers of Nubians with tributes. As these motifs return in the 'Register of Um-Nefer', they merge with a set of stereotypes, from the choice of papyrus over stone relief and the play on the epithet of the god Osiris ('Wen-nefer') to the appearance of Thutmosis III instead of Rameses II.
159. E. M. Forster, *Aspects of the Novel* (Harmondsworth: Penguin, 1970), p. 162, and 'Objects', p. 599.
160. Virginia Woolf, *To the Lighthouse* (London: Dent, 1967), p. 57. The allusion is to the supposed curse of Tutankhamun. See Parkinson, 'Old Objects', pp. 203–4.
161. 'Register of Um-Nefer', p. 6.
162. *Letters*, vol. I, pp. 236–8 (p. 237): to Goldsworthy Lowes Dickinson, 28 July 1916, and ibid., pp. 292–4 (p. 292): to Siegfried Sassoon, 3 August 1918.
163. Gaps left by the censor can be found on pages 2, 8 and 10 of this particular issue of *The Gnome*.
164. Quoted in Bush, *Ideographic Modernism*, p. 15. A common trope; see for instance Marguerite Yourcenar: 'Des prêtres égyptiens m'ont montré leurs antiques symboles, signes plutôt que mots, efforts très anciens de classification du monde et des choses, parler sépulcral d'une race morte.' *Œuvres Romanesques* (Paris: Gallimard, 1989), p. 312.
165. Virginia Woolf, 'On Not Knowing French', in *The Essays of Virginia Woolf*, vol. V: 1929–32, ed. Stuart N. Clarke (London: Hogarth Press, 2009), pp. 3–9 (pp. 3–4).
166. *Diary*, vol. II, p. 96.
167. J. H. Willis Jr, *Leonard and Virginia Woolf as Publishers: The Hogarth Press, 1917–41* (Charlottesville: University Press of Virginia, 1992), p. 68.
168. Rose Macaulay, *The Writings of E. M. Forster* (Letchworth: Garden City Press, 1938), p. 149. On reading Egypt in light of *Passage*, see Halim, *Alexandrian Cosmopolitanism*, p. 121; Allott in Forster, *Alexandria*, p. xvii; Mohammed Shaheen, *E. M. Forster and the Politics of Imperialism* (London: Palgrave Macmillan, 2004), pp. 70–4; and Peter Childs, '*A Passage to India*', in *The Cambridge Companion to E. M. Forster*, ed. David Bradshaw (Cambridge: Cambridge University Press, 2007), pp. 188–208. Peter Morey's 'Postcolonial

Forster', in that same *Companion*, fails to mention the novelist's Egyptian writings at all (pp. 254–73).
169. E. M. Forster, *A Passage to India* (Harmondsworth: Penguin, 1979), p. 46.
170. Ibid., p. 301.
171. Forster, 'Gippo English', p. 2, and *Passage*, p. 249.

3

MONUMENTS IN VIRGINIA WOOLF AND HOPE MIRRLEES

In late September 1919, a small monument was unveiled in Cookham, in Berkshire, to commemorate sixty-two local servicemen who had lost their lives in the First World War. A Celtic cross, a popular symbol in the years following the conflict, was carved from brick and flint, raised on a stepped base, inscribed with a list of names, and placed on the village green.[1] Working from a photograph in 1922, the former official war artist Stanley Spencer, who himself had served in the Balkans and whose older brother was listed among the casualties on the monument, turned the scene of the dedication into the subject for a painting (Figure 3.1). Spencer lived in Petersfield at the time, in a room that overlooked the churchyard. 'I am in immediate communication with the dead,' he observed. 'They are buried in the side of a bank, so that they only have to push the gravestones a little bit forward and lo! they are in my room, like extinct gentlemen – a very Cookhamesque place, as you can see.'[2] *Unveiling Cookham War Memorial* shows what such communication with the dead may have looked like: far from pompous, it is intimate and unhurried. No dignitaries crowd the scene on the village green. Instead, locals in their Sunday best gather near the Celtic cross to commemorate the community's losses, their bodies pressed together, their hands holding leaflets, their necks bent, their entranced faces turned in all directions, except towards the viewer. On a grass patch nearby, four young men lie down, seemingly unaffected by the day's proceedings. With their uncannily long legs, these four slain men, who symbolise soldiers who fell in action, distort the painting's

Figure 3.1 Stanley Spencer, *Unveiling Cookham War Memorial*, 1922. Private Collection. Estate of Stanley Spencer, Bridgeman Art Library.

perspective, creating the illusion of bodies piled not only into the narrow frame but on to each other, as if magnetically pulled into the monument's orbit.

At the time, war memorials were often enclosed to protect them from accidental damage through contact with passers-by or grazing animals.[3] The absence of a fence around Cookham's Celtic cross, by contrast, seems to encourage such contact – a way of communicating with the dead. In Spencer's rendition of this moment of disclosure, five young girls are pulled so near the monument that they can touch it. One of them even mounts its stone base, climbing up alongside a Union Jack that has just been pulled to the ground.

As one critic suggested, she might be kissing the stone out of respect for the dead, though her face is hidden by a bonnet.⁴ It takes a moment to spot these girls in the crowd, a delay that might be intended. Dressed in white, they appear to merge with the white stone, like 'little alive parts of the Memorial', as the artist noted.⁵ These 'alive parts' of the monument recur, as a motif, across the war archive. On an undisclosed day in 1915, three soldiers, including a British and an Indian man, climbed a pedestal in a French village left in ruins, and stood for their picture (Figure 3.2). Shortly after the Armistice celebrations, Desmond MacCarthy told Virginia Woolf of how he had seen a jubilant crowd gather in front of Buckingham Palace, as men 'climbed all over the Victoria memorial, pulling themselves up by her nose and breasts'.⁶ Woolf herself would witness masses of people moving down the Strand a year later, drawn, as if hypnotically, to the brightly lit Cenotaph on the night of its unveiling – 'a lurid scene', she recalled in her diary, 'like one in Hell'.⁷ This chapter explores such bodily encounters with and around war monuments in modernist writing. In a second step, it asks how these writings themselves began to function as memorial objects, encountered in much the same affective ways as monuments: the ephemeral leaflets in Spencer's *Unveiling Cookham War Memorial* might have been thrown out the next day, but heftier memorial volumes, printed and bound, would have appeared in their place to preserve the memory of the village men who had died in the war.

That modernism was so spellbound not only with the acts but with the objects of remembrance might be self-evident, for the thriving of this kind of experimental literature coincided in part with what Samuel Hynes influentially described as a period of 'monument making'.⁸ The First World War had prompted a loss of life on an unprecedented scale, with conservative estimates of 17 million casualties worldwide.⁹ To direct the memory of that sacrifice into a tangible form, more than 40,000 memorials were erected in England alone.¹⁰ This was a relatively new phenomenon at the time. Until the late nineteenth century, monuments had typically honoured the victories of armies instead of the loss of soldiers.¹¹ However, as Jay Winter's *Sites of Memory, Sites of Mourning* has shown, death at a scale as experienced in the First World War called for such designated spaces to grieve a lost generation.¹² To this day, war memorials, such as the one Spencer painted in Cookham, remain at once an enduring material legacy of the conflict *and* strangely unnoticed sites. Already in 1927, not even a decade after the Armistice, the Austrian modernist writer Robert Musil pointed to this paradox, noting how 'conspicuously inconspicuous' sculptures tend to be: 'There is nothing in the world as invisible as a monument.'¹³ For Musil, a memorial's endurance over time negated its ability to leave an impression: visible but unseen, once positioned centrally in village life but now scarcely noticed. The reason for this invisibility is that the feelings that inspired the erection of a monument lost their intensity and finally passed

Figure 3.2 Soldiers stand as statues in France, 1915. Bibliothèque Nationale de France (Rol 44369).

('We rely on its being overcome after a certain lapse of time,' Musil's fellow countryman Sigmund Freud noted of the mourning process in 1917).[14]

This chapter will shed light on a time when the names listed on war monuments still evoked an array of memories, feelings and associations. While emerging after 1918, these affects, too, are part of the history of the First

World War. The Armistice did not spell the end of the war experience. Rather, as Eric Leed has argued, it marked 'the beginning of a process in which that experience was framed, institutionalized, given ideological content and relived in political actions as well as fiction'.[15] Much of that process took place around memorials. My argument is that, like Spencer, two modernist writers, Virginia Woolf in her 1922 novel *Jacob's Room* and Hope Mirrlees in her 1920 poem *Paris*, probed scenes of tactile contact with memorial objects – monuments, gravestones, statues *and* books – as a way of mediating loss. These objects were accorded such a central place in the mourning process because the war dead had been absent from England. Where a Victorian death scene occurred in a familiar setting, with the body of the deceased elaborately laid out for a final farewell, men in industrial warfare were blown to shreds and quickly buried near the battlefield.[16] Many bodies, including 200,000 in the British army alone, were simply never recovered.[17] As a result, families had no physical object – no body, no grave – on which to focus their grief. Monuments addressed this need, offering, as Joy Damousi has observed, 'a material attachment to the dead'.[18] For some survivors, then, mourning involved an affective engagement with memorial objects such as books and sculptures. 'Touching war memorials, and in particular, touching the names of those who died,' Jay Winter contends, 'is an important part of the rituals of separation.'[19]

This hands-on aspect of the mourning process offers a compelling entry point into modernist literature because it unsettles one of its key proponents – the modernist interest in what Woolf famously termed 'the dark places of psychology'.[20] Grieving provided the ultimate occasion for modernist writers to turn *inward*: Woolf, for one, started, but left unfinished, a piece on the psychology of war widows for *The Times*. I seek to foreground how modernist representations of grieving are at the same time marked by a turn *outward*, as objects, and the bodies that encounter them, were moved to centre stage. To the modernists, remembrance was in part premised on affective proximity and tactile perception. As an associative process, memory, for these writers, attached itself to things, sights, sounds or smells – Proust's illustrious *madeleine* – which evoke reminiscence when met later on.[21] '[A] sight will only survive in the queer pool in which we deposit our memories', Virginia Woolf, an admirer of Proust, noted in 1928, 'if it has the good luck to ally itself with some other emotion by which it is preserved. Sights marry, incongruously, morganatically (like the Queen and the Camel), and so keep each other alive.'[22] '[T]here is nothing to take the place of childhood,' the ageing protagonist in 'Mrs Dalloway in Bond Street' muses in a similar vein. 'A leaf of mint brings it back: or a cup with a blue ring.'[23] I aim to trace the ways in which memorials, from tombstones to memoirs, likewise 'ally' themselves with the war dead.[24] For survivors, placing a hand on a cold stone, or picking up a book from a shelf, triggered a memory of a life vanished in war – 'brings it back'.

This chapter will focus on two women writers, Virginia Woolf and Hope Mirrlees, in the implicit assumption that women assumed (often critically) the leading role in the war's culture of mourning.[25] In Woolf's Britain, there were 240,000 war widows by late 1918; Mirrlees's France counted more than twice as many.[26] I will argue that *Jacob's Room* and *Paris: A Poem* reflect on mourning and remembering as tangible processes. In these writings, memories of the war dead are evoked through visceral engagement with gravestones and statues, with what Woolf's narrator terms 'a rush of friendship for stones'.[27] If Woolf's and Mirrlees's characters so obsessively fixate on what things feel like and are made of – stone, marble, paper, earth, wax, glass, bronze – it is because these materials outlast human life and are meant to take its place, implying the possibility of continued engagement for the men and women left behind. In a second step, I treat these texts themselves as enduring material objects. My claim is that the war created a preoccupation with the materiality of the book, which had its own set of implications for the mourning process. Mirrlees's *Paris: A Poem* and Woolf's *Kew Gardens*, to which I also briefly turn, were published at the Hogarth Press, the publishing house Leonard and Virginia Woolf set up in their drawing room at Hogarth House in 1917. As material objects, these books were much more solid and seemingly permanent than loose papers and manuscript pages; they were also uniquely shaped by the material realities of warfare and therefore treasured rather than discarded. As such unique objects, I argue, books were encountered affectively, like memorials made from stone, ensuring a continued existence to the brief life remembered in and through their pages. In closing, I zero in on two such publications: *Poems by C. N. Sidney Woolf*, which the Woolfs printed in early 1918, and *The Collected Poems of Rupert Brooke: With a Memoir*, which Woolf reviewed for the *Times Literary Supplement* that summer. As I argue more generally throughout this book, these stone and paper memorials ultimately contribute to a deeper understanding of how the material culture of war helped modernist writers make sense of different aspects of the war experience. In their writing, personal loss and the memory of the war dead were mediated in entangled ways: through the mind, those 'dark places of psychology' that we know so intrigued the modernists, and through the body, as it affectively encountered the physical world.

STATUES AND TOMBSTONES IN *JACOB'S ROOM*

Virginia Woolf's war experience was marked by hardship.[28] Even for a civilian, the war's dangers were far from remote. From the downs above Asheham House, Woolf was able to discern the pounding on the Flanders front, and the distinctive white bridge over the Thames, near her home in Richmond, became a target for night-time air raids. Those raids saw the family camp out in the basement kitchen, with Virginia and the servants Lottie Hope and Nelly Boxall in camp beds, and their apprentice at the press, Barbara Hiles, under a table. To mitigate the servants' alarm, as Hiles remembered, Virginia Woolf would try 'to make them laugh by joking about Leonard who was precariously balanced on top of the table'.[29] The war claimed the bodies of many young men they knew, wounding their acquaintance Josiah Wedgwood in Gallipoli and ending the lives of Leonard's brother and two of Virginia's cousins. The fighting also wounded Nick Bagenal, who married Hiles, and whose experiences in the trenches interested Woolf 'extremely'.[30] They lost their loyal servant Nelly when she left to care for her sister, who had just given birth, and her brother-in-law, who had been wounded at the front. In July 1918, their neighbour died from influenza. In fact, Virginia Woolf lived across from the Richmond mortuary and felt moved by 'the extraordinary number of coffins one sees about'.[31]

These experiences deepened Woolf's pacifist politics, which had been shaped by her upbringing.[32] Leonard Woolf, by contrast, admitted he would have signed up for military service, from 'an irresistible desire to experience everything', if it had not been for his, and his wife's, poor health.[33] In mid-April 1920, Virginia Woolf began writing her lost generation into a novel, *Jacob's Room*, which traces the life of its titular character, Jacob Flanders, from his childhood in Scarborough to his death in the First World War. For her, Jacob's generation included Thoby Stephen, her brother who had died young, in 1906, of typhoid fever contracted in Istanbul. 'Of course I see something of Thoby in him, as I suppose was intended,' Lytton Strachey confessed to Woolf of the novel's protagonist.[34] Writing family members and friends into *Jacob's Room* – Leonard Woolf as Simeon, Ethel MacNeil as Betty Flanders, Lytton Strachey as Richard Bonamy, Madame Gravé as a French tourist – developed into something of an old trick for the author, so much so that she wondered whether she dealt 'openly in autobiography & called it fiction'.[35] An attempt to lay Thoby to rest among the war dead of his generation may explain why the writing process had been so difficult and protracted, interrupted by insecurities, illness and other writing assignments. 'My book is an eyesore,' she confessed in private in February 1921. 'I wake in the night twitching with horror at the thought of it.'[36]

Despite having a clear model in doomed young men such as Thoby Stephen or Rupert Brooke – given the descriptions of Jacob as 'the most beautiful man we have ever seen', 'beautifully healthy, like a baby after an airing' – Woolf's protagonist eludes the reader's grasp.[37] The novel opens on a beach with Jacob's mother, a widow, looking for her 'tiresome little boy', whose room is always found empty, the air 'listless', and who, as was his habit, is late to dinner.[38] Years later, in the Cambridge train station, Mrs Norman wishes to point out Jacob to her son, but as she turns around he 'had already gone', disappeared in a crowd on the platform.[39] If getting to know Jacob is 'mostly a matter of guess work', as the narrator admits, then still 'over him we hang vibrating'.[40] Woolf's earliest readers picked up on this. For Leonard Woolf and Robert Trevelyan, the characters were 'ghosts' and 'shadowy' respectively; Roger Fry wished 'a bronze body might somehow solidify beneath the gleams & lights'.[41] These absences are replicated in the novel's elliptical form. Its fragmented vignettes, beginning *in medias res*, make a mockery of the Victorian *Bildungsroman*, which progresses, with such exhaustive detail, from birth to death.[42] 'The effort of breaking with complete representation', Woolf noted of her 'disconnected' design, 'sends one flying into the air.'[43]

Instead, we know Jacob through the possessions that clutter his rooms in Cornwall, where he vacations as a boy; Scarborough, where he grows up; Rugby and Cambridge, where he receives his education; and Covent Garden, where he settles into professional life. 'Let us suppose that the Room will hold it together,' Woolf had scribbled on the first page of a holograph draft of the novel dated 15 April 1920.[44] At Trinity College, Cambridge, we follow the narrator into Jacob's room at the top of a staircase in Nevile's Court. '[R]eaching his door one went in a little out of breath,' she remarks, 'but he wasn't there':

> Jacob's room had a round table and two low chairs. There were yellow flags in a jar on the mantelpiece; a photograph of his mother; cards from societies with little raised crescents, coats of arms, and initials; notes and pipes; on the table lay paper ruled with a red margin – an essay, no doubt – 'Does History consist of the Biographies of Great Men?' There were books enough. [...] His slippers were incredibly shabby, like boats burnt to the water's rim.[45]

Despite Woolf's familiar boast to Mansfield that she had wanted 'only thoughts and feelings – no cups and tables' in her third novel, this scene offers no such discerning mind or sensing body, only clutter.[46] Through this muddle, the reader gets a sense of Jacob, who 'wasn't there': intelligent, a bit sloppy, sociable, a caring nature, a reader. His possessions will gain in significance once Jacob loses his life in the First World War. In the closing scene to the novel, his mother sifts through his things – bills, unanswered letters, old shoes – remembering the life behind them, while, in an earlier draft, the 'room waved behind her tears'.[47] Memory, as Woolf alleged in the *Times Literary Supplement* in 1917, attaches itself to 'the strangest odds and ends that have become somehow part of it'.[48] At the time Woolf was writing the novel, in 1921, 300,000 British and Imperial servicemen were still missing in action.[49] If there is a point to this room emptied of its inhabitant, symptomatic of Jacob's characteristic absences throughout the novel, then it is that he, too, will vanish in the haze of war, leaving his possessions behind.[50] Absence anticipates loss. For Paul Saint-Amour, Woolf is 'one of our central anatomists' of precisely this historical feeling: 'the sense that something terrible, even annihilating, is at hand'.[51] Jacob's reading habits at Cambridge already suggest such a foreclosed futurity. The books in his room serve as a *memento mori*: hefty volumes on the sack of Rome; short poems by Keats, who 'died young'; lives of the Duke of Wellington; a *Manual of the Diseases of the Horse*.[52]

Jacob's death occurs offstage, for Woolf had what she termed a 'prejudice' against the war in fiction.[53] Modernist novels in fact rarely confront death.[54] Yet, the bodies of the novel's older men carry the traces of what such a sacrifice might have entailed. Jacob's father died young; his uncle, Morty, was lost, possibly in the Third Anglo-Burmese War, 'last heard of – poor man – in Rangoon'.[55] The other men who populate Jacob's surroundings were left maimed from their service to the nation, from Mr Curnow, who had lost an eye in an unspecified explosion, and old George Garfit, who had fought in the Crimea, to 'old Jevons with one eye gone, and his clothes the colour of mud' and the appropriately named Captain Barfoot, who 'was lame and wanted two fingers on the left hand, having served his country' (though he is retired, there still is 'something military in his approach').[56] In real life, too, as she struggled with the manuscript of *Jacob's Room*, Woolf could not help but notice the many 'stiff legs, single legs, sticks shod with rubber, & empty sleeves' across London: 'at Waterloo I sometimes see dreadful looking spiders propelling themselves along the platform – men all body – legs trimmed off close to the body.'[57]

Jacob, meanwhile, is portrayed as 'the most beautiful man we have ever seen', in a line reminiscent of Rupert Brooke.[58] At Cambridge, following the narrator's directive to look closely, the reader catches a glimpse of Jacob among his contemporaries, as they walk into King's College Chapel:

> Look, as they pass into service, how airily the gowns blow out, as though nothing dense and corporeal were within. What sculptured faces, what certainty, authority controlled by piety, although great boots march under the gowns. In what orderly procession they advance. Thick wax candles stand upright; young men rise in white gowns; while the subservient eagle bears up for inspection the great white book. An inclined plane of light comes accurately through each window, purple and yellow even in its most diffused dust, while, where it breaks upon stone, that stone is softly chalked red, yellow, and purple. Neither snow nor greenery, winter nor summer, has power over the old stained glass.[59]

For Woolf, foreboding was a kind of falsification.[60] Yet, this scene is rife with imagery of death, its young men so vulnerable to erasure. As the narrator announces, 'there is no need to think of them grown old'.[61] Striding into the chapel, they seem to be made not of substance but of air, with their gowns blowing out in the wind as if 'nothing dense or corporeal were within' – a passage that surely prompted Leonard Woolf's description of the novel's characters as ghosts. The image may in fact have found its source in Thomas

Hardy's spectral Oxford fellows – 'In the gloom it was as if he ran against them without feeling their bodily frames' – in *Jude the Obscure*.[62] The sense of lightness, of immateriality, serves as a symbol of the fragile existence of these students (Hardy's dons are, in fact, already dead). Such ephemeral images proliferate in the novel, from dead leaves lifted by the wind to the 'brief lives' of paper flowers floating in finger-bowls at London restaurants.[63] Death looms large behind these descriptions. For a *TLS* reviewer, Jacob seemed like 'a little marching soldier'.[64] Rather than entering King's College Chapel, it appears that Woolf's Cambridge men, strapped in 'great boots' and marching in 'orderly procession', enter into armed service and thus advance towards a sure death.

At the same time, the 'sculptured faces' and the light breaking upon the imperishable stone of King's College Chapel suggest something more solid, more permanent. Unlike the precariousness of life, stone endures. This tension, as Elaine Scarry has argued, creates an idea of solidness in the reader's mind: 'the mental image of a wall', she writes, taking Proust as her example, 'can be coaxed into solidity by the passing of a transparent surface over it.'[65] Woolf gets her reader to imagine the solidity of the chapel by making it appear as a backdrop to transparent bodies and to the play of shadow and light. The impression conjured up by this trick – 'the glide of the transparent over the assertedly solid' – is one of durability.[66] King's College Chapel will last, like 'the great blocks of stone' at Stonehenge, which a young Woolf once described as 'the stark remains of an age I cannot otherwise conceive; a piece of wreckage washed up from Oblivion'.[67] An earlier draft of the novel had in fact opened not with Jacob, missing on the beach, but with a description of 'The Rock', 'one of those tremendously solid brown, or rather black, rocks which emerge from the sand like something primitive'.[68] Here, too, the feel and firmness of stone – and its longevity – is evoked through a juxtaposition with transparent substances: 'a hollow full of water' on the top; 'a blob of jelly stuck to the side'.[69] A persistent thought across Woolf's oeuvre, the durability of certain materials was also a topic for much debate in the years following the war, when local memorials were usually set in the hardest material available to a community (stone over bronze, granite over sandstone).[70]

In this scene at King's, then, we encounter Jacob at a moment of metamorphosis: at once transparent body and sculptured face, a ghostlike figure moving against the backdrop of a chapel (he is also dressed in a gown white as stone). The protagonist appears like a marble statue come to life, indirectly substantiating Rainer Maria Rilke's belief that a sculpture was as much an inert object as a living thing.[71] Walking into Westminster Abbey in the early 1930s, Woolf had been struck by a similar notion that its sculptured dignitaries were uncannily alive: 'From every corner, from every wall, somebody leans or listens or bends forward as if about to speak. [...] Their hands nervously grasp their sceptres, their lips are compressed for a fleeting silence, their eyes lightly closed as if for a moment's thought.'[72] If Woolf's Cambridge students advance, like soldiers, towards their death, then they already take on the material qualities of the statues to be erected in their honour – resembling the 'little alive parts' of the stonework in Spencer's *Unveiling Cookham War Memorial*. Anticipating the war's culture of commemoration, the narrator again and again carves the novel's young men out of blocks of marble, from Curnow, a boy in Cornwall who sits 'immobile as stone', to Nick Bramham, a painter whose head appeared like 'the work of a sculptor, who had squared the forehead, stretched the mouth, and left marks of his thumbs and streaks from his fingers in the clay'.[73] An impression of stasis and impending death permeates the descriptions of these men made of stone, 'standing forever stiff and pathetic', as D. H. Lawrence once fittingly wrote of a memorial to an Anzac soldier.[74]

Throughout Woolf's novel, the elusive Jacob Flanders is depicted in precisely these terms. '[T]hat he exists, that he stands as does a monument is certain,' E. M. Forster observed in the *New Criterion* in 1926.[75] We find Jacob at St Paul's Cathedral, among 'ghosts of white marble', and on Trafalgar Square, passing 'Nelson on his column surveying the horizon'.[76] Elsewhere in London, Florinda compares him to 'one of those statues' in the British Museum, as does Fanny Elmer, whose notion of Jacob as 'statuesque, noble, and eyeless' draws on 'the battered Ulysses' of the Elgin Marbles.[77] In Olympia, as he travels through a country Woolf once described as made 'of a beauty of stone and earth rather than of woods and greenery', Jacob sits himself down 'in the quarry where the Greeks had cut marble for the theatre'.[78] Spying him from a distance, Sandra Wentworth Williams gets his head 'exactly on a level with the head of Hermes of Praxiteles' and thinks the comparison 'all in his favour'.[79] So convincing is Jacob as a Greek sculpture that a French tourist on her way to join her husband in Constantinople perches 'on a block of marble with her kodak pointed at his head' and snaps a picture.[80] In fact, in a move similarly revealing of the intimacies between stone and untimely death, Woolf herself was often likened to a sculpture following her suicide: for Osbert Sitwell, she resembled a Roman patrician bust; Frances Partridge remembered her as a statue from the Acropolis, as if she 'had stepped down from her pedestal and was taking a stately walk'.[81]

Woolf's gendered critique of war revolves around these men chiselled in stone: war memorials, she believed, permit and glorify sacrifice in the name of the belligerent nation state rather than mourn the short, sharp lives behind them. Statues mediate not only memories, but ideologies. In *Jacob's Room*, and in later essays such as 'A Sketch of the Past', 'Thoughts on Peace in an Air Raid' and *Three Guineas*, she levels a challenge at a patriarchal society that sends its young men into war (for her, famously, 'a preposterous masculine fiction').[82] In the novel, she terms this system the 'Greek myth' – a set of values, such as sacrifice, duty to the nation, love of country and hero worship, which were inculcated in young boys through a love of the antique world.[83] '[W]e have been brought up in an illusion,' Woolf remarks through her protagonist.[84] Ancient Greece provided the inspiration for these ideals, the source for this illusion: Jacob is compared to ancient statues; taught Greek and Latin from an early age; adorns his Cambridge room with 'a Greek dictionary with petals of poppies pressed to silk between the pages' and 'photographs from the Greeks' (probably of the Elgin Marbles); and travels through Greece, Baedeker in hand, on a European tour.[85] The need to protect ancient artefacts, and the pursuit of the patriarchal values these artefacts emblematised, lead Jacob blindly into war. Woolf's assessment of the Greek myth may be read to target the notorious consternation, early on in the war, at Germany's destruction of Leuven's University Library, Ieper's Cloth Hall and Reims Cathedral.[86] These were places of learning and cultural achievement meant to be above the political upheaval of the day, that is, to be protected and delivered to the next generation (Jacob, too, has 'a sense of old buildings' and sees himself as their 'inheritor').[87] The notion that the protection of such places never justifies war sounds as a familiar refrain through modernist war writing, encompassing not only Virginia Woolf's *Jacob's Room*, but also a text as different as Ezra Pound's *Hugh Selwyn Mauberley*, in which the poet famously regrets the death of a myriad of men 'For two gross of broken statues, / For a few thousand battered books'.[88] The reference is to a generation of dead men, perhaps even to Pound's friend, the French Vorticist sculptor Henri Gaudier-Brzeska, whose single life, Pound revealingly lamented, 'was worth more than dead buildings'.[89]

That the female narrator in *Jacob's Room* is critical of such ideological thinking – of placing young men in front of dead buildings – is evident from her protagonist's visit to the Acropolis on his Grand Tour:

> The yellow columns of the Parthenon are to be seen at all hours of the day firmly planted upon the Acropolis; though at sunset, when the ships in the Piraeus fire their guns, a bell rings, a man in uniform (the waistcoat unbuttoned) appears; and the women roll up the black stockings which they are knitting in the shadow of the columns, call to the children, and troop off down the hill back to their houses.
>
> There they are again, the pillars, the pediment, the Temple of Victory and the Erechtheum, set on a tawny rock cleft with shadows [...] The extreme definiteness with which they stand, now a brilliant white, again yellow, and in some lights red, imposes ideas of durability [...] But this durability exists quite independently of our admiration. Although the beauty is sufficiently humane to weaken us, to stir the deep deposit of mud – memories, abandonments, regrets, sentimental devotions – the Parthenon is separate from all that.[90]

The scene is in all likelihood set in May 1914, though a date is not specified. As the firing guns, uniforms, black stockings and mud make clear, war is on the horizon. Yet, certain places, which stand with 'extreme definiteness', are above the tumult of the day. '[F]irmly planted', these ruins exist independently of our involvement, seemingly unaffected by the passing of time, which is here reflected in the changing light. Like in the scene at King's College Chapel, the grazing of light and shadow against the pillars – what Scarry termed 'the glide of the transparent over the assertedly solid' – creates an image, in the reader's mind, of the Parthenon as rock-hard and therefore enduring, 'likely to outlast the entire world', as the narrator continues.[91] On her own travels in Greece, Woolf noted that a statue of Apollo in Olympia appeared 'to look across & above the centuries'.[92] By repeatedly describing Jacob as sculpted from marble, then, the novelist predicts not only her protagonist's early demise but also his extended life as an object and an idea: Jacob will be made to take up his place in the mythology that drove him to war in the first place, as one more memorial among the broken statues and battered books. As Laura Wittman has argued, a 'tendency to stylise death, to make it beautiful' underlies many of the First World War's commemorative projects.[93] Cleansed from the horrors of warfare in this way, Jacob's monument will serve as a model for duty and a promise of glory to future generations, thereby keeping alive the war spirit (a genuine fear, as debates from the early 1920s illustrate).[94] In this scene on the Acropolis, we catch a glimpse of precisely such a future, as young boys *troop off* down the hill at the close of day. Likewise, in *Mrs Dalloway*, Peter Walsh comes across a commemoration ceremony in London, with boys marching, guns in their hands, 'on their faces an expression like the letters of a legend written round the base of a statue praising duty, gratitude, fidelity, love of England'.[95]

As the Parthenon passage also proposes, with its image of mothers knitting black stockings, it is the women in Woolf's writings who are left behind to encounter these memorials – who are made to be receptive to the memories and ideologies they evoke. As scholars such as Douglas Mao and Paul Saint-Amour have shown, Woolf is an excellent historian of affectively charged encounters with objects, of 'fingers curl[ing] round something hard – a full drop of solid matter' in 'Solid Objects' or of women's 'odd affinities [with] trees, or barns' in *Mrs Dalloway*.[96] In *Jacob's Room*, such odd affinities are centred around women's visceral engagement with old stones, as if they were practising – Jacob is not even dead yet – the role of mourners in which they will be cast.[97] That such is their fate is already clear from the cameo appearance, in Betty Flanders's letter to Jacob, of an old Miss *Wargave*, who is in and out of the narrative in a split instant, yet whose unusual name (like *Flanders*) carries all the associations of the coming conflict. Similar rehearsals of grief pervade the novel. Mrs Lidgett, a cleaner at St Paul's Cathedral, takes a seat beneath Wellington's sarcophagus, folding her hands and half closing her eyes:

'A magnificent place for an old woman to rest in, by the very side of the great Duke's bones, whose victories mean nothing to her, whose name she knows not, though she never fails to greet the little angels opposite.'[98] Fanny Elmer strays 'between the white tombs' of a 'disused' St Pancras graveyard, much like Florinda, Jacob's lover, who keeps a photograph of her father's tombstone in her pocket, and the novel's female narrator, who catches sight of a mason's van in oncoming traffic, loaded with 'newly lettered tombstones recording how someone loved someone who is buried at Putney'.[99] In turn, Miss Marchmont is found sitting in the British Museum reading room, under the gilt names of great men which 'stretched in unbroken file round the dome', and on her teabreak, as is her habit, passes by the Elgin Marbles, 'look[ing] at them sideways, waving her hand and muttering a word or two of salutation'.[100]

Through these women's embodied responses to old stones – 'the emotion of the living breaks fresh on them year after year', as the narrator declares of the Parthenon columns – Woolf's critique of the Greek myth comes into its own.[101] Some women in the novel appear not as readily won for the cause of war, never as easily fooled. Woolf recruits these women to interact with monuments in ways that were not intended – not, that is, the 'thanks and applause' expected by the statues of statesmen in St Paul's, as Woolf quipped in 'Abbeys and Cathedrals', but a response less akin to wilful submission and more resembling rage, ridicule or quiet, everyday resignation.[102] In *Jacob's Room*, Greek women knit while sitting on the Parthenon columns; Mrs Lidgett rests below Wellington's tomb yet fails to recognise the famous Duke; feminists in the British Museum reading room curse at the male names carved in the dome ('"Oh damn," said Julia Hedge, "why didn't they leave room for an Eliot or a Brontë?"').[103] In doing so, these women find fault with the monument's hero-worshipping powers, challenging its 'need to reaffirm the nobility of the warrior' and 'to highlight soldiers' sacrifice and civilian debt', which Jay Winter identified as central themes of commemoration in the First World War.[104] These stones rather begin to bear a resemblance to what David Bradshaw, in a discussion of *Mrs Dalloway*, termed 'anti-monuments'.[105] In another such gesture hostile to the Greek myth, Clara Durrant reads out the inscription on the Wellington Monument in Hyde Park, a bronze statue of Achilles dedicated to the memory of Arthur Wellesley and cast from cannons captured in the Napoleonic Wars. She does so 'with a foolish little laugh'. The railing around the statue is 'full of parasols and waistcoats; chains and bangles; of ladies and gentlemen, lounging elegantly, lightly observant'.[106] Not a single thought seems wasted on Wellesley's victory at Waterloo.

Among these affects – Mrs Lidgett's resignation, Julia Hedge's anger, Clara Durrant's derision – we may count Betty Flanders's quiet resilience, which is no less disparaging of war. For her, a widow in her prime, memories, not ideologies, are stored in ancient stones (like the Parthenon columns which, as the narrator suggests, hold the capacity 'to stir the deep deposit of mud – memories, abandonments, regrets, sentimental devotions').[107] Betty Flanders is a practised mourner. Her husband, Seabrook Flanders, lies buried in the Scarborough churchyard, and his widow's visit to his grave can be read as a gesture anticipating her son's early demise (note how Jacob is once more absent from the scene and how his brother's voice merges with funeral bells):

> True, there's no harm in crying for one's husband, and the tombstone, though plain, was a solid piece of work [...] Seabrook lay six foot beneath, dead these many years; enclosed in three shells; the crevices sealed with lead, so that, had earth and wood been glass, doubtless his very face lay visible beneath, the face of a young man whiskered, shapely, who had gone out duck-shooting and refused to change his boots. [...] [H]e had merged in the grass, the sloping hillside, the thousand white stones, some slanting, others upright, the decayed wreaths, the crosses of green tin, the narrow yellow paths, and the lilacs that drooped in April, with a scent like that of an invalid's bedroom, over the churchyard wall. Seabrook was now all that; and when, with her skirt hitched up, feeding the chickens, she heard the bell for service or funeral, that was Seabrook's voice – the voice of the dead [...]
>
> 'Wouldn't you like my knife, mother?' said Archer.
>
> Sounding at the same moment as the bell, her son's voice mixed life and death inextricably, exhilaratingly.[108]

Woolf had a penchant for graveyard scenes; she once authored a piece, now lost, on the Protestant cemetery at Lisbon.[109] As with Jacob's visit to the Acropolis and procession into King's College Chapel, she draws attention to the material textures of the site, which suggest 'ideas of durability': the solid tombstone, the lead coffin (shelled, as a safeguard against grave-robbers), the tin crosses and the 'thousand white stones' may themselves be subject to decay, but long outlive the ephemeral life accorded to humanity. While Seabrook Flanders may have died young and any trace of his body may have vanished after these many years – 'Had he, then, been nothing?' Mrs Flanders muses – material objects such as headstones and crosses have come to take his place.[110] These are the kind of 'artifacts', as Allyson Booth has argued, capable of standing as 'substitutes for the body'.[111] Woolf's focus on the natural surroundings in particular – a more stable category, in the face of time, than man-made materials – works to further emphasise this intransience, not only of the material environment but of the memory of Seabrook by association (in another graveyard scene in the novel, a man is remembered 'so long as his tombstone endures').[112] In fact, merging with the lilacs and the thousand white stones, Seabrook enjoys a continued existence of sorts – he is 'now all that'.[113]

Because of the widow's trust in such afterlives, touching the headstones, crosses and flowers means getting closer to her dead husband. The sense of touch offers an illusion of proximity, of a strongly felt presence (had earth and wood been glass, she believes, she might have caught a glimpse of his whiskered face).[114] Woolf's description resonates with Freud's 1917 theory of grief: namely that 'the existence of the lost object is psychically prolonged'.[115] To understand that her husband merged with the earth is to account for the widow's habit, elsewhere in the novel, of 'press[ing] her finger here and there into the soft earth' as the church bells toll ominously, or of 'rubb[ing] the turf with her toe' on Dods Hill, Scarborough's Roman fortress.[116] Such intimacy with the material world, from the earth's surface to the graveyard's stones, dislodges a flood of memories: of Seabrook breaking horses, farming fields, running 'a little wild'.[117] For Woolf, then, writing in the wake of war, gravestones and statues figured centrally in the act of grieving. Remembering the war dead was an entangled process, the work not only of the mind, but, entwined with it, of the body as it interacted with the material world. Modernists were fascinated with that world's solidness, its promise of permanence. When in the novel Fanny Elmer has not seen Jacob in over two months, while he travels through Europe just before the outbreak of war, she receives 'a fresh shock of Jacob's presence' on catching a glimpse of the battered Ulysses in the British Museum.[118] His life may ultimately be fragile and painfully short; a lingering memory will be locked in the statues and tombstones erected in his absence, encountered in visceral, at times ambivalent, ways by the women who survived the war. In modernist writing, memory is marked, in part, by such affective gestures – the moment of receiving 'fresh shocks'.

THE BOOK AS OBJECT: *PARIS: A POEM* AND *KEW GARDENS* AT THE HOGARTH PRESS

The notebook in which Virginia Woolf began *Jacob's Room* was wrapped in gold, red and blue coloured paper, left over from a small book she had just published at the Hogarth Press: Hope Mirrlees's *Paris: A Poem*. Woolf and Mirrlees had been acquaintances for some years by the time the poem appeared in 1920. The novelist thought the poet 'eccentric', but her work 'brilliant', and counted her (together with Katherine Mansfield) as one of her 'literary ladies'.[119] If Woolf favourably reviewed Mirrlees's first novel, *Madeleine*, for the *Times Literary Supplement*, she reserved particular praise for *Paris*, which, like *Jacob's Room*, grapples with the memories and ideologies mediated through stone memorials. Part of what drew Woolf to this vanguard text was the way in which it dealt with its topic through the use of experimental typography, with which Woolf, as the typesetter for the poem, became intimately acquainted.[120] Through such typographical tricks as capitalisation and alignment, the page sought to mirror the tombstones and memorial plaques it represented, thus calling attention to the poem's own materiality. In tracing this shift in focus from the poem to the book,

I want to suggest that the war urged modernist writers to reflect on how books themselves, like old stones, are solid and durable objects, with long shelf lives. The influence of the war in occasioning this shift, as I will show, is also apparent in another early Hogarth Press publication, Woolf's *Kew Gardens*, which was affected by the war's paper shortages. In my final section below, I will argue that this *material turn* to the book – as an object that lasts and outlasts us – had its own implications for the memorial culture that developed in the war's wake.

Hope Mirrlees spent her war years in Paris. Fleeing a Cambridge that increasingly came to house cadets instead of students, she had moved to the French capital with Jane Ellen Harrison, her tutor in Classics at Newnham College. Mirrlees was Harrison's 'favourite pupil', at least according to Woolf, who also wrote the professor into *Jacob's Room*.[121] The unorthodox duo found the French capital, as Harrison wrote, 'wounded' but 'less unbearable for the nightmare becomes real'.[122] Woolf had noted a similar sentiment in her *TLS* review of the Cambridge scholar E. M. Spearing's war memoir, who as a volunteer in France had felt 'something of the excitement of a student plunged from books into practical work'.[123] In Paris, the war came palpably close to the scholar and the student: they even escaped three bombs in late 1914 during Zeppelin raids on the city. Their shared life played out in and around the Hôtel de l'Élysée, where they lived, and the École des Langues Orientales, where they took classes in Russian. There were occasional visits to Gertrude Stein, Alice B. Toklas and Sylvia Beach.[124] There may even have been, early in the war, a trip to the front to see Mirrlees's brother Reay – 'a trim officer', as Woolf knew him.[125] We know that Mirrlees and Harrison went to the British Embassy to inquire about permits, but it is unclear whether the two women were successful in obtaining them and ever ventured as far as the trenches.

These wartime sights and scenes loom large in Mirrlees's work. *Paris: A Poem* is her account of a *flânerie* through Paris on a single day and night in the spring of 1919, when world leaders met at Versailles for the Peace Conference.[126] The overwhelming impression is of Paris as a city of the dead. Woolf's typesetting mistake is revealing in this respect: in the original Hogarth Press edition, she dated the poem 1916, instead of 1919, and later had to correct 160 copies by hand. *Paris: A Poem* opens in a metro station, an underground setting reminiscent of the troglodyte world of the trenches and of the grave (a site which the reference to the 'Black-figured vases in Etruscan tombs' immediately brings to mind).[127] For more than four years, in the French army alone, an average of 900 men had been killed every day.[128] Their spectral presence, like that of Woolf's young men walking into King's College, haunted the city. The 'Holy Ghost', 'the ghost of Père Lachaise', the 'blue ghosts of king-fishers' and 'Old Hesiod's ghost' convene across the poem's meandering lines, as does 'the soul of a brother killed at Sebastopol', while the Louvre is 'melting into mist / It will soon be transparent'.[129] Meanwhile, young children are depicted as the uncanny reincarnation of their dead fathers: in the Tuileries, 'Little boys in black overalls', their hands sticky with mud, go 'round and round on wooden horses' of the carousel; other children, whose 'amulets' and 'Blue smocks' denote their soldier-fathers returned to life, play in the streets as the spring day around them brings the rebirth of the natural world.[130] Taken together, Mirrlees's ghosts and reincarnated soldiers evoke the contemporary interest in spiritualism, which surged after the war, as is also clear from buried references in *Jacob's Room* (from Mrs Flanders discerning the 'voice of the dead' and Jacob reading Plato's tract on the immortal soul to the brief appearance of a Mrs Stuart, who 'kept a parrot, believed in the transmigration of souls, and could read the future in tea leaves').[131] In a 1926 essay, Mirrlees even went so far as to invent an 'aural kaleidoscope' with which she could tune into 'the old fragments of human speech blown in from the waste places of the universe to be lost again for another thousand years'.[132]

At the same time, *Paris: A Poem* envisions a more embodied contact with the dead than through séances – a feeling Mirrlees once described as 'a sudden *physical* conviction (like fingering for the first time the antiquity one had so often gazed at through the glass case in the museum)'.[133] In the wake of hostilities, as *Paris: A Poem* and *Jacob's Room* illustrate, modernist writing developed a keen preoccupation with characters counting back the days and years through such affective engagement with effigies of the war dead. Mirrlees's poem, too, is thickly populated with dummy figures, from the chalk drawing of a *poilu* and the wax model in a department store window to 'Pigeons [...] turned to stone', the Louvre's Assyrian statues, and the sculptures of the grey sphinx of the Tuileries, the Roman boy Spinario and Léon Gambetta, who was War Minister during the Paris Siege.[134] Memories and myths work through these sculpted stones. When the *flâneuse* comes across middle-class women taking up collection for war victims, her mind wanders to the tombstone of a soldier who was killed in action in the Battle of the Marne:

> The unities are smashed,
> The stage is thick with corpses....
>
> Kind clever *gaillards*
>
> Their *eidola* in hideous frames inset with the brass motto
>
> MORT AU CHAMP D'HONNEUR;
> And little widows moaning
>   *Le pauvre grand!*
>   *Le pauvre grand!*
>
> And petites bourgeoises with tight lips and strident voices
> are counting out the change and saying *Messieursetdames*
> and their hearts are the ruined province of Picardie....[135]

Grief is a complex phenomenon: it deranges the mind; it unnerves the body. If scholars continue to read Mirrlees's *flânerie* as a psychogeography – of a wandering woman who 'wade[s] knee-deep in dreams' – then this mourning scene rather pulls bodies and physical sense-impressions into a sharper focus: the stage thick with corpses; the *grand* and lifeless *gaillard*, both strapping fellows; the sensing, living bodies of the little widows and *petites bourgeoises* who are burdened with the task of remembering.[136] Such a bodily preoccupation recalls the famous figure of the mother – kneeling, head down, arms folded over her chest, back bent with sorrow – in Käthe Kollwitz's *Trauernde Eltern*. The sculpture, which bore Kollwitz's facial features and which she had placed in front of her son's war grave in Flanders, gave shape to her own notion of mourning as a 'need to kneel down and let him pour through, through me. Feel myself altogether one with him.'[137] As Richard Cork notes, the emotional resonance of the two grieving parents lies in their positioning: mother and father mourn in physical proximity to their son's grave and to each other, yet they kneel on separate blocks, creating a 'tension between their ability to share suffering and an equally evident awareness of each mourner's isolation'.[138] In Mirrlees's grave scene, too, bodies figure so prominently – the little widows, the *pauvre grand* – because grief was partially envisioned as a bodily experience, the affective attachment of a mourner to a gravestone that triggers a memory of her dead husband, who had been so 'kind', so 'clever'.

Such a reading resonates closely with the poem's obsessive interest in material textures, as the reader learns that things are made from rubber, ivory, paper, chalk, bronze, marble and brass. The point these details raise is straightforward: in contrast to the immaterial presence of the war dead haunting the city, material objects have a weight to them and occupy a physical place in the world. Made from such durable materials, gravestones and statues can be touched long after the dead have passed away, thus allowing for the retrieval of a memory of the vanished lives they symbolise. The solidity of the material object, and its relative confidence in the face of time, I argue, is further supported by the visual look of Mirrlees's page – on a par with the effect evoked by Woolf's juxtaposition of ghostlike students moving against the backdrop of King's College. For, Mirrlees's page mirrors the grave it represents: its inscription is centred between two prose passages aligned evenly along the right and left margins, conveying the impression of a text framed like the actual lettering on a tombstone.[139] The inscription, MORT AU CHAMP D'HONNEUR, is further set with capital letters, as it would be on a grave, which is a much more radical typographical gesture than it may appear at first (Seabrook's tombstone lettering, in *Jacob's Room*, is simply replicated, in lower case, as 'Merchant of this city', though Woolf once confessed to an unorthodox interest in the 'surface oddity' of epitaphs).¹⁴⁰ Mirrlees's typographical experimentation draws attention to the material dimensions and contours of the memorial object under poetic consideration. Similar 'tricks of type', as one reviewer called them somewhat disparagingly, also serve to represent three memorial plaques which the *flâneuse* spots on the buildings where once lived, and died, famous Parisians.¹⁴¹ A reader in 1920 would be forgiven for thinking of more recent loss:

>   MOLIERE
>   EST MORT
> DANS CETTE MAISON
> LE 17 FEVRIER 1673
>
>   VOLTAIRE
>   EST MORT
> DANS CETTE MAISON
> LE 30 MAI 1778
>
>   CHATEAUBRIAND
>   EST MORT
> DANS CETTE MAISON
> LE 4 JUILLET 1848

As Robert Musil wrote, 'You can walk down the same street for months' and one day still be surprised to notice 'a not-at-all tiny metal plaque' indicating that 'from eighteen hundred and such and such to eighteen hundred and a little more the unforgettable So-and-so lived and created here'.¹⁴² Mirrlees's *flâneuse*, by contrast, notices these plaques at once, and so does her reader: their indelible letters jump off the page. 'MOLIERE / EST MORT' is centrally aligned, cast in capitals and stretched across two lines, as it would appear off the page, in order to awaken readers to the specific physical proportions of the object under consideration. From three extant proof pages held at the University of Toronto, which show Mirrlees's suggestions on Woolf's typesetting, it is apparent just how much importance the poet accorded to the visual look of the page ('slightly larger spaces between the words' reads one such comment).¹⁴³

Molière, Voltaire, Chateaubriand: the dead just pile themselves into these meandering lines. For Sean Pryor, *Paris* is an occasional poem: Mirrlees's typographical experimentation emerged out of its singular historical moment.¹⁴⁴ Mirrlees was never the most prolific author – in a letter addressed to Alice B. Toklas she called herself 'pen & ink-shy' – and the fact that she at no time appears to have returned to these vanguard 'tricks of type' certainly can be read as proof of their historical significance.¹⁴⁵ In other words, an attempt to represent the war's memorial culture in part prompted Mirrlees's experimentation, much as was the case for Apollinaire, who had loved seeing how the spirit behind his calligrams also shaped military press releases.[146] The French avant-garde poets – Mirrlees spoke excellent French – were clearly an inspiration, as reviews in the *Athenaeum* and *TLS* also understood (comparing the author's free verse, for instance, to 'an experiment in Dadaism').[147] While the premise of the poem recalls Apollinaire's *Zône* and Cendrars's *Les Pâques à New York*, and certain allusions appear to be lifted from Cocteau's *Le Cap de Bonne Espérance*, *Paris* still presented a novelty to an English readership.[148] It famously pre-dated Eliot's 'The Waste Land'. Woolf, for one, confessed to being much impressed by Mirrlees's adoption of what the former termed 'the very latest style'.[149]

Mirrlees's 'tricks of type' do not only emphasise the physicality of memorial objects such as gravestones and plaques. They also signpost, at the level of discourse, the materiality of the text, which exists, as Johanna Drucker noted of this kind of vanguard experiment, 'in its own right on an equal status with the tangible, dimensional objects of the real world'.[150] In doing so, Mirrlees appears to suggest an initial way, explored further below, in which books like *Paris: A Poem* might themselves be encountered as a kind of memorial object. Books preserve the past. Her 1962 biography of an Elizabethan antiquary, *A Fly in Amber*, was named for a phrase – a strange relic from the past – that uses the longevity of stone as a symbol for preservation. Books, too, possessed a certain longevity and a capacity to safeguard (her dead subject, she suggested in the preface, would 'survive his biographer, who is already an old woman').[151] Certain passages in *Paris: A Poem* draw awareness to this notion of the poem *as object*, among other media, with the power to provoke memory and loss: a fading photograph of a French soldier ('*eidola* in hideous frames inset with the brass / motto'), paintings of bereaved women (Jacques-Louis David's *Portrait of Madame Récamier* and Enguerrand Quarton's *Pietà of Villeneuve-lès-Avignon*), a music score from a Handel opera ('dim-in-u-en-do' for the dying) and advertisement posters for a service that dyes clothes black for mourning ('DEUIL EN 24 HEURES').[152] By implication, Mirrlees positions the text of the poem alongside these paintings, music scores, posters and photographs – as more than a set of disembodied lines, as an object proper taking up its rightful place in the material memorial culture of war. After all, *Paris: A Poem* was an object. It was printed in the drawing room at Hogarth House in February 1920, and Virginia Woolf once admitted, in a line equally revealing of the awareness Mirrlees's poem creates, that the books they print 'cease to be literature in an early stage of the process'.[153] Typesetting the poem was Woolf's responsibility, since her husband's tremor, which had kept him out of the army, also kept him from handling the more intricate parts of the printing process. Setting *Paris: A Poem* in type was, according to Julia Briggs, 'the single most difficult task

Woolf ever undertook as a printer'.[154] Leonard Woolf, in turn, worked the hand-press. They sewed the separate pages together, bound them in a booklet, covered it with harlequin patterned paper in gold, blue and red, and corrected a few printing errors by hand (leaving her, as Woolf wrote on 24 April 1920, '[h]alf blind').[155]

Mistakes were not uncommon, for the Hogarth Press in its early years was, Mirrlees later recalled, 'delightfully intricate & amateurish'.[156] 'Printing at Hogarth', Woolf herself observed a year after the founding of the press in 1917, 'must look like something seen through opera glasses upside down.'[157] The Woolfs had been self-taught, after being denied entry to the St Bride's School of Printing.[158] For their first publication, for instance, they had not properly locked the type in its chase, with the result that the ink was not black enough (though Vanessa Bell, Woolf's sister, found the 'greyness of the wood cuts [better] than the extreme blackness').[159] Such missteps – alongside the colourful wrappers, the typographical experiments, the handprinting, the annotations by hand – lent a makeshift character to Hogarth Press editions from the early, war-ridden years, transforming them into curiously affective objects.[160] Whoever purchased a copy – and 152 out of 175 copies were indeed sold – was more likely to treasure than to discard Mirrlees's poem, a fact, as I go on to explore below, that has its own implications for the memorial culture that developed in the early post-war years. In the late 1930s, John Lehmann spotted a few unsold copies of *Paris: A Poem* among piles of books at the Hogarth Press's London offices, 'all different shapes and sizes and many of them in the prettily designed paper covers'. They were 'little books almost entirely forgotten'.[161] Even unread, they continued to exist, and to appeal. Lehmann persuaded Leonard Woolf to let him have them for his personal collection. (Much later, Barbara Hiles likewise admitted that her copy of Mansfield's *Prelude*, for which she had helped set the type at the Hogarth Press, by then already many years ago, was among her most cherished possessions.)[162]

In fact, the war underwrote this modernist curiosity in the materiality of the book in a variety of ways – from a poet's experimentation with the visual look of the page in an attempt to convey the war's memorial objects to radical choices made by the printer as a consequence of the conflict's paper shortages. The latter is clear from Virginia Woolf's *Kew Gardens*, an early Hogarth Press publication from 1919 (which Mirrlees, too, purchased and read when it was collected in *Monday or Tuesday* two years later). Like *Jacob's Room* and *Paris: A Poem*, the short story resorts to the same imagery in its investigation of the war dead: two strollers in London's Kew Gardens, who 'look half transparent' as the 'substance' of their bodies dissolves in the midday light, debate the invention of a little machine with which a widow could summon the spirits of the war dead.[163] The war shaped not only the timely interest in spiritualism within its pages, but the book as a handprinted object, in ways that struck contemporary reviewers. 'The stories are not to be had through the booksellers,' E. M. Forster wrote in the *Daily News*. 'Those who would experiment in them should write to the Hogarth Press.'[164] Set up and printed by the Woolfs in 150 copies in November and December 1918, *Kew Gardens* is such a curiously affective object partly because of the war's paper shortages.[165] Virginia Woolf herself had noted a 'great shortage' of paper, which made up the main cost of early Hogarth Press editions.[166] For the marbled covers of *Kew Gardens*, coloured by hand at the Omega Workshops, Virginia Woolf paid Roger Fry 25/-, a sum the former found 'extortionate'.[167] Since the paper was only enough to cover half of the copies, the Woolfs turned to Vanessa Bell to make more instead of buying from the Omega Workshops. '[T]here need be no likeness,' Woolf advised her (just as the woodcuts Bell had produced were also permitted to be 'without reference to the story'), explaining the lack of uniformity in the 150 copies of the first edition of *Kew Gardens*.[168] As Woolf found Fry's coloured paper 'very nice' but 'so thin', she first covered the booklets in cheaper pink wallpaper for support, before wrapping them with Fry's covers.[169] The bright colours and the art-deco flower motif of the wallpaper stand out as one opens the book; together, they make for a strange, collage-like whole.

A reviewer for the *Times Literary Supplement*, Harold Child, appreciated these makeshift qualities, highlighting the woodcuts and the 'blotched, spotted, streaked, speckled and flushed' cover in his review. For him, the experimental character of *Kew Gardens* – he called it 'original' and 'strange' and its cover 'like no other' – was located in the material qualities of the booklet as much as in the writing it contained.[170] Not much later, when Virginia Woolf went around local shops 'with a bag of our books' (including the recently printed *Kew Gardens*), a bookseller likewise assured her that 'so long as you print things yourself I can guarantee you an immediate sale and high prices'. Having someone else do the printing for them would be a different matter, he added. 'Its the personal touch.'[171] In more ways than one, the war accounts for what makes these early Hogarth Press publications such curiously affective objects: from Mirrlees's use of typographical experimentation to represent the war's memorial culture in *Paris: A Poem* to Woolf's unique responses to paper shortages in *Kew Gardens*. The effect these experiments generated, then and now, was to alert the reader to the material properties of the book. As such unique objects, handprinted and bound, books were thought of as having extended shelf lives, reaching far beyond the limits imposed on human existence. As Patrick Collier put it simply, books, unlike periodicals, 'come home to stay'.[172] In my final section, I go on to show that the fact of these extended *material* lives was harnessed to retrieve the memory of the war dead. For the wartime modernist, a book might equally, as Allyson Booth argued of the tombstone, 'ensure permanence of epitaph'.[173]

PAPER TOMBS: *POEMS BY C. N. SIDNEY WOOLF* AND *THE COLLECTED POEMS OF RUPERT BROOKE: WITH A MEMOIR*

Remembering in and after the First World War, Laura Wittman contends, was an act that took form across a variety of media.[174] If the war urged the modernists to think of the book as a material object, with the capacity to outlast the people who wrote and printed it, then the book may also keep hold of lives and function as a memorial, one made not from stone but from paper. Like graves and monuments, books in the Greater War period were used in visceral ways for precisely this reason. Towards the end of *Jacob's Room*, for instance, at an inn in Olympia, Woolf's elusive protagonist meets the beautiful Sandra Wentworth Williams, an older Englishwoman travelling in Greece and the Ottoman Empire with her husband. She lends him her copy of Tchekov, 'a little book convenient for travelling'.[175] They fall in love. In Athens, on a moonlit walk around the Acropolis, Jacob returns the gesture, offering Sandra his treasured copy of John Donne's *Poems* – something 'hard and durable to keep for ever'.[176] Moments later they vanish into the night, as the narrator, tellingly, loses trace of her protagonist, who in the spring of 1914 is already so close to death. On his return to London, Jacob receives a long letter from Sandra, which she has written 'with his book before her and in her mind the memory of something said or attempted, some moment in the dark on the road to the Acropolis which (such was her creed) mattered for ever'.[177] For Sandra, the memory of Jacob, and of an unwitnessed moment in Athens, attaches itself to Donne's *Poems*.

Years later, by which time Jacob has perished in combat, Sandra Wentworth Williams finds the volume on a shelf in Milton Dower House, her country home:

> There were ten or twelve little volumes already. Strolling in at dusk, Sandra would open the books and her eyes would brighten (but not at the print), and subsiding into the armchair she would suck back again the soul of the moment; or, for sometimes she was restless, would pull out book after book and swing across the whole space of her life like an acrobat from bar to bar. She had had her moments.[178]

Throughout, Woolf's novel is stuffed full of throwaway papers: receipts, letters, 'long pink spills from an old newspaper', 'one of those scribbles' falling out of a book after twenty years, 'the unpublished works of women' (dried by the fireside 'for the blotting-paper's worn to holes and the nib cleft and clotted').[179] The book in this scene, however, is much less ephemeral, bound and covered and placed on a shelf in a stately home: not 'the sheet that perishes', as the narrator in *Jacob's Room* puts it, but 'the sheet that endures'.[180] Its material form, 'hard and durable', is key to this quest for permanence. It is primarily as a material object that Sandra Wentworth Williams encounters the book anew: 'her eyes would brighten (but not at the print)'. Unlike Jacob, who has died young, Donne's *Poems* can still be held and felt.

In a way reminiscent of Betty Flanders at Seabrook's grave earlier in *Jacob's Room*, or of the 'little widows' standing at the tombstones of 'kind, clever *gaillards*' in *Paris: A Poem*, Sandra Wentworth Williams's affective encounter with Donne's *Poems* triggers a memory: she would 'suck back again the soul' of that unwitnessed moment with Jacob on the Acropolis. At times, holding these books, she even 'swing[s] across the whole space of her life'. By the same token, as Jacob parts ways with Mr Floyd early on in the novel, he is gifted his tutor's *Byron* 'to remember him by'.[181] What Woolf illustrates through these scenes is that the book – not merely its contents but its affective associations as an object once belonging to the deceased or the absent – was understood as an important tool for memory. As in fiction, so in life: when Thoby Stephen died in 1906, the author forwarded his copy of Milton to his friend from university, her future husband Leonard Woolf, then still in Ceylon (a similar instinct underlay her desire to publish Thoby's letters in a memorial volume, which never materialised).[182] In fact, retrieving the past through books is what drew Woolf so distinctly to memoirs and biographies: *Life of Christina Rossetti* was like 'a magic tank' to her, with the past and its inhabitants miraculously sealed within it; of Henry James's *Memoirs*, she wrote that it helped 'summon back the past'.[183] That the physicality of old books comes into play in these preserving and excavating efforts is clear from Woolf's idea, in 1899, to paste her early diary pages on to the leaves 'of some worthy & ancient work' bought at a St Ives curiosity shop (she had not glanced at the title page but had confined herself 'wholly to the outward aspect of the book').[184] The author often compared books to tombstones.[185]

At the Hogarth Press, Leonard and Virginia Woolf also printed a memorial volume to the war dead. *Poems by C. N. Sidney Woolf* was meant to stand in for Cecil Woolf's life in the way that *Poems by John Donne* stood in for Jacob Flanders. On 2 December 1917, Leonard Woolf had received a telephone call informing him that his younger brother, Cecil, a brilliant historian at Trinity College, Cambridge, had been killed in the Battle of Cambrai. '[I]n the dull, static greyness of one's day', Woolf remembered almost fifty years later, 'it was as if one had suddenly received a violent blow on the head.'[186] Woolf's other sibling, Philip, had also been seriously wounded and was evacuated to London. Cecil and Philip Woolf, who had been 'absolutely inseparable' since childhood, had joined the Hussars early in the war and in late November 1917 found themselves in the trenches near Bourlon Wood, seemingly abandoned and in low spirits.[187] To inspire his men with confidence, their major foolhardily climbed into No Man's Land and was severely wounded. While carrying him back later that night, Philip and Cecil were hit by a shell that fell between them.[188] Cecil died and was buried outside Bapaume in the only grave in his plot not adorned with a cross but inscribed with words chosen by his mother: 'YOUR DAYS WERE ALL TOO SHORT BELOVED FOR A LIFE SO NOBLY LIVED'.[189] Philip survived his brush with death, though he never completely recovered, Leonard Woolf observed.[190] In September 1939, Philip, who rarely spoke about his war experiences, visited his brother's burial place in France. By his son's account, the encounter with the grave brought back memories that had long faded: 'it was all as real and horrific to him as it had been in November 1917.'[191]

Cecil Woolf also made it into print, a memorial of a different kind. Virginia Woolf wrote him into *Jacob's Room*, as another model for her protagonist, alongside Thoby Stephen and Rupert Brooke.[192] After his release from hospital, Philip – who 'still talks of "we" & "our" things', as Virginia Woolf noted in her diary – also brought over the manuscripts of Cecil's poems from his time at Trinity College, Cambridge.[193] The Woolfs had been setting Katherine Mansfield's *Prelude* in type, which was to become the second publication of their recently founded Hogarth Press. Putting it aside, they published *Poems by C. N. Sidney Woolf* instead. Only a small number of copies – one scholar has counted as few as five – were printed, for private circulation, on their hand-press at Hogarth House in March 1918.[194] According to J. H. Willis Jr, publishing the poems was meant as a therapy for Philip, who helped set the type and wrap the books in white paper.[195] For Virginia Woolf, too, the reasons for printing *Poems by C. N. Sidney Woolf* had been practical rather than aesthetic: giving Philip an occupation would be 'a good thing to do', she noted, though the poems themselves were 'not good'.[196] The resulting volume was an understated production: covered with white wrappers (instead of the usual colourful covers the Hogarth Press would quickly become known for); slim at only nineteen pages; and printed in simple black lettering on an otherwise white, empty page. The impression thus conveyed is, appropriately, minimalist, much like the timeless effect war memorials (including the Cenotaph) aspired to at the time through their simple designs and white stone.[197] *Poems by C. N. Sidney Woolf* is a tomb in its own right. Even as a 'small book', as Virginia Woolf called it, it stood a much greater chance of surviving than Cecil Woolf's loose manuscript pages.[198] As a bound volume it was ensured a continued existence, so that it could be encountered from the future, prompting an image of Cecil to emerge from the fog into memory – that he very much loved learning and art, and all manner of people, but never as much as horses.[199] The thought fascinated Woolf: books hold the capacity to bring back 'the unknown and the vanished', as she noted in 'Street Haunting', 'whose only record is, for example, this little book of poems, so fairly printed, so finely engraved, too'.[200]

'It seems an odd time to do this sort of thing', Roger Fry had admitted to Virginia Woolf about starting book publishing at the Omega Workshops in the early war years, 'but I think it's as necessary as ever to keep certain things going.'[201] Producing memorial tributes in print, then, was a compelling reason to start, or keep going, a small press in wartime. This idea must also have inspired John Middleton Murry in founding the Heron Press, named after Katherine Mansfield's brother, who had been killed in the fighting around Ploegsteert Wood in 1915.[202] Similar acts of commemoration followed the publication of Cecil Woolf's *Poems* at the Hogarth Press, including volumes dedicated to Ferenc Békássy, a Hungarian student of Maynard Keynes at King's College, Cambridge, who fell in July 1915, and to Julian Bell, Woolf's favourite nephew, who was killed in the Spanish Civil War ('the war all over again', as Leonard had observed on receiving the news of his death, 'when one was rung up to be told that Rupert was dead, or one's brother killed').[203] That there was a real taste for such books is unmistakable from a reference to the phenomenon in Evelyn Waugh's *Brideshead Revisited*, in which Lady Marchmain hires an All Souls don to compile 'a memorial book for circulation among her friends, about her brother Ned, the eldest of three legendary heroes all killed between Mons and Passchendaele; he had left a quantity of papers – poems, letters, speeches, articles'.[204] When Woolf herself drowned, in the winter of 1941, her long-time friend Ethel Smyth had her letters typed and bound – 'sometimes her script was cryptic' – to ensure them a long life.[205] Such a long life meant that the image projected had to be as accurate as possible, which, Woolf feared, was not always the case. A few months after the publication of Cecil Woolf's memorial volume, she reviewed Edward Marsh's *The Collected Poems of Rupert Brooke: With a Memoir* for the *Times Literary Supplement*. Brooke had died from septicaemia, aged twenty-eight, while on active service in the Dardanelles. He lay buried on the Greek island of Scyros, in a grave covered with great pieces of white marble, later replaced by a proper tomb. Printed by Sidgwick & Jackson, Marsh's memoir is another such tomb; it presents Brooke as a scholar, a traveller, a soldier who (quoting from the poet's letters) marches through war-ridden France 'full of thought of how human life was a flash between darknesses'.[206] Marsh's Brooke – 'a young Apollo' – is painted in the tradition of the Greek myth.[207] (Churchill had famously described the poet, in his obituary in *The Times*, as a young man 'with classic symmetry of mind and body'.)[208] These descriptions are of a piece with portrayals of Jacob as statuesque, announcing and justifying his early death. Such adulation, Woolf posited, ultimately leads men into war; it is a form of rhetoric bound up with the interests of the patriarchal state. For these reasons, she despised Marsh's book. Privately, she called it 'sentimental', 'superficial and affected'.[209] In the *TLS*, she was more diplomatic, stating that it was difficult to get a biography right, especially since so many of the people who knew the poet well had themselves died in action.

Why had Woolf been so bothered by this distorted image? When young people die, she wrote in the *TLS*, '[t]hey leave so little behind them that can serve to recall them with any exactitude. A few letters, written from school or college, a fragment of a diary – that is all.'[210] *The Collected Poems of Rupert Brooke* was meant to stand in the place of such absences: the solid codex, rather than the ephemeral papers, entailed the capacity to preserve an image of Brooke for the future. Objects strangely linger when witnesses have long gone. Woolf suggested James Strachey, who had known Rupert Brooke intimately, write his biography instead, to be printed at the Hogarth Press. Had the book existed – it never materialised – then it would have occupied a place on the shelf alongside *Poems by C. N. Sidney Woolf* to be picked up in much the same visceral way one touches a war sculpture or a gravestone. As I have argued, Woolf and Mirrlees were interested in how memory was triggered not only through the work of the mind, but through a 'fresh shock' and 'a sudden *physical* conviction'. Modernist writing from around the war years sought comfort in the thought that we remember the dead through such objects, through such affective attachments. For some modernists, the war even prompted an understanding of printed texts themselves as material objects, so solid and seemingly imperishable in the face of the flight of years that they may preserve and recall the bright young men – Jacob Flanders, Thoby Stephen, Cecil Woolf, Julian Bell, Rupert Brooke – entombed in their pages.

Notes

1. On the popularity of the Celtic cross, see Jay Winter, *Sites of Memory, Sites of Mourning: The Great War in European Cultural History* (Cambridge: Cambridge University Press, 1995), p. 92.
2. Quoted in Richard Cork, *A Bitter Truth: Avant-Garde Art and the Great War* (New Haven and London: Yale University Press in association with Barbican Art Gallery, 1994), p. 263.
3. On the absence of a fence, see Winter, *Sites of Memory*, p. 96, and Laura Wittman, 'Memorials: Embodiment and Unconventional Mourning', in *The Edinburgh Companion to the First World War and the Arts*, ed. Ann-Marie Einhaus and Katherine Isobel Baxter (Edinburgh: Edinburgh University Press, 2017), pp. 149–65 (p. 156).
4. Cork, *A Bitter Truth*, p. 263.
5. Quoted in Toby Spencer, *British Culture and the First World War: Experience, Representation and Memory* (London: Bloomsbury, 2014), p. 260.
6. *The Letters of Virginia Woolf*, vol. II: 1912–22, ed. Nigel Nicolson and Joanna Trautmann (London: Chatto & Windus, 1980), pp. 296–8 (p. 297): to Vanessa Bell, 19 November 1918.
7. *The Diary of Virginia Woolf*, vol. II: 1920–24, ed. Anne Olivier Bell and Andrew McNeillie (London: Penguin, 1981), pp. 79–80. In all, 1.25 million mourners came to see the Cenotaph in the week following its dedication on 11 November 1920. See Alice Kelly, *Commemorative Modernisms: Women Writers, Death and the First World War* (Edinburgh: Edinburgh University Press, 2020), p. 194.

8. Samuel Hynes, *A War Imagined: The First World War and English Culture* (London: Pimlico, 1992), p. 269.
9. Kelly, *Commemorative Modernisms*, p. 8. Many more died from influenza in the 1918–19 pandemic – from 50 to 100 million casualties – but few monuments were erected in their memory. This was in all likelihood the case because of the transnational circulation of the virus, which did not lend itself to appropriation in terms of national identity. For the statistic, see Anne Rasmussen, 'The Spanish Flu', in *The Cambridge History of the First World War*, vol. III, ed. Jay Winter (Cambridge: Cambridge University Press, 2014), pp. 334–57 (p. 355).
10. K. S. Inglis, 'The Homecoming: The War Memorial Movement in Cambridge, England', *Journal of Contemporary History* 27.4 (1992), 583–602 (p. 592).
11. Bruce Scates and Rebecca Wheatley, 'War Memorials', in *Cambridge History of the First World War*, vol. III, pp. 528–56 (p. 529).
12. Winter, *Sites of Memory*, chapter 4.
13. Robert Musil, 'Monuments', in *Posthumous Papers of a Living Author* (London: Penguin, 1995), pp. 64–8 (p. 64). See also Henri Gaudier-Brzeska's claim that 'critics always ignore [sculpture] – place it always last'. Quoted in Ezra Pound, *Gaudier-Brzeska: A Memoir* (Hessle: Marvell Press, 1960), p. 30.
14. 'Mourning and Melancholia', in *The Standard Edition of the Complete Psychological Works of Sigmund Freud*, vol. XIV, trans. James Strachey (London: Hogarth Press and the Institute of Psycho-Analysis, 1957), pp. 243–58 (p. 244). See also Winter, *Sites of Memory*, p. 93: memorials 'were built as places where people could mourn. And be seen to mourn. Their ritual significance has often been obscured by their political symbolism which, now that the moment of mourning has long passed, is all that we can see.'
15. Eric Leed, *No Man's Land: Combat and Identity in World War I* (New York: Cambridge University Press, 2009), p. xi.
16. See, for instance, Kelly, *Commemorative Modernisms*, pp. 6–7, and Joanna Bourke, *Dismembering the Male: Men's Bodies, Britain and the Great War* (London: Reaktion, 1996), p. 216. The publication of images of corpses in the press was prohibited.
17. Bourke, *Dismembering the Male*, p. 229.
18. Joy Damousi, 'Mourning Practices', in *Cambridge History of the First World War*, vol. III, pp. 358–84 (p. 371). See also Katie Trumpener, 'Memories Carved in Granite: Great War Memorials and Everyday Life', *PMLA* 115.5 (2000), 1,096–103 (p. 1,101) on memory as 'sensorily palpable'.
19. Winter, *Sites of Memory*, p. 113.
20. Virginia Woolf, 'Modern Fiction', in *The Essays of Virginia Woolf*, vol. IV: 1925–28, ed. Andrew McNeillie (London: Hogarth Press, 1994), pp. 157–65 (p. 162). For scholarship on Woolf and material culture, see for instance Douglas Mao, *Solid Objects: Modernism and the Test of Production* (Princeton: Princeton University Press, 1998) and Ruth Hoberman, 'Woolf and Commodities', in *Virginia Woolf in Context*, ed. Bryony Randall (Cambridge: Cambridge University Press, 2012), pp. 449–60. To date, there is no such scholarship on Hope Mirrlees.
21. As Proust wrote, 'the greater part of our memory exists outside us'. See *In Search of Lost Time: In the Shadows of Young Girls in Flower*, trans. James Grieve (London: Penguin, 2002), p. 222.
22. Virginia Woolf, 'The Sun and the Fish', in *Essays*, vol. IV, pp. 519–24 (p. 519).
23. Virginia Woolf, *Mrs Dalloway's Party: A Short Story Sequence*, ed. Stella McNichol (London: Hogarth Press, 1973), p. 19.

24. Allyson Booth has also examined how modernist writers 'endow material objects with the luminous ability to evoke memories', but her focus fell on how these objects were discarded – not kept and encountered anew – to erase memories of the past. *Postcards from the Trenches: Negotiating the Space between Modernism and the First World War* (New York: Oxford University Press, 1996), p. 127.
25. 'It was women who assumed the burden of the mourning work in many communities, not least because they made up the bulk of the survivors.' Damousi, 'Mourning Practices', p. 360.
26. For these numbers, see ibid., p. 361.
27. Virginia Woolf, *Jacob's Room* (Oxford: Oxford World's Classics, 2008), p. 194.
28. For scholarship on Woolf's war, see Karen Levenback, *Virginia Woolf and the Great War* (Syracuse: Syracuse University Press, 1999); Alex Zwerdling, *Virginia Woolf and the Real World* (Berkeley: University of California Press, 1986); and Mark Hussey, *Virginia Woolf and War: Fiction, Reality, and Myth* (Syracuse: Syracuse University Press, 1991).
29. The words are Barbara Bagenal's (née Hiles), who 'particularly remembers one noisy night when the bridge was bombed'. See *Recollections of Virginia Woolf*, ed. Joan Russell Noble (London: Peter Owen, 1972), p. 150. See also *Letters*, vol. II, p. 185: to Vanessa Bell, 6 October 1917.
30. See Barbara Bagenal in Noble, *Recollections*, p. 151.
31. *Letters*, vol. II, pp. 258–61 (p. 259): to Vanessa Bell, 15 July 1918. Woolf believed 'the war has taught us a proper sense of proportion with respect to human life'. *The Diary of Virginia Woolf*, vol. I: 1915–19, ed. Anne Olivier Bell (London: Penguin, 1979), p. 7.
32. Leslie Stephen abominated war, forbidding his sons to go into the army. See Jane Lilienfeld, 'Woolf: War and Peace', in *Woolf in Context*, pp. 159–69.
33. Leonard Woolf, *Beginning Again: An Autobiography of the Years 1911 to 1918* (London: Hogarth Press, 1964), p. 177.
34. *Virginia Woolf and Lytton Strachey: Letters*, ed. Leonard Woolf and James Strachey (New York: Harcourt, Brace & Co., 1956), p. 144: to Virginia Woolf, 9 October 1922. 'She has given so much of him in *Jacob's Room*.' See Vanessa Bell, *Sketches in Pen and Ink: A Bloomsbury Notebook*, ed. Lia Giachero (London: Hogarth Press, 1997), p. 57.
35. *Diary*, vol. II, p. 7. For the real-life identity of Woolf's characters, see Richard Shone, *Bloomsbury Portraits: Vanessa Bell, Duncan Grant and their Circle* (New York: E. P. Dutton, 1976), p. 39, and the notes to Virginia Woolf, *Jacob's Room*, ed. Stuart N. Clarke and David Bradshaw (Cambridge: Cambridge University Press, 2020), pp. 413, 417, 656. I will refer to the notes in this edition as Clarke and Bradshaw, *Jacob's Room*.
36. *Diary*, vol. II, p. 92.
37. Woolf, *Jacob's Room*, pp. 100, 124. On Jacob as Brooke, see also Anne Fernald, *Virginia Woolf: Feminism and the Reader* (New York: Palgrave Macmillan, 2006), p. 192.
38. Woolf, *Jacob's Room*, pp. 3, 49.
39. Ibid., p. 37.
40. Ibid., p. 98.
41. *Diary*, vol. II, pp. 186, 214; *Letters*, vol. II, p. 588: to R. C. Trevelyan, 23 November 1922.
42. Vincent Sherry, *The Great War and the Language of Modern* (New York: Oxford University Press, 2003), p. 272: 'The disjoining of serial plot into single, vignette-like instants accrues to an effect of discontinuity that leaves, increasingly, a feeling of incompleteness in the reader's understanding of and relation to Jacob.'

43. *Diary*, vol. II, p. 179. See Woolf's letter to Logan Pearsall Smith quoted in *Virginia Woolf: Interviews and Recollections*, ed. J. H. Stape (London: Palgrave Macmillan, 1995), p. 55.
44. Clarke and Bradshaw, *Jacob's Room*, p. 314.
45. Woolf, *Jacob's Room*, pp. 48–9.
46. Quoted in Clarke and Bradshaw, *Jacob's Room*, p. xl. On Woolf's own cluttered rooms, see for instance Vita Sackville-West in Stape, *Interviews and Recollections*, p. 80.
47. Clarke and Bradshaw, *Jacob's Room*, p. 743. Virginia Woolf found Charlotte Brontë's 'little personal relics, the dresses and shoes of the dead woman' so moving, because their fate is 'to die before the body that wore them'. *The Essays of Virginia Woolf*, vol. I: 1904–12, ed. Andrew McNeillie (London: Hogarth Press, 1986), pp. 5–9 (p. 7). Of the emptied rooms in Hampton Court, Woolf likewise noted, in 1903, that Henry VIII and the little Edward VI 'might have revived in ones mind, if the old chairs & tables had been left in their places'. See *A Passionate Apprentice: The Early Journals 1879–1909*, ed. Mitchell A. Leaska (London: Hogarth Press, 1990), p. 174.
48. Virginia Woolf, 'Mr Sassoon's Poems', in *The Essays of Virginia Woolf*, vol. II: 1912–18, ed. Andrew McNeillie (London: Hogarth Press, 1987), pp. 119–22 (p. 121). Dora Carrington similarly noted on the death of her brother at the Somme: 'I hate coming home because everywhere in the house I see his things and in my rooms all his school books, the queer boxes, and carved things he made, drawings of engines, and frigates. [...] And here, with all his things, I cannot forget hardly for a moment in this house.' See *Letters and Extracts from her Diaries* (London: Jonathan Cape, 1970), p. 107.
49. Kelly, *Commemorative Modernisms*, p. 14.
50. See also Booth, *Postcards*, p. 24, on 'architectural space as a visual strategy for displaying absence'. For her, architecture 'supplies a vocabulary and a set of images through which civilians can begin to articulate war' (p. 43).
51. Paul K. Saint-Amour, *Tense Future: Modernism, Total War, Encyclopaedic Form* (New York: Oxford University Press, 2015), p. 93. '[W]e are witnessing the preparation of cannon fodder,' writes Alex Zwerdling in '*Jacob's Room*: Woolf's Satiric Elegy', *ELH* 48.4 (1981), 894–913 (p. 896).
52. Woolf, *Jacob's Room*, p. 55, much like the ram skull he carries in from the beach in the novel's opening pages. On the Stephen siblings, and Woolf's characters as collectors, see Mao, *Solid Objects*, pp. 28–9; Hoberman, 'Woolf and Commodities', pp. 455–6; Clarke and Bradshaw, *Jacob's Room*, p. 354.
53. Woolf's 1917 review of *Before Midnight*, quoted in Levenback, *Woolf and the Great War*, pp. 22–3. On the absence of combat in *The Years*, Woolf wrote: 'I couldnt bring in the Front as you say partly because fighting isnt within my experience, as a woman; partly because I think action generally unreal. Its the thing we do in the dark that is more real; the thing we do because peoples eyes are on us seems to me histrionic.' See *The Letters of Virginia Woolf*, vol. VI: 1936–41, ed. Nigel Nicolson and Joanna Trautmann (London: Chatto & Windus, 1983), pp. 122–3 (p. 122): to Stephen Spender, 30 April 1937.
54. Alan Warren Friedman, *Fictional Death and the Modernist Enterprise* (Cambridge: Cambridge University Press, 1995), p. 18: 'Subverting suspense, modern novels become circular and self-reflexive, returning repeatedly and ultimately to terminal events they rarely confront or transcend. Modernists elide the dying process [...] base it in materiality.'
55. Woolf, *Jacob's Room*, p. 189.
56. Ibid., pp. 137, 28, 31.

57. *Diary*, vol. II, p. 93.
58. Woolf, *Jacob's Room*, p. 100. On the cultural trope of beautiful yet doomed young men, see Marina Mackay, *Modernism, War, and Violence* (London: Bloomsbury, 2017), pp. 7–8.
59. Woolf, *Jacob's Room*, p. 38.
60. Virginia Woolf, 'A Sketch of the Past', in *Moments of Being: Autobiographical Writings*, ed. Jeanne Schulkind (London: Pimlico, 2002), pp. 78–160 (p. 144): 'We had no kind of foreboding that he was to die when he was twenty-six and I was twenty-four. That is one of the falsifications – that knell I always find myself hearing and transmitting – that one cannot guard against, save by noting it. Then I never saw him as I see him now, with all his promise ended. Then I thought only of the moment; him there in the room; just back from Clifton; or from Cambridge; dropping in to argue with me.'
61. Woolf, *Jacob's Room*, p. 55. The reference is to Laurence Binyon's 'For the Fallen'.
62. Thomas Hardy, *Jude the Obscure* (London: Penguin, 1998), p. 80. Woolf knew Hardy through her father and was rereading him in 1921, when she worked on *Jacob's Room*.
63. Woolf, *Jacob's Room*, pp. 114, 111. The image returns in 'The Art of Fiction': 'Mr Forster has the art of saying things which sink airily enough into the mind to stay there and unfurl like those Japanese flowers which open up in the depths of the water.' *Essays*, vol. IV, pp. 599–603 (p. 600). On dead leaves as a trope in Woolf, see David Bradshaw, '"Vanished, Like Leaves": The Military, Elegy and Italy in *Mrs Dalloway*', *Woolf Studies Annual* 8 (2002), 107–25.
64. Quoted in Levenback, *Woolf and the Great War*, p. 44.
65. Elaine Scarry, *Dreaming by the Book* (Princeton: Princeton University Press, 2001), p. 12.
66. Ibid., p. 17.
67. *A Passionate Apprentice*, p. 199.
68. Woolf, *Jacob's Room*, p. 6.
69. Ibid., p. 6.
70. For instance, see *To the Lighthouse* (London: Dent, 1967), p. 41: 'The very stone one kicks with one's boot will outlast Shakespeare.' For an opposite approach, see Marco Caracciolo, 'Leaping into Space: The Two Aesthetics of *To the Lighthouse*', *Poetics Today* 31.2 (2010), 251–84. For the debate on war memorials, see Scates and Wheatley, 'War Memorials', pp. 550 and 552: 'National memorials were [...] built to last. Ancient and enduring stone was the medium of commemoration – bronze, the Canadian Battlefield Memorial Commission warned, would only be melted down by the next invading army.'
71. See Rainer Maria Rilke, *Auguste Rodin*, trans. Jessie Lemont (New York: Sunwise, 1919), p. 42: 'stone pulsates like a spring in which there is an eternal motion, a rising and falling, a mysterious stir of an elemental force.' Of *The Citizens of Calais*, for instance, Rilke writes, 'These sculptural forms seen from a distance [...] catch on their surfaces as with a mirror its moving distances so that a great gesture seems to live and to force space to participate in its movement' (p. 73). The names of the fallen would go up on the walls of King's College Chapel. As Virginia Woolf's cousin, H. A. L. Fisher, wrote in 1917, 'the chapels of Oxford and Cambridge display long lists of the fallen, and no institutions have suffered greater or more irreparable losses than have these ancient shrines of learning and piety'. Quoted in Winter, *Sites of Memory*, p. 463.
72. Virginia Woolf, 'Abbeys and Cathedrals', in *The Essays of Virginia Woolf*, vol. V: 1929–32, ed. Stuart N. Clarke (London: Hogarth Press, 2009), pp. 301–6

(p. 303). On statues in Woolf, see also Diane F. Gillespie, 'A City in the Archives: Virginia Woolf and the Statues of London', in *Woolf and the City: Selected Papers of the Nineteenth Annual Conference on Virginia Woolf*, ed. E. F. Evans and S. E. Cornish (Clemson: Clemson University Press, 2010), pp. 55–62, and Scott Cohen, 'The Empire from the Street: Virginia Woolf, Wembley, and Imperial Monuments', *Modern Fiction Studies* 50.1 (2004), 85–109.
73. Woolf, *Jacob's Room*, pp. 72, 157. This was a common trope at the time. Dora Carrington, who designed woodcuts for the Hogarth Press, remembered her brother's 'chiseled bronze head' after he had died at the Somme (her father, on his deathbed, resembled 'the marble bishops in the cathedral'). See Carrington, *Letters and Extracts*, pp. 107, 122.
74. D. H. Lawrence, *Kangaroo* (London: Martin Secker, 1923), p. 213.
75. E. M. Forster, *Abinger Harvest* (London: Edward Arnold, 1961), p. 128.
76. Woolf, *Jacob's Room*, pp. 86, 121. Leonard Woolf described Thoby Stephen, the model for Jacob, as a 'monolithic character' in *Sowing: An Autobiography of the Years 1880–1904* (London: Hogarth Press, 1960), p. 123.
77. Woolf, *Jacob's Room*, pp. 108, 238.
78. Ibid., p. 200. Virginia Woolf, 'On Not Knowing Greek', in *Essays*, vol. IV, pp. 38–53 (p. 40).
79. Woolf, *Jacob's Room*, p. 200.
80. Ibid., p. 209.
81. Stape, *Interviews and Recollections*, pp. 51, 93.
82. Woolf rehearses this point throughout her career. In 'A Sketch of the Past', she asks what her cousin would have been without 'Winchester, New College and the Cabinet': 'What would have been his shape had he not been stamped and moulded by that great patriarchal machine? Every one of our male relations was shot into that machine at the age of ten and emerged at sixty a Head Master, an Admiral, a Cabinet Minister, or the Warden of a college. It is as impossible to think of them as natural human beings' (p. 155). In *Three Guineas*: 'There they go, our brothers who have been educated at public schools and universities, mounting those steps, passing in and out of those doors, ascending those pulpits, preaching, teaching, administering justice, practising medicine, transacting business, making money. It is a solemn sight always – a procession, like a caravanserai crossing a desert. [...] most of them kept in step, walked according to rule, and by hook or by crook made enough to keep the family house, somewhere, roughly speaking, in the West End, supplied with beef and mutton for all, and with education for Arthur.' See *A Room of One's Own* and *Three Guineas* (London: Penguin, 2000), p. 183. For war as a 'preposterous masculine fiction', see *Letters*, vol. II, pp. 76–7 (p. 76): to Margaret Llewelyn Davies, 23 January 1916.
83. For a discussion of the Greek myth, see Christine Froula, *Virginia Woolf and the Bloomsbury Avant-Garde: War, Civilization, Modernity* (New York: Columbia University Press, 2005), pp. 64–5, and Levenback, *Woolf and the Great War*, pp. 91–2.
84. Woolf, *Jacob's Room*, p. 189.
85. Ibid., pp. 48–9. Thoby Stephen had likewise been inducted into the 'great patriarchal machine'; it was through him, tellingly on his return from public school, that the author first heard about the Greeks. See Woolf, 'Sketch', pp. 155 and 131: 'The day after he came back from Evelyns, the first time, he was very shy; and odd; and we went walking up and down the stairs together; and he told me the story of Hector and of Troy. [...] Those stories went on all through Evelyns, through Clifton, and through Cambridge. I knew all his friends through those stories.' Woolf began her study of Greek at King's College, London, in 1897, with

George Warr and Janet Case. She found it 'an immensely difficult language'. See 'The Perfect Language', in *Essays*, vol. II, pp. 114–19 (p. 115).
86. See Modris Ekstein, *Rites of Spring: The Great War and the Birth of the Modern Age* (Boston: Houghton Mifflin, 2000), p. 158. Ekstein quotes Henry James on the destruction of Reims: 'the most hideous crime ever perpetrated against the mind of man'. Guillaume Apollinaire, *Correspondance Générale*, vol. II, ed. Victor Martin-Schmets (Paris: Honoré Champion, 2015), pp. 571–4 (p. 574): to Madeleine Pagès, 18 July 1915: 'Voilà une autre façon pour les Allemands d'aimer les Arts. Quand ils n'incendient pas de cathédrale française ils volent les poètes français.'
87. Woolf, *Jacob's Room*, p. 57.
88. Ezra Pound, *Hugh Selwyn Mauberley* (London: Ovid Press, 1920), p. 13.
89. Pound, *Gaudier-Brzeska*, p. 54. The sculptor had sent the poet a postcard of the ruins of Reims. As Pound writes, 'Gaudier's ancestors had been masons and stone carvers for generations and had worked on the cathedral of Chartres. Brodzky himself had discovered an almost exact portrait of Gaudier, carved on some French cathedral façade' (p. 76).
90. Woolf, *Jacob's Room*, p. 205.
91. Ibid., p. 206.
92. *A Passionate Apprentice*, p. 319.
93. Wittman, 'Memorials', p. 154.
94. On these debates, see Scates and Wheatley, 'War Memorials', p. 533. Some people advocated 'living memorials', such as libraries and community housing, instead of monuments that glorify war. See also ibid., p. 540, on how statues of unmaimed bodies diverted attention from the horror of war.
95. Virginia Woolf, *Mrs Dalloway* (London: Penguin, 1996), p. 57.
96. Ibid., p. 168. Virginia Woolf, 'Solid Objects', in *The Mark on the Wall and Other Short Fiction* (Oxford: Oxford World's Classics, 2001), pp. 54–9 (p. 55).
97. See also Woolf, 'Abbeys and Cathedrals', p. 303: 'Even the stone of the old columns seems rubbed and chafed by the intensity of the life that has been fretting it all these centuries.'
98. Woolf, *Jacob's Room*, pp. 86–7.
99. Ibid., pp. 156, 154.
100. Ibid., pp. 143, 147.
101. Ibid., p. 224.
102. Woolf, 'Abbeys and Cathedrals', p. 302.
103. Woolf, *Jacob's Room*, p. 145.
104. Winter, *Sites of Memory*, p. 85.
105. Bradshaw, 'Military, Elegy and Italy in *Mrs Dalloway*', p. 108. On the failure of memorialisation, see also Trumpener, 'Great War Memorials and Everyday Life', p. 1,098; Kelly, *Commemorative Modernisms*, p. 205.
106. Woolf, *Jacob's Room*, p. 233.
107. Ibid., p. 205.
108. Ibid., pp. 15–16.
109. For Woolf's own grave visits, see *A Passionate Apprentice*, pp. 67, 74, 116, 139, 271, 294. In April 1928, two days after Jane Harrison's death, Mirrlees and Woolf met, in the rain, in the graveyard behind Mecklenburg Street: 'We kissed by Cromwell's daughter's grave, where Shelley used to walk, for Jane's death,' Woolf wrote. Quoted in Annabel Robinson, *The Life and Work of Jane Ellen Harrison* (Oxford: Oxford University Press, 2002), p. 305.
110. Woolf, *Jacob's Room*, p. 15. At the time of writing, Woolf designed a tombstone for Thoby, drawing on Catullus' elegy for his brother who had died near Troy:

'Julian Thoby Stephen / 1881–1906 / atque in perpetuum frater / ave atque vale'. See Lyndall Gordon, *Virginia Woolf: A Writer's Life* (London: Virago Press, 2006), p. 216.
111. Booth, *Postcards*, p. 41.
112. After the publication of the novel, Lytton Strachey and Dora Carrington wrote a letter to Woolf from Tom Gage, in which they claimed he had lost his job as a lavatory attendant at Oxford Circus because of her use of his name. Bertha Ruck, who is also listed among the names on the graves, threatened to sue.
113. See Chapter 4 for a discussion of this trope in Anand, Hardy and Eliot. In *Paris*, too, 'The lovely Spirit of the Year / Is stiff and stark / Laid out in acres of brown fields, / The crisp, straight lines of his archaic drapery / Well chiselled by the plough ...'. Hope Mirrlees, *Paris: A Poem* (London: Faber & Faber, 2020), pp. 6–7. Woolf pointed to this scene as an example of the 'glaring' mistakes in the novel: 'What about lilacs in April, fountains in Neville's Court, tulips in August, etc.' *Letters*, vol. II, pp. 577–8 (p. 578): to C. P. Sanger, 30 October 1922.
114. On glass and transparency in war writing, see Booth, *Postcards*, chapter 7.
115. Freud, 'Mourning and Melancholia', p. 245.
116. Woolf, *Jacob's Room*, pp. 261, 182. The first quote is from a draft of the novel and did not make it into the published text. The novel opens with a similarly affirmative gesture, as Betty Flanders 'press[es] her heels rather deeper in the sand' (p. 3). Jacob, on the other hand, 'flopped in the mud' on a hunting trip (p. 137).
117. Ibid., p. 15.
118. Ibid., p. 238.
119. Quoted in Michael Swanwick, *Hope-in-the-Mist: The Extraordinary Career and Mysterious Life of Hope Mirrlees* (Montclair: Temporary Culture, 2009), p. 4 ('eccentric'). *Letters*, vol. II, pp. 384–5 (p. 385): to Margaret Llewelyn Davies, 17 August 1919 ('brilliant'). *Diary*, vol. I, p. 244 ('literary ladies'). For Woolf's account of a dinner with the Mirrleeses – 'a rich warm hearted British family' – see *Diary*, vol. II, p. 48.
120. For Laura Marcus, the strong sense of design in Woolf's fiction is partly due to 'her feeling for the shape and materiality of the book given to her by the processes of printing and binding'. See 'Virginia Woolf and the Hogarth Press', in *Modernist Writers and the Marketplace*, ed. Ian Willison, Warrick Gould and Warren Chernaik (New York: St. Martin's Press, 1996), pp. 133–42 (p. 133).
121. *Letters*, vol. II, pp. 384–5 (p. 385): to Margaret Llewelyn Davies, 17 August 1919. Harrison is a model for old Miss Umphelby, who saunters along the Backs quoting Virgil. Woolf, *Jacob's Room*, p. 53. She also features in *A Room of One's Own*, p. 15: 'a bent figure, formidable yet humble, with her great forehead and her shabby dress'. Harrison was recruited by Masterman for the propaganda effort.
122. The words are Harrison's, quoted in Jessie Steward, *Jane Ellen Harrison: A Portrait from Letters* (London: Merlin Press, 1959), p. 155. 'We have bought a house about 1 ½ miles out of Cambridge, and are camping out there just now for a week, just for a treat before it's turned into a Hospital, for which purpose we have lent it for the duration of the War. It's on the top of one of Cambridge's two hills.' Undated letter by Mirrlees to Alice B. Toklas in the Stein Papers, Beinecke Library, Yale University (box 116, folder 2469, YCAL MSS 76).
123. Virginia Woolf, 'A Cambridge V.A.D.', in *Essays*, vol. II, pp. 112–14 (p. 112).
124. Mirrlees's letters to Stein are kept in the Stein papers at Yale (box 116, folder 2469, YCAL MSS 76).
125. Quoted in Robinson, *Jane Ellen Harrison*, p. 236.
126. Leonard Woolf had meant to attend Versailles. See *Diary*, vol. I, p. 221.

127. Mirrlees, *Paris*, p. 3.
128. Alexandre Lafon, 'War Losses (France)', in *1914–1918 Online: International Encyclopedia of the First World War*, ed. Ute Daniel et al., <https://encyclopedia.1914-1918-online.net/article/war_losses_france> (last updated 8 October 2014).
129. Mirrlees, *Paris*, pp. 19, 11, 14, 6, 18, 14.
130. Ibid., pp. 4, 7. In the poem, men (and boys) are often dressed in *bleu horizon*, the colour of the French army uniform. Women go dressed in black. Ibid., pp. 17, 20, 10, 7. On war and the motif of the merry-go-round, see also Aristarkh Vasilyevitch Lentulov's *A Victorious Battle* (1914) and Mark Gertler's *Merry-Go-Round* (1916).
131. Woolf, *Jacob's Room*, p. 104. On the resurgence of spiritualism in the war's wake, see Damousi, 'Mourning Practices', pp. 382–4; Bourke, *Dismembering the Male*, pp. 231–5; Winter, *Sites of Memory*, chapter 3.
132. Hope Mirrlees, 'Listening to the Past', in *Collected Poems*, ed. Sandeep Parmar (Manchester: Carcanet, 2011), pp. 85–9 (p. 85).
133. Ibid., p. 85.
134. Mirrlees, *Paris*, p. 4.
135. Ibid., p. 11.
136. Ibid., p. 16. See for instance Oliver Tearle, *The Great War, The Waste Land and the Modernist Long Poem* (London: Bloomsbury, 2019), chapter 2.
137. Quoted in Winter, *Sites of Memory*, p. 111. See also Kollwitz's 1919 *Gedenkblatt für Karl Liebknecht* on this moment of touch. Kollwitz obsessively rehearsed the theme of the mother grieving for her dead child in a series of seven woodcuts, *Krieg*. See Cork, *A Bitter Truth*, pp. 270–1.
138. Ibid., p. 296.
139. On the uniformity of the wartime headstone, see Bourke, *Dismembering the Male*, p. 225. Leonard Woolf's protagonist 'wonder[s] why we do it', visiting graves and laying down flowers on a November day, 'yet keeps coming back'. See Leonard and Virginia Woolf, *Two Stories* (Richmond: Hogarth Press, 1917), p. 10.
140. Woolf, *A Passionate Apprentice*, p. 314.
141. 'Paris: A Poem by Hope Mirrlees, London: The Hogarth Press', *Times Literary Supplement*, 6 May 1920, p. 10.
142. Musil, 'Monuments', p. 64.
143. The proofs have been digitised: <https://digitalcollections.vicu.utoronto.ca/RS/pages/view.php?ref=6456&k=>.
144. Sean Pryor, 'A Poetics of Occasion in Hope Mirrlees's *Paris*', *Critical Quarterly* 61.1 (2019), 37–53 (p. 38): 'its singular form meets the felt singularity of its historical moment'. See Peter Howarth, *The Cambridge Introduction to Modernist Poetry* (Cambridge: Cambridge University Press, 2012), p. 16 on 'the fragmentedness of modernist forms as a direct *reflection* of the sense of cultural crisis' ('A poem without an obvious order is symptomatic of the madness of the war').
145. Stein Papers, Beinecke Library, Yale University (box 116, folder 2469, YCAL MSS 76).
146. *Correspondance*, vol. II, pp. 900–2 (p. 900): to Jeanne-Yves Blanc, 30 October 1915.
147. Swanwick, *Hope-in-the-Mist*, p. 3: 'all her life, people were to comment on the perfection of her spoken French'. 'New Books and Reprints', *Times Literary Supplement*, 6 May 1920, p. 286. According to the *Athenaeum* reviewer, Mirrlees 'adopted the idiom of the younger French poets'. See Pryor, 'Poetics of Occasion', p. 38.

148. Mirrlees herself acknowledges the influence of Cocteau, and may have attended his reading of *Cap* at Adrienne Monnier's Paris bookshop. On these influences, see Clair Wills, 'On Hope Mirrlees', *London Review of Books*, 10 September 2020, pp. 36–7.
149. *Letters*, vol. II, p. 392: to Violet Dickinson, 21 October 1919.
150. Johanna Drucker, *The Visible Word: Experimental Typography and Modern Art, 1909–23* (Chicago: University of Chicago Press, 1994), p. 49.
151. Hope Mirrlees, *A Fly in Amber: Being an Extravagant Biography of the Romantic Antiquary Sir Robert Bruce Cotton* (London: Faber & Faber, 1962), p. 13. See also Woolf on the 'eternity of print' in 'The Modern Essay', in *Essays*, vol. IV, pp. 216–27 (p. 221).
152. Mirrlees's interest in painting is also clear from her comparison of *Jacob's Room* to Matisse: 'It is astonishing how certain pages are *exactly* like Matisse – the same seductive virtuosity, the tip of pen or brush the antenna through which one feels the world.' See Beth Rigel Daugherty, 'Letters from Readers to Virginia Woolf', *Woolf Studies Annual* 12 (2006), 1–212 (p. 27).
153. They had asked for a story for their new venture in 1918, but Mirrlees had 'nothing that is short & suitable'. Quoted in Julia Briggs, 'Modernism's Lost Hope: Virginia Woolf, Hope Mirrlees and the Printing of *Paris*', in *Reading Virginia Woolf* (Edinburgh: Edinburgh University Press, 2006), pp. 80–95 (p. 81). *Letters*, vol. II, p. 436: to Lady Ottoline Morrell, 18 July 1920. Of Mansfield's *Prelude*, Woolf wrote that the booklets 'surprised us when done by their professional look – the stiff blue cover pleases us particularly. I must read the book through after dinner, partly to find possible faults, but also to make up my mind how much I like it as literature.' *Diary*, vol. I, p. 165.
154. Briggs, 'Modernism's Lost Hope', p. 83. When in 1922 the Woolfs had finished setting a similarly typographically complex poem, T. S. Eliot's 'The Waste Land', Virginia admitted it was 'much to our relief'. *Diary*, vol. II, p. 259.
155. Ibid., p. 33.
156. Quoted in Stanley B. Olson, 'The History of the Hogarth Press: 1917–23; A Biographical Study with Critical Discussion of Selected Publications' (unpublished doctoral thesis, Royal Holloway College, 1972), p. 8. For Lehmann, too, it started out 'in the tiniest way possible'. See Noble, *Recollections*, pp. 23–4.
157. *Letters*, vol. II, pp. 277–8 (p. 278): to Barbara Bagenal, 20 September 1918.
158. Woolf, *Beginning Again*, p. 233.
159. *Letters*, vol. II, pp. 172–3 (p. 173): to Dora Carrington, 12 August 1917. The ink was not quite black enough; tiny white dots appeared in the lettering. In locking the type in its chase, so the local Richmond printer advised them, one had to make sure it was exactly level. Woolf, *Beginning Again*, p. 238.
160. Leonard Woolf also uses the word 'curious' to describe early Hogarth Press editions in *Beginning Again*, p. 235. However, my argument challenges Leonard Woolf's own assertion that they were only interested in the 'immaterial inside of a book'. Leonard Woolf, *Downhill All the Way: An Autobiography of the Years 1919–39* (New York: Harcourt, Brace & World, 1967), p. 80.
161. John Lehmann, *Thrown to the Woolfs* (London: Weidenfeld & Nicolson, 1978), pp. 11–12.
162. Bagenal (née Hiles) in Noble, *Recollections*, p. 151.
163. Virginia Woolf, *Monday or Tuesday* (Richmond: Hogarth Press, 1921), pp. 71, 77.
164. E. M. Forster, 'Review of Kew Gardens', *Daily News*, 31 July 1919, p. 2.
165. They had started typesetting on 7 November 1918, a few days before the Armistice, and had finished by the second week of December. The proofs were printed on 17 December 1918.

166. *Letters*, vol. II, pp. 353–4 (p. 354): to Janet Case, 4 May 1919. On 11 March 1918, Woolf 'overheard a long conversation with a parson, who had discovered a shop in Paddington full of Elzevirs. He denounced the government, particularly for its waste of paper. They should abolish all newspapers, & stick a sheet in the p. office, if there happened to be any news.' See *Diary*, vol. I, pp. 126–7. We know little of where the Woolfs got their paper during World War I. The details are clearer for World War II, as recorded by Lehmann in *Thrown to the Woolfs*: 'The chief trouble of the Hogarth Press during the war was finding paper [...] we bought up a certain amount of paper at the outbreak of war (not much because we didn't dare take too big a risk), but by the middle of 1940 there was scarcely any of that left. Unfortunately, in the twelve months that were chosen as a yardstick by the Paper Control we had ordered comparatively little; and when it came to being allowed only forty per cent of that we were reduced to something well under ten tons a year' (p. 85). They go from twelve titles in 1940 to just four in 1945.
167. *Letters*, vol. II, pp. 349–50 (p. 349): to Duncan Grant, 17 April 1919. On further difficulties regarding the choice of paper for woodcuts, see J. H. Willis Jr, *Leonard and Virginia Woolf as Publishers: The Hogarth Press, 1917–41* (Charlottesville: University Press of Virginia, 1992), pp. 31–2.
168. *Letters*, vol. II, p. 350 and pp. 298–300 (p. 298): to Vanessa Bell, 26 November 1918.
169. Ibid., p. 298.
170. Harold Hannyngton Child, 'Kew Gardens', *Times Literary Supplement*, 29 May 1919, p. 293.
171. *Letters*, vol. II, pp. 376–8 (p. 378): to Vanessa Bell, 17 July 1919. William Rothenstein, too, had found that the handprinting of *Two Stories* gave the book a more human quality. See Willis Jr, *Hogarth Press*, p. 18.
172. Patrick Collier, *Modern Print Artefacts: Textual Materiality and Literary Value in British Print Culture, 1890–1930s* (Edinburgh: Edinburgh University Press, 2016), p. 15.
173. Booth, *Postcards*, p. 45.
174. Wittman, 'Memorials', p. 150. On the modernist interest in epitaphs, obituaries and memorial plaques, see Marysa Demoor, 'From Epitaph to Obituary: The Death Politics of T. S. Eliot and Ezra Pound', *Biography* 28.2 (2005), 255–75.
175. Woolf, *Jacob's Room*, p. 195.
176. Ibid., p. 224.
177. Ibid., p. 236.
178. Ibid., p. 224.
179. Ibid., pp. 55, 208, 123.
180. Ibid., p. 126. See also Woolf's essay on Rossetti: 'some of the poems you wrote in your little back room will be found adhering in perfect symmetry when the Albert Memorial is dust and tinsel.' 'I Am Christina Rossetti', in *Essays*, vol. V, pp. 208–17 (p. 213).
181. Woolf, *Jacob's Room*, p. 23. Scholars have read this choice as another premonition of Jacob's death, like Byron's, in war: 'The coincidence of Byron dying, like her brother Thoby and like Rupert Brooke (also in war but not dying in battle), from a fever caught in Greece, is something that would not have escaped VW's attention.' Clarke and Bradshaw, *Jacob's Room*, p. 347.
182. Victoria Glendinning, *Leonard Woolf: A Biography* (New York: Free Press, 2006), p. 103.
183. Woolf, 'I Am Christina Rossetti', p. 208; 'The Old Order', in *Essays*, vol. II, pp. 167–76 (p. 173). Other essays include 'Geraldine and Jane', 'The Captain's Death Bed' and 'Jane Austen'.

184. *A Passionate Apprentice*, p. 159.
185. See for instance Virginia Woolf, 'The Lives of the Obscure', in *Essays*, vol. IV, pp. 118–45 (pp. 118, 121).
186. Woolf, *Beginning Again*, p. 197.
187. See *Letters of Leonard Woolf*, ed. Frederic Spotts (London: Weidenfeld & Nicolson, 1989), pp. 219–20: to Violet Dickinson, 15 December 1917. While in training at Mayfield, they would often visit Leonard and Virginia at Asheham House.
188. Woolf, *Beginning Again*, p. 182. Cecil Woolf died on 29 November 1917 in a field hospital.
189. See the records of the Commonwealth War Graves Commission, <https://www.cwgc.org/find-records/find-war-dead/casualty-details/291390/woolf,-cecil-nathan-sidney/>.
190. Quoted in Levenback, *Woolf and the Great War*, p. 34 (letter to the author).
191. Ibid., p. 34. 'Philip very rarely spoke about his experiences.' Woolf, *Beginning Again*, p. 182. For some, Philip is a model for the struggling returned soldier in *Mrs Dalloway*. See Levenback, *Woolf and the Great War*, p. 74.
192. See Woolf, *Jacob's Room*, p. 117 for mention of the Twentieth Hussars. On *Jacob's Room* and Cecil Woolf, see Clarke and Bradshaw, *Jacob's Room*, pp. 294, 303, 514–16.
193. *Diary*, vol. I, p. 92.
194. Willis Jr, *Hogarth Press*, p. 24. The British Library, Beinecke Library and Washington State University Library each hold a copy. It is the rarest Hogarth Press publication.
195. Ibid., p. 23.
196. *Diary*, vol. I, pp. 123, 124.
197. The Cenotaph is a good example here. See Scates and Wheatley, 'War Memorials', pp. 537–8. See also Bourke, *Dismembering the Male*, p. 227 on the starkness of war cemeteries.
198. *Diary*, vol. I, p. 123.
199. See Philip Woolf's preface to the volume, as quoted in a contemporary review: 'Four Young Poets', *Times Literary Supplement*, 23 January 1919, p. 40. The reviewer called *Poems* 'a privately printed little volume'.
200. Virginia Woolf, 'Street Haunting', in *Essays*, vol. IV, pp. 480–91 (p. 487). See also 'Reading', in *The Essays of Virginia Woolf*, vol. III: 1919–24, ed. Andrew McNeillie (London: Hogarth Press, 1988), pp. 141–61 (p. 144): 'making something that will endure and wear a brave face in the eyes of posterity'.
201. Quoted in Jeremy Greenwood, *Omega Cuts* (Woodbridge: Wood Lea Press, 1998), pp. 14–15. On the Woolfs' own reasons for starting a press, see Woolf, *Beginning Again*, p. 233; *Letters*, vol. II, pp. 59–60: to Margeret Llewelyn Davies, 22 February 1915. Woolf noted in 1919: 'Everyone is setting up private presses now.' *Letters*, vol. II, pp. 378–80 (p. 379): to Janet Case, 23 July 1919.
202. Memorial albums, ranging from the professionally printed to the hand-made, were very common at the time. See Scates and Wheatley, 'War Memorials', p. 549; Erica Grossi, 'The Photo Albums of the First World War: Composing and Practising the Images of the Time of Destruction', in *War Time: First World War Perspectives on Temporality*, ed. Louis Halewood, Adam Luptak and Hanna Smyth (Abingdon: Routledge, 2019), pp. 132–52.
203. Quoted in Lehmann, *Thrown to the Woolfs*, pp. 58–9. On *Julian Bell: Essays, Poems and Letters*, see Willis Jr, *Hogarth Press*, pp. 333–5.
204. Evelyn Waugh, *Brideshead Revisited* (London: Penguin, 1987), p. 105. 'Mr Samgrass's deft editorship had assembled and arranged a curiously homogeneous

little body of writing – poetry, letters, scraps of a journal, an unpublished essay or two' (p. 134).
205. Ethel Smyth in Stape, *Interviews and Recollections*, pp. 174–5.
206. *The Collected Poems of Rupert Brooke: With a Memoir* (London: Sidgwick & Jackson, 1918), p. cxxviii.
207. Ibid., pp. xxvii, cvii, cxxiii.
208. W. S. C., 'Death of Mr Rupert Brooke: Sunstroke at Lemnos', *The Times*, 26 April 1915, p. 5.
209. *Diary*, vol. I, p. 171; *Letters*, vol. II, pp. 268–9 (p. 268): to Katherine Cox, 15 August 1918, where she also admits that 'it was one of the most repulsive biographies I've ever read'. Marsh gives no sense of how Brooke was 'jealous, moody, ill-balanced' (*Diary*, vol. I, p. 171); how his adulation was undesired (see 'The New Crusade', in *Essays*, vol. II, pp. 201–3). See also Levenback, *Woolf and the Great War*, p. 25: 'In the case of Rupert Brooke, she recognized that superficial popular adulation distorted the real complexity of both his being and his vision of the war, and in regard to its mythology, she knew that misrepresenting the lived experience of the war on the front widened the chasm between civilians and combatants.'
210. Virginia Woolf, 'Rupert Brooke', in *Essays*, vol. I, pp. 277–84 (p. 278).

4

MULK RAJ ANAND IN THE MUD

A photograph buried in the collection of the Bibliothèque Nationale de France shows eight Indian men, dressed in turbans, digging through the rocky earth (Figure 4.1). The photograph was taken in September 1914, in all likelihood in France, where 138,608 Indians would arrive to fight in the first year of war.[1] More details are hard to come by. While it is unclear what these men were digging – a well, an irrigation ditch, a grave, a trench – their movements appear old and practised. Hailing from the rural northern provinces of Undivided India, as did so many recruits at the time, these eight men had been accustomed to working the land long before they enlisted in the British army, boarded a ship and stepped ashore in France in the midst of a global conflict. The power relations implicit in such a trajectory, and implicit in this scene in the French countryside, are obscured in the photograph, with the British officer overseeing the work and the white photographer taking a picture both positioned just outside the frame. This chapter reads affective moments of contact with the soil in relation to these power imbalances in Mulk Raj Anand's First World War trilogy. In *The Village*, *Across the Black Waters* and *The Sword and the Sickle*, composed in the late 1930s and early 1940s, Anand explores engagements with the land in a literal and abstract sense, moving from scenes of men working the fields in the Punjab, and crawling through the mud of northern France, to men handling the documents, such as land revenue notices and military files, that governed these movements. My argument is that the encounter with the land, and with the documents that determined its ownership, serves as

Figure 4.1 Indian soldiers digging, September 1914. Bibliothèque Nationale de France (Rol 42667).

an image in these novels for the loss of agency, thus functioning as an implicit critique of the power structures of empire. In the photograph, too, the backs of these Indian soldiers are turned to the camera, their faces indistinct.

India was Britain's proudest possession in an empire that would be at its largest in the years following the taking of this photograph, after Britain acquired German overseas possessions in the Treaty of Versailles. As an army recruiter in Anand's *The Village* observes, 'the sun never sets on the kingdom of George Panjam'.[2] For modernist novelists, then, India was a source of much fascination. It may appear strange to locate a history of modernist engagement with the material culture of the late British Empire in soil and mud. Other objects and materials came more readily to the modernist mind: Darjeeling tea, for which Wallace Stevens developed a taste and which led him to pick up a correspondence with the Associated Tea Syndicate in West Bengal; the Delhi muslins and Indian cashmere scarfs in Oscar Wilde's *The Picture of Dorian Gray* and Marcel Proust's *Swann's Way*; the portrait of Laurence Binyon that Manmohan Ghose hung up in his room at Oxford; Tipu's Tiger and the Dancing Shiva bronze in the collection of the Victoria & Albert Museum, where Herbert Read worked as curator; the Tukojirao III Gold Medal E. M. Forster received from a maharaja on his departure from India, and which he kept, and treasured, for more than thirty years; the opal necklace in Mrs Ramsay's jewel-case in *To the Lighthouse*, which her Uncle James had brought from India; and the alabaster models of the Taj Mahal, which Virginia Woolf recalled adorned her grandmother's drawing room.[3] Colonialism and commodity culture, as Leonard Woolf understood, were mutually constitutive phenomena.[4] Yet, while these commodities, souvenirs and antiquities found their way into the modernist novel, the engagement of modernist writers with colonial material culture has surprisingly been underexplored (unlike that of their Victorian predecessors).[5] One reason for this scarcity, as we have seen, can be found in the modernists' own instructions to turn to the *mind within* rather than the *world without*. In the mid-1920s, Virginia Woolf told Mulk Raj Anand about her by-then infamous dislike of Bennett, Galsworthy and Wells for merely writing, as the Indian noted, 'about tables and chairs and haberdashery stores' (Anand would later pick up on Woolf's metaphor, asserting that Victorian literary conventions, like 'the heavy, solid, well-polished furniture of that age', were 'dead weight' for the modern novel).[6] 'Hindus', so Woolf told Anand, of a direction her own fiction took, 'have the advantage of always looking inwards'; Indian literature had a sense of 'unfathomable depths'.[7]

Among these riches, why mud? When E. M. Forster first arrived in India, as a young man in 1912, he noted how 'unspectacular' the princely state of Dewas was: 'No antiquities, no picturesque scenery, no large rivers or mountains or forests, no large wild animals [...] Only agriculture. Flat or rolling fields.'[8] Unlike splendid objects or traded commodities, soil offers a fresh perspective on the lifeworld of Indians living and working on the land, both in India and eventually in a war in Europe. Elleke Boehmer and Antoinette Burton have reconstructed these rare historical passages of Indians to the West, but their focus has been on princes, students and the educated middle classes and, as a result, their scenes were set on the crowded streets of London.[9] Mulk Raj Anand himself, who moved to London in the interbellum and enrolled in a doctoral programme in philosophy at University College, fell into this category. The First World War, however, would occasion a sea-change in this history of movement: not only did the number of Indians travelling to Europe rise exponentially – from 10,000 arrivals around the turn of the century to a number around fourteen times as high in the war period – these travellers, as sepoys, mostly had a working-class background.[10] Mud, then, sheds light on the experience of these men in the farming fields of northern India and the battlefields around Ypres, Festubert, Loos and Neuve Chapelle – providing access, that is, to subaltern realities of colonialism and of war, entangled categories that pivot around the question of land, as it was ploughed, tilled, furrowed, harvested, seized, defended, torn apart, excavated, lost. A cursory glance at the *Oxford English Dictionary* illustrates these broader political meanings: *soil* is both the face of the earth and, since the late Middle Ages, one's native land ('son of the soil'); *land*, in turn, is a portion of the earth's surface initially marked off by natural boundaries (as opposed to sea) and later also demarcated by political boundaries (as in territory). Etymologically, these words started out as tangibly concrete materials that make up the earth's surface and have since acquired additional meanings that gravitate towards the political realm.

This chapter will trace the move suggested in the etymology of these earthly categories – from the concretely tangible to the political – in a war trilogy Anand wrote at a time when 'anti-war books', as he put it, had been 'dominant in the minds of all the writers in the West'.[11] *The Village*, the first volume in the trilogy, introduces Lal Singh, 'Lalu', a young farmer from the colonial Punjab with a penchant for planting his feet firmly in the moist soil of the fields. Running as a motif throughout the novel, these visceral encounters, I will argue, figure as an assertion of the right to place, confirming Leela Gandhi's influential thesis that affect was central to anti-colonial thought (though shifting her focus on friendship and community toward literal moments of touch).[12] I will read these moments alongside scenes of sepoys covered in mud, digging and delving through No Man's Land, and fearing burial under yielding trench walls in *Across the Black Waters*, which depicts Lalu's brief career in the First World War. Considered together in this light, Anand's encounters with mud come into their own as sites for a critique of a particularly colonial war experience. Through an engagement with the soil, what both novels show is that the sepoy, robbed of any sense of agency, was a cog in the machines of war and empire. In Anand's writings, this feeling of impotence also convenes around Indians' use of documents that governed their lives, from land deeds and revenue notices verifying the ownership of their fields to the military files that dictated their movements across the war front. Illiterate, farmers and sepoys handled these documents in a way that, so I will argue, similarly threw their limited agency – over themselves, over their lands – into sharp relief.

Working the Land: *The Village* and *Across the Black Waters*

The First World War cast a long shadow across the life and fiction of Mulk Raj Anand. Born in Peshawar, in the Punjab, in 1905, the author was too young to enlist in the Indian Expeditionary Force at the outbreak of hostilities in 1914. However, he knew many who went on to fight in France, Flanders and Mesopotamia. From a young age, Anand had grown up among these men in cantonments across the Punjab, where his father served as the head clerk of the 38th Dogra Regiment. Peshawar, Mian Mir, Nowshera, Amritsar, Ludhiana: Anand later remembered that the 'army gave no chance to the family to settle down in one place'.[13] As such, he became intimately acquainted with the world of the British Indian barracks. Living in London in the mid-1920s, his then-girlfriend Irene Rhys, much impressed by his gift for storytelling, convinced

Anand to begin a 'confession', for which he drew inspiration from James Joyce and a draft of which he would later share with Virginia Woolf.[14] The initial memoir developed into a set of autobiographical novels, *Seven Ages of Man*, in which Anand returned to the sights and scenes of his Punjab childhood, so 'indelibly fixed on [his] mind'.[15] These early reminiscences throw the spotlight on the 'humble, poor sepoys' he grew up with: 'I learnt a great deal of what I know now from these people, the gift for making things, of telling a tale as well as making tea.'[16]

That the First World War constituted the background to Anand's formative years is clear from the first two volumes of his fictionalised reminiscences, *Seven Summers* and *Morning Face*. Anand's father was probably never sent to Europe but instead ordered to the depot in Malakand at the outbreak of war in what Indians at the time termed *Vilayat* (foreign country, typically Britain). He sent his family to live in Amritsar. '[W]e stared wide-eyed and uncomprehending at the troop movements and the packing of our own luggage,' his son would write of those early days of war.[17] For children, as Manon Pignot has argued, 'the war often became truly tangible not at the moment when it was declared, but when the father went away'.[18] It is difficult to distinguish between what Anand's mind remembered and what it conjured into being, but from these autobiographical novels an image of the war in the Punjab nonetheless begins to take shape. The young boy slept badly in the absence of his father and because his mother insisted on lighting earthen saucer lamps to appease the spirit of the household deity; prices soared in the local bazaars; his uncle told tall tales of a German Kaiser 'jealous of the British Empire' and of 'Indian sepoys at Messines and Festubert'.[19] From these stories – early on Anand heard of corpses 'littered across the trenches' – the boy learned about 'the contrast between life and death' and fostered his initial aversion to the British Empire.[20] This tension manifested itself as a conflict with his father, the Angrezi's loyal servant; the situation reached its tipping point in Anand's late teenage years, when his arrest occasioned his father to turn his hand on his mother for failing to keep their son in check. Fleeing from such abuses, and from the increasingly fraught state of affairs in the post-war Punjab, Anand arrived in London in 1925.

War gave Mulk Raj Anand his subject. In much of what he wrote from the mid-1920s, and continuing into the 1930s and 1940s, the author compulsively returned to the First World War, a conflict he had only experienced secondhand.[21] His most sustained engagement with the war came in the form of a trilogy he drafted in the late 1930s as Europe geared up to another world war. Setting the scene in Nandpur, in the Punjab, *The Village* introduces 'Lalu', the son in a Sikh farming family whose fortunes slowly dwindle through debts to the local landlord and moneylender. The novel opens as the preparations for the harvest are under way in Lalu's village, a turn in the season that brings on his father's reminiscences of resistance to the British ruler and of the consequent loss of parts of their land to a landlord appointed by the British. These entangled realities – land, dispossession, empire, war – set the theme for the trilogy. Written in 1938 in the Woburn Buildings in London (where, incidentally, W. B. Yeats had also received the Indian poet Sarojini Naidu years before), the novel drew on Anand's memories of his mother's village. Lalu's father, too, was modelled after Anand's maternal grandfather, Nihal Singh:

> *The Village* was inspired by the experience of my mother's family whose land had been taken away by the big-landlord of the village. The poor peasantry was completely sold out as a result of British legislation. The novel was welcomed for its revelations about the hitherto unknown lives on the land. The British critics wondered how I could sustain such energetic expression living in London. I replied that I could write in the language of the people because I lived in my mother's village.[22]

Anand had already been in London for more than a decade by the time he began his novel. Still, recalling childhood visits to his mother's village, the author insisted that 'the contours of those rich fields in the Central Punjab have always come back to me' – he had a penchant for moving between worlds.[23] 'Unknown lives on the land', instead of the Anglo-Britons and maharajas in J. R. Ackerley's *Hindoo Holiday* and E. M. Forster's *A Passage to India*, offered a relatively unexplored topic, with its own virtues, for modernist and Indian fiction in English.[24] As Valentine Dobrée once encouragingly remarked to Anand, over coffee and brandy in Francis Meynell's flat in the 1920s, 'I was always fascinated by the ghettos of every town, when I visited India as a young girl. Emily Eden lived among the princes. No one has noticed the villagers.'[25]

Anand *did* notice the villagers. 'Out of every 10 Punjabis', the historian M. S. Leigh counted in the early 1920s, '9 live in villages, and 6 make their living by agriculture.'[26] While early on in Anand's novel the first symbols of modernity – trains, canals, a power house – make their appearance and prompt their own set of anxieties, the village is still overwhelmingly oriented towards the tilling of the land, a source of income and belonging. 'For a colonized people', writes Frantz Fanon in *The Wretched of the Earth*, 'the most essential value, because the most concrete, is first and foremost the land: the land which will bring them bread, and above all, dignity.'[27] In the novel, Lalu's father senses 'a kinship with the familiar earth', and his mother, too, throws her gaze out across the countryside, 'every patch of which was familiar'.[28] Their son, Lalu, was born in the fields, literally, and appears as deeply rooted in the local landscape:

> The thud, thud of his strokes mingled with the involuntary gasps of 'hum, hum' that issued from his throat at the end of each thrust, straining

> his breath. He had rolled back the sleeves of his cotton tunic, for he was absorbed in the effort to dig the ditch deeper, and he struck at the curve [...]. [F]or a long moment his mind was a blank. He was only conscious of the mounds of moist earth yielding to his blade and breaking up into smaller mounds or crumbling away into particles where they were upturned. And he could only feel his burning face smart with the white heat of the lowering sun and the irritation of the sweat pouring across the skin.[29]

Passages such as this litter the novel and give rise to a shift in our attention from the mind, here 'blank', to matter. As he digs a ditch, we learn not of *how* Lalu feels, but of *what* he feels: mounds of moist earth, his face burning in the sun, sweat trickling across his skin. The sense of touch emphasises Lalu's harmony with his surroundings, his feet stuck in the dark earth and his breathing adjusted to the rhythm of the hoe striking the land. The repetition, 'thud, thud' and 'hum, hum', formally drives home that sense of affinity. 'Hum' also recalls the Hindi word for 'we' (हम), suggesting not only an attachment of a singular man to his land but to other men through it – a subtle reference, then, to the burgeoning wish for an Indian nation. Rabindranath Tagore, whom Anand knew well and whose poems he would go on to recite on the BBC, offered a similar, if perhaps better-known image of agricultural labour in the opening stanzas to *Gitanjali*, where it is suggested that God can be found 'there where the tiller is tilling the hard ground [...] He is with them in sun and in shower, and his garment is covered with dust.'[30]

Especially in these late colonial writers, visceral images of working the land, from Anand's 'mounds of moist earth yielding' to Tagore's 'tiller on the dusty soil', become emblematic of a character's emotional attachment to the local landscape. We find the young protagonist expressing a similar sentiment en route to a fair, while he contemplates the grasslands of the Punjab:

> His eyes lingered over the furrows of the newly ploughed fields. He felt they were not deep enough, and thought with some satisfaction that he himself had ploughed the family fields better. As he lay back in the cart, he could almost feel the fresh, moist, upturned sod clinging to his feet, cool and crumbling. He was irritated by it at times and yet he liked it. It was just the feeling he had when he used to practise wrestling. He liked walking behind the plough [...] He looked deep through the moonshine, into the vast, open bare fields for some hidden meaning, some intricate subtlety which held him in thrall. But the iteration of the hedgeless layers which spread for miles and miles and miles held no secret, apart from the memory of the feel of the moist earth on his feet, and the sense of a vague inner largeness, as if he had increased in stature since he had begun working on the land. And yet, because he had not been this way

for months, he looked deeper and deeper into space, led on by a strange curiosity, till his gaze was frustrated by the meeting of the earth and the sky, of the darkness and light, in the single line of the horizon.[31]

Lalu's immersion in the landscape is, in the first instance, a literal affair, figured through the sense of touch. Reiterated twice in this short passage, the motif of the 'fresh, moist, upturned sod clinging to his feet' recurs throughout the novel to symbolise the character's attachment to the landscape. The feeling of belonging appears to be growing still, as suggested through the piling up of words ('deeper and deeper', 'miles and miles and miles').[32] At the same time, peering out over the expanse of the land and peering into the future, Lalu aches for the wider world. The tension between literal rootedness (his feet planted in the mud) and figurative rootlessness (his gaze frustrated by the horizon) anticipates Lalu's escape to Europe, and to war, at the end of the novel.

Lalu's and his family's attachment to the local land is all the more poignant because, being deep in debt, they stand to lose it. The pervasiveness of families plunged into financial crisis in *The Village* is explained through a combination of factors, including drought and disease, extravagant expenditure on marriage ceremonies, and, perhaps most significantly, land redistribution under British rule ('Only I can never forget that those *ferungis* took the Punjab by a fraud,' Lalu's father recalls. 'We lost ten of the twenty-five acres we had inherited, through that thuggery by the *Sarkar*').[33] In a detail indicative of these intimate ties between local debt and imperial politics, the landlord of Nandpur suffers from leukoderma, a condition that sees patches of the skin lose their pigment, making 'his face the colour of an Englishman's in the tropics'.[34] Malcolm Darling, a former assistant commissioner of the Punjab with whom Anand was in touch at the time of writing his trilogy, remains perhaps the most eloquent historian of this particularly Punjab predicament of the time: that one of the most prosperous provinces in British India was also one of its most indebted.[35] As he wrote in *The Punjab Peasant in Prosperity and Debt*, 'the bulk of the cultivators of the Punjab are born in debt, live in debt, and die in debt'.[36] A civil servant, Darling became a surprisingly pivotal figure in the history of modernist engagement with India: acquaintance of Anand; head of the BBC Indian Section; long-time correspondent of E. M. Forster, whom he recommended as tutor to the Raja of Dewas State (an experience that would feed into both *A Passage to India* and *The Hill of Devi*). In mid-war, Darling joined the Punjab co-operative department, to arbitrate and set up co-operative credit programmes which helped alleviate the peasant's debts. There is a case to be made that Hercules Long, the likeable yet caricatured deputy commissioner in *The Village*, was inspired by Darling, who features by name elsewhere in Anand's fiction.[37]

The realities of debt, especially in the veiled ways they were linked to land redistribution under British rule, underline the political motives at the back of

Anand's affective encounters with mud and soil. For, one way of reading Lalu's rootedness in the earth is as an assertion of the right to place, in the face of a reality that increasingly sees him lose a sense of ownership over himself and his land. Through a substance as sticky as mud, sticking to Lalu's bare feet, Anand critiques the ironic gap between affective and abstract claims to the land (the latter, the landlord's, symptomatic of Britain's wider claim to India). His insistence that he is a *son of the soil* – the repeated planting of his feet in the moist mud gestures to a kind of belonging – underscores just how out of place the British were in India, how illegitimate their rule. 'Nationalism is not only frenzy and struggle with all its necessary demand for the destruction of those forces which condemn you to the status we call colonial,' the Caribbean novelist George Lamming once observed, writing of this affective sense of ownership. 'It is the private feeling you experience of possessing and being possessed by the whole landscape of the place where you were born.'[38] Such a reading of the novel is in tune with its descriptions of natural surroundings, especially the flora foreign to the British eye: the mango groves, the kikar, banyan and casuarina trees (the latter, as J. R. Ackerley wrote, 'lives for ever, each branch thrusting down a new root into the earth').[39] If Chinua Achebe could famously claim the palm tree as a subject fit for poetry, then this was perhaps precisely because its unfamiliarity to a Western reader becomes a subtle point of uneasiness about their own presence in such far-away climates, as it does in Anand's work.[40] Already long before the publication of *The Village* or *Seven Summers*, these exotic images from nature had figured a way to raise a simple point about dispossession in Indian literature written in English: that the local population is best equipped to interpret, and as such morally positioned to lay claim to, its natural surroundings. In 'A mon Père', which the Indian poet Toru Dutt translated from the French, 'The flowers look loveliest in their native soil / Amid their kindred branches; plucked, they fade'; and 'Our Casuarina Tree' turns the memory of Dutt's Bengal garden, reaching out to her 'far, far away / In distant lands', into a symbol of exile.[41] Ironically, and indicative of just how far the work of empire reached, the British in India appropriated and named much of the local plant life that later developed into a figure for resistance. Virginia Woolf, for instance, recalled how the botanist C. B. Clarke, who often visited the family at Hyde Park Gate, had given his name to 'three excessively rare Himalayan ferns'.[42]

The First World War exacerbated the colonial subject's sense of impotence and, in doing so, provided further incentive to politicise affective encounters with the land and its natural surroundings. At a local fair, Lalu comes across a recruiter for the British Indian army, who is cleverly placed alongside a quack selling an elixir for eternal life to indicate, as Saros Cowasjee argued, that 'British power in India rests on a fraud'.[43] Because of the burdens of debt in the province, Punjab farmers enlisted in great numbers mainly for material gain – a salary of 11 rupees.[44] Malcolm Darling and Santanu Das have each shown that military service in colonial India was closely bound up with the agricultural economy, from farmers sending their sons to the army to help pay off the property to the lack of recruits in the summer of 1915, in the middle of harvest time, when men were needed on the land.[45] M. S. Leigh, the first historian of the Indian war engagement, similarly observed that the army offered a 'welcome career' to men 'willing to add to the family income by seeking employment away from home'.[46] In addition to a monthly salary and a pension, Indian veterans in the First World War, especially those higher up in the military hierarchy or those who had exhibited unprecedented gallantry, could expect to receive a plot of land as a reward for their service – a promise readily made and obsessively rehearsed in conversations across Anand's early writings.[47] This promise was, however, rarely fulfilled.

In part to alleviate the family's debts (and to evade the police), Lalu enlists in the army as recruit no. 12444 in 2 Platoon, B Company in the 68th Rifles. With remarkable ease, the farmer – 'the primitive natural son of the soil', as the narrator reminds us at this stage, 'who had furrowed the slumbrous earth and felt a sense of power in the sweating sinews of his flesh' – finds kinship among the sepoys.[48] Colonial India delivered an estimated 1,440,437 men to the war effort, many of them, like Anand's Lalu Singh, from farming backgrounds.[49] Nearly a third of these recruits originated from the Punjab, and many others came from the North-West Frontier, the United Provinces of Agra and Oudh, and Nepal.[50] Indian troops first arrived late in September 1914 and saw major engagements in Ypres, Neuve Chapelle, Festubert and Loos. By the end of the next year, Indian infantry soldiers would have been withdrawn from Europe to be deployed closer to home in Mesopotamia. *Across the Black Waters*, Anand's sequel to *The Village*, tracks Lalu's circuitous route to the European front. As Saros Cowasjee reveals, Lalu's fictional unit – 68th Rifles in *The Village* and, by mistake, 69th Rifles in *Across the Black Waters* – faithfully follows the career of the 57th Wilde's Rifles in the Ferozepore Brigade (one of the brigades in the Lahore Division of the Indian Corps).[51] The Wilde's Rifles embarked in Karachi on 24 August 1914, landed in Marseille a month later, and, via Orléans, arrived just in time for the First Battle of Ypres. On 22 October, the Rifles moved up to the trenches near Wytschaete, where the first casualties occurred; by late November they were engaged in action around Festubert.[52]

Across the Black Waters picks up where *The Village* left off: Lalu's ship departs at the end of the latter novel and docks at the beginning of the former, having travelled the roughly 6,000 miles between Karachi and Marseille. Anand's title is a reference to that month-long journey between the ports: under Hindu practice, orthodox Brahmins were forbidden to go abroad by sea, that is, to cross the black waters, *kālāpānī*.[53] The novel charts Lalu's tentative first steps through the rear areas and trenches of France and Flanders, culminating in his capture by the Germans around Festubert in early January 1915. Anand had started a rough draft of *Across the Black Waters* in Barcelona and Madrid in the winter months of 1937, while he was fighting in the Spanish Civil War, and reworked the manuscript in England late in 1939, by which time Britain had entered another world war.[54] The belatedness of Anand's interest in the war was in no way exceptional: Ahmed Ali (much like Vera Brittain and David Jones) was also still writing about the war years, in *Twilight in Delhi*, published by the Hogarth Press in 1940. For his novel, Anand drew on a variety of sources: published histories of the Indian war engagement, his own experience of trench warfare in Spain, his recollections of those who had fought in World War I, and collective memory (like the countless films and conversations over the years, in *Brideshead Revisited*, which had introduced 'the mud of Flanders' to a younger generation and had made it into 'part of one's experience, at second hand').[55] In a 1999 interview with the *New Indian Express*, the author even admitted he spent several months in Flanders 'to get the feel of the situation' before embarking on the writing process.[56] Evidently, Anand wrote with some knowledge of affairs, and the resulting novel, as Santanu Das maintains, is the most sustained and persuasive literary engagement with the Indian war experience.[57]

Transplanted away from home and into war, Lalu learns to navigate this new world through its objects – upon arrival, he is himself objectified, in a moment often recorded at the time (as in Apollinaire's correspondence: 'Passing through Marseille, I stopped for an hour to see the Hindu troops who had just disembarked').[58] Window shopping, the sepoys in the novel are mesmerised by what they see behind the glass: 'big carcasses of cows and goats hanging down from hooks in butchers' shops' and 'wax effigies of men and women dressed in silken dresses, strange shaped hats and coats'.[59] Back home in the Punjab, a young Anand, in any case his alter ego in *Seven Summers*, similarly relied on commodities to construct an 'idea of Englishness':

> My mind devoured the pictures of Englishmen in raincoats, of Englishwomen in lingerie and of English children in Eton collars and school kits and of all the appurtenances of Anglo-Indian existence – boots, shoes, hats, pistols, forks and knives, push bikes, motor bikes, cricket bats and the rest in the catalogues of Whiteway Laidlaw and Company and other firms, which flooded in by every mail for the British officers from Bombay, Calcutta and London and which my father kept for us to play with when he sorted the mail for the post orderly in the mornings. These wonderful products of western civilization illuminated the course of my imaginings so intensely that I built up a vivid dreamworld Vilayat on the basis of this rubbish and went about dressed in

paper clothes cut to the English pattern and ordered about dummy figures of fuel wood as if I were a full-blown Sahib.[60]

The young protagonist in Anand's *Seven Summers* bears a passing resemblance to James Ramsay, at the opening of Virginia Woolf's *To the Lighthouse*, 'sitting on the floor cutting out pictures from the illustrated catalogue of the Army and Navy Stores'.[61] Through images of objects from catalogues both boys navigate their feelings, from aspirations for a future in England ('I built up a vivid dream-world Vilayat') to love for one's mother (as James 'endowed the picture of a refrigerator as his mother spoke with heavenly bliss').[62] In *Across the Black Waters*, Indian sepoys similarly learn of the Europeans through the rubbish they left behind, as when they arrive in a new section of the front and can tell, by 'the greater profusion of empty tins and damp cigarette packets', that this part of the line had been occupied by a British regiment.[63] War objects were put to use to communicate feelings across the kind of language barriers explored in Chapter 2. For instance, we encounter Lalu and his friends in a café behind the front, 'in a crowded, smoky room full of the babble of tongues', where a French officer produces a piece of shrapnel and places it between the sepoys on the table.[64] Failing to cross the linguistic divide, with his 'broken English', the officer resorts to the object to reveal that he had been impressed by, and was grateful for, the bravery the Indian sepoys had displayed under shell fire during a recent German offensive.[65] If the officer's English and gestures make a pantomime of war, as Lalu playfully insinuates, then the piece of shrapnel on the table between them (as well as the drinks the officer pays for) carries his message across.

Like damp cigarette packs and pieces of shrapnel, trench mud was endowed with a range of meanings, only much more critically. From the moment of his arrival, Lalu stamps his feet 'to see if the impact of the earth of France was any different from the feel of Hindustan', in a gesture reminiscent of 'the feel of the moist earth on his feet' in *The Village*.[66] What catches the sepoys' attention, as soon as these former farmers begin travelling around France, is the richness of its soil and the wonder of its agricultural methods and equipment: 'freshly ploughed fields' and 'machine ploughs, steel implements, sheep, pigs, cows, chickens, beetroot, potatoes and apple wine'.[67] To Lalu, the inhabitants of France and Flanders are 'wonderful cultivators'.[68] This is also the sense that emerges from a remarkable archive of sepoy correspondence.[69] For instance, as one Indian soldier wrote (or dictated to a scribe) from a camp in Rouen to a friend in India: 'I believe France is the home of beauty. Here everything is beautiful. The hills are covered with beautiful pastures from top to bottom all over the country. The soil is rich for fruits.'[70] A fellow sepoy, Saif Ali, was equally surprised by what he found abroad, adding in a letter drafted in Urdu in mid-August 1915, 'The country is very fine, well watered and fertile. The fields are very large, all gardens full of fruit trees. [...] Even vegetables need no watering, because every week at least three or four good showers fall.'[71] It is unlikely Anand ever saw these letters, but the writer must have gathered similar impressions from sepoys returning home to the Punjab. Some of these veterans, Malcolm Darling noted, began growing vegetables and cultivating gardens against religious advice: 'The war killed many splendid men from the Punjab, but in widening the minds of those who served abroad and returned it gave the province something of value to balance its loss.'[72]

Descriptions of the marvel of the French countryside – seeing 'the beautiful lands beyond the black waters' is cited in *The Village* as a principal motivation for enlisting – begin to fade from the novel as soon as Lalu's unit draws near No Man's Land. Here, the war unsettled village communities and tore apart the landscape.[73] By the time of the Armistice, 25,000 miles of trenches will have been dug, a ditch, as Paul Fussell points out, sufficient to circle the earth.[74] However, this early on in the conflict, the trenches still rather resembled shallow holes providing but little cover and situated on wet clay ground.[75] Indians often found themselves, one historian notes, 'waist deep with water or liquid mud'.[76] Trained on the dry ground of the North-West Frontier, sepoys were initially ill-equipped for warfare in the soft French and Flemish soil; the parapets and alcoves they constructed regularly collapsed.[77] In *Across the Black Waters*, too, the day's work is a muddy affair: crawling through No Man's Land to repair barbed wire, clearing 'masses of mud' from shell holes and craters, repairing the parapet which had been shattered by enemy fire, and draining trenches turned into 'nullahs, with tributary rivulets flowing down into them from the communication trenches'.[78] This mud is far from the substance Virginia Woolf spotted on her travels in Florence before the war – 'Perfectly pure mud, with a fringe of grass, runs along the Arno' – but instead contains dirt, leaves, rats and rotting corpses.[79] Many of the tasks carried out in the novel, at night and out of sight of the enemy, are made difficult because of 'the ruts and shell holes in the waterlogged earth, the puddles, pools, the mud, the slime, the slippery craters, and the stakes'.[80] To be sure, the period between late October 1914 and mid-March 1915, comprising the world of Anand's novel, counted only eighteen dry days.[81]

Much like in *The Village*, Anand locates a form of dissent in confrontations with these waterlogged conditions: the literal erasure of the self, as it becomes mud-stained, signifies a figurative threat to individual agency in a colonial war context. *Across the Black Waters* stages embodied encounters with the muddy matter of the trenches to raise a point about the sepoy's impotence:

> the parapet was lined with the yawning, dirty, mud-besmeared hulking forms of sepoys, rubbing their glued heavy eyes and scratching their ritualistic tuft knots under their turbans, baring their cheeks over-grown

> with bristling moustaches from under the wraps, even as they puffed and blew the stale smoke of their breath and spat on their hands to warm them before adjusting the cold steel of their rifles into position.[82]

And,

> Lalu dug his feet on a raised pitch which he had constructed for himself and sought to secure himself against the damp by scratching mounds of earth from the front wall of the trench to fill up the puddles. The trench face yielded: the soil was soft and liquid ... This seemed curious to Lalu who somehow naively expected everything here to be hard. But the earth didn't seem to be a part of this war, from the way it let itself be torn up.[83]

'Since the war takes place outdoors and always within nature,' Paul Fussell has argued, 'its symbolic status is that of the ultimate anti-pastoral.'[84] Nature was both destructed and itself destroyed. The impact of artillery fire on the French landscape equalled 40,000 years of natural erosion.[85] Indeed, if Lalu digs 'his feet on a raised pitch', and scratches 'mounds of earth from the front wall of the trench', which then gives way, these two gestures are much less affirmative than the 'fresh, moist, upturned sod clinging to his feet' in *The Village*. Both passages move the sensing body of the sepoys to the forefront – digging their feet into the sludge, warming their hands, touching the cold steel of their rifles – only to have it vanish in mud. As Santanu Das has argued, in his landmark *Touch and Intimacy in First World War Literature*, trench mud offered 'one of the most powerful encounters of the human subject with the immensity and chaos of inert matter'.[86] 'Soft and liquid', Lalu is surprised to find, the substance confuses the tenuous boundaries between subject and object – a particularly modernist apprehension – so that it is difficult to determine where the mud ends and the 'mud-besmeared hulking forms of sepoys' begin. More radically, it carries a 'threat, both physical and psychic, of *dissolution into formless matter*'.[87] Trench mud serves as a constant reminder of a looming death, of the body itself becoming object-like – and serves as a threat, as well, to any form of individual agency within the war machine. This fear is hinted at in the novel as the sepoys sleep in muddy dugouts, duck away from shell fire or dig trenches; it is finally fulfilled when Daddy Dhanoo drowns in a sinkhole, his body 'invisible under the muddy water'.[88]

The contemporary fear of dissolution into formless matter perhaps appeared unusually pressing for Indian sepoys, given the racial dimension implicit in the motif of mud in war and colonial writing.[89] Trench mud constitutes what Jahan Ramazani has termed an 'anti-individuating element': like rain, it covers friend and foe alike, at times to the point where they become indistinguishable.[90] In his discussion of poetic cosmopolitanism in the war canon, Ramazani points to a telling moment in Siegfried Sassoon's memoir, in which the poet recalls a desire to wipe the mud from a dead German's 'blond [...] gentle face' – a moment that is intimate, yet at the same time can be interpreted as carrying racial anxieties of a skin turned dark.[91] For the Indian sepoys in Anand's novel, mud engenders a loss of self twice over: in equal measure, these colonial soldiers disappear in a crowd of 'mud-besmeared hulking forms' and stand out, with the mud emphasising their darker skin. In doing so, the First World War provides an unlikely source for E. M. Forster's famous description of Chandrapore in *A Passage to India*: 'The very wood seems made of mud, the inhabitants of mud moving. So abased, so monotonous is everything that meets the eye, that when the Ganges comes down it might be expected to wash the excrescence back into the soil.'[92] Throughout Anand's novel, the sepoys are in fact objectified – their bodies viewed as unfamiliar, their silhouettes likened to 'strange characters of the *Arabian Nights*'.[93]

In *The Village* and *Across the Black Waters*, then, visceral forms of contact with mud mark moments of suspended agency: from farmers losing ownership of their land in British India to sepoys perceived merely as unfamiliar bodies and made to crawl through the mud of No Man's Land. Read together in this way – the 'furrows of the newly ploughed fields of the Punjab' alongside the winding trenches of Flanders and northern France – an engagement with soil and mud begins to function as a site for a critique of the colonial experience of war, in particular, and may explain why both novels were banned in the Punjab.[94] To be sure, trench mud is a common motif in the war canon, ranging from Mary Borden's 'The Song of Mud', Ivor Gurney's 'To His Love' (inspired by Walt Whitman's 'The Compost') and Helen Saunders's 'A Vision of Mud' to Wyndham Lewis's October 1917 letter to Ezra Pound: 'If you wish to visualize me these times, imagine a bulging figure covered with mud, with haversacks, field-glasses etc. hanging round it, plodding through a spacious and sinister desert, at the head of a small party of signallers, loaded in their turn with coils of wire, lucas lamps, telephone-cases etc. – all suffused with mud.'[95] So widespread are these passages that Paul Fussell was prompted to read the anti-pastoral as the war's literary symbol par excellence, at least 'so long as we are in the presence of English materials'.[96] Anand offers a corrective to Fussell's Eurocentrism, showing that the anti-pastoral takes on a stronger resonance as a form able to contain the experiences of the disempowered colonial subject. In *Untouchable*, his first and best-known novel, the author had already recruited the motif of dirt for a similarly radical purpose, this time to uncover divisions not outside but within Indian society (issues not of race but of class). *Untouchable* brings the story of a class of sweepers and latrine cleaners whose touch, because of the nature of their work, was thought to pollute and who thus were expected to remain at a remove from other people, existing 'beyond polluting distance'.[97] The novella's political message revolves around moments where the sweeper-protagonist enters 'into a sentient, living, quivering contact' with others, crossing the divide erected between his status as untouchable and his beautiful, sensing body.[98]

INTERLUDE: BURIAL RITES IN ANAND, BROOKE, HARDY AND ELIOT

The ultimate encounter with the soil is burial, when the earth receives the lifeless body; it is the sepoy's fear of dissolution into formless matter profoundly realised. Daddy Dhanoo, an old hand in Lalu's unit in *The Village* and *Across the Black Waters*, fears dying in Europe because he wishes to be cremated according to Hindu rites instead of being buried in the French soil: 'He had always insisted on the performance of the last rites on his dead body,' the narrator explains, 'and his dread of the impossibility of this in a foreign land had been his only objection to the orders of the Sarkar to cross the black waters.'[99] In the fighting around Messines, Dhanoo is ultimately wounded and drowns in a sinkhole in No Man's Land, 'floating in the water, while the rest of his body was submerged with the weight of his equipment'.[100] It is suggested his body is never recovered, left to rot instead, and therefore never buried, let alone cremated. For this reason, the sepoys in *Across the Black Waters* believe his ghost haunts the trenches.[101] That Anand himself was familiar with the Hindu and Sikh rites of dying and mourning Daddy Dhanoo had been refused by historical circumstance is evident from his fictional reminiscences. Growing up in and around Amritsar, he had seen it all many times: lifting the ill from their bed and lowering them to the ground before their last breath (for, as he writes, 'from dust you came and to dust you must return'), bathing and draping the body of the deceased, breaking the skull of the dead so that the soul may have its exit, cremating it outside Lohgarh Fort gate, collecting the ashes and bones from the funeral pyres on the thirteenth day and ceremonially casting away the remains of the dead on the banks of the Ganges in Hardwar.[102] When Anand's alter ego in *Morning Face* learns of the many Indian soldiers dying in the European war, he, too, wonders if the Hindu dead are cremated over there or simply buried like Christians and Muslims.[103]

Little could Anand have known at the time that the War Office in fact ensured that the Indian casualties in the First World War received the appropriate rites, where possible. While technically prohibited under French and British law, Hindus (whose bodies had been recovered from the battlefields) were cremated at Hardelot, Boulogne, Marseille and Brighton, and their ashes cast into the English Channel.[104] Muslim soldiers, meanwhile, were buried facing Mecca on military cemeteries or near Woking Mosque, gathered 'like pearls in their alien graves', as the Indian poet Sarojini Naidu remarked.[105] Verses from the Quran were recited, gravestones were inscribed in Urdu, and their names, according to Muslim custom, would be remembered for a thousand years.¹⁰⁶ One soldier in the Indian Corps, Saddler Ibrahim, had been moved so much by the care which the British government had exhibited in burying his deceased Muslim friend that, as he wrote from Brighton, 'I shall remember all my life, and [it] will bind me in complete loyalty'.¹⁰⁷ By 1930, more than 550,000 colonial soldiers, like Saddler Ibrahim's friend, had been buried in marked graves, most of them in Belgium and France.¹⁰⁸ The practice had been established long before the Great War, in the *little wars* that gave the British Empire its contours. Bodies of British soldiers and civilians had been rarely, if at all, repatriated, but had been returned instead to the black earth near where they died.¹⁰⁹ In Virginia Woolf's *Freshwater*, a play she first conceived in 1919, the Victorian poet Alfred Lord Tennyson recommends Woolf's great-aunt take the necessary precautions for her travels to the colonies, adding, by way of explanation, 'You can't go to India without your coffins'.¹¹⁰

The death of Rupert Brooke is a case in point, and a familiar one at that. The poet died a soldier, but not from a wound on the battlefield. En route to Gallipoli, he passed away from an infected mosquito bite and was buried among the olive groves on the Greek island of Scyros. According to a contemporary source, his coffin, covered with flowers and an English flag, was lowered into an improvised grave dug by the son of the Prime Minister, Lieutenant Asquith. The grave was covered with stones and adorned with a white oak cross spelling out his name (there had been no time to engrave a brass plate).¹¹¹ Later on, these ad hoc provisions were replaced by a marble tomb, which became a site for pilgrimage in the 1920s – encountered anew in ways that I explored in Chapter 3. 'Few people trouble to know much about his poetry', Virginia Woolf wrote of Rupert Brooke in the *Times Literary Supplement*, 'but everyone takes an intelligent interest in his death.'¹¹² In part, the reason for such intelligent interest was the uncanny way in which Rupert Brooke's 'The Soldier', a poem written in November and December 1914, appears to have anticipated its author's death in the following year. 'The Soldier' suggests a way the British learned to cope imaginatively with the prohibition against repatriation home. For Brooke, the land abroad where a soldier is buried *becomes* England: 'If I should die, think only this of me: / That there's some corner of a foreign field / That is for ever England' (a word compulsively repeated six times over in the sonnet).¹¹³ Such symbolic ownership – as the English body merges with, and claims, the foreign field – is part and parcel of the work of empire Anand critiques in *The Village*. For this reason, soil was often retrieved from the battlefield and put to both private and public use. Soil from Verdun was placed before French war memorials and soil from a French battlefield was scattered on the grave of the Unknown Warrior in Westminster Abbey, before it was covered by a slab of black marble from a quarry near Namur.¹¹⁴

To be sure, modernist writers, including Anand, had their own version of this tradition, in which the merging of the deceased body with the foreign land became an occasion for a condemnation of Britain's expansionist politics, rather than its consolidation. One of them is Thomas Hardy, a favourite of Anand's.[115] In 'Drummer Hodge', a poem about a nameless, young agricultural labourer's swift burial in the Second Boer War, there is no such suggestion of symbolic ownership, no appropriation and celebration as in Brooke's 'The Soldier': 'They throw in Drummer Hodge, to rest / Uncoffined – just as found: / His landmark is a kopje-crest / That breaks the veldt around'.[116] '[I]n the country one knows everybody, or about everybody, for miles round,' Thomas Hardy had noted in a letter in late December 1899, '& many husbands & sons have disappeared from our precincts, & are continually talked about by their relatives, naturally enough. I wrote a little poem about the ghost of one who was killed the other day.'[117] Had young Hodge died in that close-knit agrarian community, as he probably assumed he would, we could have drawn up an image of his burial. Instead, he fell in the Boer War and was flung into a grave without the expected ceremonial rites and far removed from his Wessex home. The strangeness of that place of burial – a landscape the Drummer 'never knew' – is emphasised by Hardy's use of foreign words. Kopje-crest, veldt and Karoo are perhaps to Hardy what the casuarina tree was to Anand and Dutt, that is, symbols of a familiarity with the local landscape which the ruler lacked but the ruled possessed. Hardy's critique of empire, and of the little wars that were its making, manifests itself at the turning point in the poem, as the final stanza reveals that this alien natural world now feeds on, and benefits from, the decaying body: 'His homely Northern breast and brain / Grow to some Southern tree', thus serving, in John Paul Riquelme's casual verdict, as 'fertilizer for foreign plants'.[118]

This notion, so unheroic an image of warfare, echoes throughout the First World War canon: in *Mrs Dalloway*, the troubled war veteran Septimus Smith envisages red flowers growing through his flesh; the corpses of dead privates, in Wilfred Owen's 'A Terre', exist to push up daisies; Joachim Ziemssen's soldier's grave, in Thomas Mann's *The Magic Mountain*, is 'thick with matted roots'.[119] In 'The Waste Land', T. S. Eliot, whom Anand knew well, turned to the merging of body and earth as a criticism of war, as is clear from the opening lines in 'The Burial of the Dead':

> April is the cruellest month, breeding
> Lilacs out of the dead land, mixing
> Memory and desire, stirring
> Dull roots with spring rain.
> Winter kept us warm, covering
> Earth in forgetful snow, feeding
> A little life with dried tubers.[120]

April is cruel because the coming of spring brings ceaseless renewal. The 'dead land' comes back to life, the world moves on – a continuity evoked in these initial lines through Eliot's use of gerunds and enjambments. What made the regeneration of the natural world so punishing in the aftermath of the war was the break with the recent wartime past it implied (when Ezra Pound edited the manuscript in Paris, in January 1922, he circled the word 'forgetful'). Pastoral images have long been a favoured mode of elegy, because perennial flowers signal immortality, especially those in red and purple, the colours of arterial and venous blood.[121] For Eliot, however, the lilac – a word, Anand points out, originating from Sanskrit – carries no such indication of resurrection to eternal life.[122] Instead, as a war veteran suggests to a man called Stetson, the land feeds on the corpses it receives, which serve as its fertiliser: 'That corpse you planted last year in your garden, / Has it begun to sprout? Will it bloom this year?'[123] Anand was much struck by this image of the sprouting corpse, reportedly citing it in a conversation with Eliot in the late 1920s.[124] 'I owe a good deal to you,' he confessed on another occasion. 'I owe my critique of Western civilization, of world civilization, to The Waste Land.'[125] As in Anand's sepoy encounters with mud, the dissolution of the *white* body, buried in the dark earth in the poetry of Hardy and Eliot, puts pressure on such constructions as war and empire, illustrating the meaninglessness of individual sacrifice to the nation state.

READING THE SOIL: ANAND'S REVENUE NOTICES AND OFFICE FILES

Empires were made, as Leonard Woolf shrewdly observed in Ceylon in 1909, from 'piles of papers'.[126] Anand's writings juxtapose visceral engagements with the land with more abstract engagements with its paperwork: the scene of Lalu's feet planted in the muddy fields of the Punjab is followed by the arrival of a debt collection letter; after having plummeted through the sludge of the battlefield, Lalu is dispatched as a clerk to the regimental office. Similar feelings of disempowerment convene around these passages, because colonial subjects (often illiterate) rarely had access to the bureaucratic documents (often out of reach) that ruled their lives. Precisely by dealing with the text as a physical object in this manner, Anand alerted his reader to the way colonial and military power operated, insidiously and invisibly, through paperwork.[127] If the war prompted a more material understanding of the text, as this book in part aims to show, then we find in Anand's representations of encounters with files and folders left unread one of that hypothesis's most compelling illustrations. To be sure, war never appears to have inspired Anand to experiment with the materiality of writing in the way of Apollinaire's collages, Mirrlees's experimental typography or Woolf's printing at the Hogarth Press (where the Indian author also briefly worked as proofreader). Much excitement for this kind of experimentation had waned by the time Anand began his trilogy in the late 1930s.[128]

Early on in *The Village*, Lalu's father receives a notice for revenue to be paid, in taxes, to the government, a moment in the novel that conveys a powerful sense of the authority of the unread text:

> 'Look at this letter,' said the old man, handing him a scroll. 'It is the notus for the revenue, isn't it?' He was mumbling eternal prayers to the great Dispenser of light and warmth, though his teeth chattered with the cold. And, somehow, he looked pathetic as he stood bent and expectant to know the meaning of the words on the paper. Lalu wiped his hands on his tehmet and took the rough printed form on which the name of his father, the details of the land and the amount of revenue were filled in. He stared hard at the paper so as to get the whole content of its meaning beyond the bare facts printed and written on the sheet in the uneven flourish of the Urdu creeds. His heart thumped out of respect for his father. A third of the earnings of the family for the year were to be paid as revenue to the Sarkar.[129]

The arrival of the land revenue notice in the mail constitutes the way the harsh realities of colonialism enter into Nihal Singh's understanding. Illiterate, the farmer fails to read the letter (later he will also sign the moneylender's ledger with a fingerprint). For him, the bureaucratic document, left unread, is a material object on to which he projects an aura of authority (while 'mumbling eternal prayers' to relieve his fears). 'Once books are placed in the hands of owners who recognize neither their language nor even their alphabet,' writes Leah Price, 'illegibility throws their material attributes into relief.'[130] Though literate, Nihal's son, Lalu, also initially stares hard to decipher the notice's implications 'beyond the bare facts printed and written on the sheet'. As Priyasha Mukhopadhyay has argued, colonial fiction regularly rehearses such scenes of non-reading, with characters engaging with 'the rough printed form' of a revenue notice rather than the words it spells out. Doing so, the document is transformed into a 'material locus around which the complex relations between power, performance, and writing amalgamate'.[131] The fate of Lalu's family, and their land, is locked in this document; being unable to read it becomes a symbol of the inscrutable ways in which colonial power operated through the printed word. In Anand's *Private Life of an Indian Prince*, a maharaja stands to lose his palace and a large piece of land in his princely state because a cousin claims it as his inheritance: 'He says that there is a document somewhere in the Sarkar's office which proves his claim.'[132] For the farmer with little to no formal education as well as the prince with no access to the governmental offices in Delhi, the bureaucratic document holds power precisely because it cannot be deciphered. The irony in such a moment, equating writing with authority, lies in the tension between the characters' physical and emotional closeness to the land and a remote authority figure's abstract hold over it – a disconnect that is often construed as political in the war canon.[133]

Notus, Tehmet, Sarkar: Anand partly shifts the balance in these scenes through the use of language, thus according a sense of agency to his characters. The author was a forerunner in this respect, often called the father of Indian literature in English.[134] He once described his style, combining English, Punjabi, Urdu and Hindi words, as 'Pigeon Indian' in that it was 'like a pigeon: a little heavy, but it flies'.[135] Anand's language in the trilogy re-enacts, in miniature, what Priya Joshi has termed narrative indigenisation, a process through which Indians imported the novel from the West and reinvented it, and in so doing 'claimed the English novel and produced it to their own ends'.[136] The result, on first hearing, may sound 'a trifle strange', as Anand noted.[137] Like no other, he understood that such estrangement could be put to subtly political uses. Italicised and transliterated, words like *notus* and *tehmet* signalled a foreignness to the British reader – Elleke Boehmer calls them 'betraying signs' of a different perspective – and thus functioned as modest forms of dissent.[138] An obscure, anecdotal moment lifted from the modernist archive illustrates this point: in a heated conversation with T. S. Eliot on colonial politics in the 1920s, Anand felt, yet suppressed, an urge to correct the poet's pronunciation of Muhammad Iqbal's name (Forster, by contrast, had a much more 'intimate' knowledge of 'Hindustani words').[139] 'I think you have got a very good command of English,' Herbert Read wrote to the Indian modernist in the 1930s, 'and some of your expressions, if not quite idiomatic, have a charm of their own.'[140]

Like empires, wars were sustained on paper. For some, warfare bore an imperfect resemblance to office work. This was a side of army life Anand was intimately acquainted with: his father, with perpetually 'ink-stained' fingers, was the head clerk of the 38th Dogra Regiment, and often brought military stationery home from the office, on which Anand learned to write.[141] If the unread letter, in *The Village*, symbolises the insidious operations of colonial rule, then the files and folders used *as physical objects* in *Across the Black Waters* similarly diagnose a sense of barred agency in the face of the military apparatus. Freshly enlisted, Lalu Singh's first confrontation with the army, at the barracks in the Punjab, is through the sight of 'trays of files' that were 'borne in and out of mysterious office rooms in which sat Sahib logs'.[142] One of these, in due time, will be his own file, to which he will be denied access, but which contains details about his past and his politics as well as a letter from the Deputy Commissioner. That such paperwork, tracking one's movements, was crucial to the success of war making was a reality relatively new to modernist writers in the war years. Hope Mirrlees, a foreigner in Paris, struggled to acquire a *permis de séjours*; Virginia Woolf recalled the 'nuisance' of getting an exemption card for Leonard ('waiting a week, examination at 8.30 at Kingston [barracks] – visits to Craig & Wright for certificates').[143] As head searcher for Egypt, E. M. Forster's job consisted in composing and then filing daily reports on the missing with the War Office in London, and Apollinaire, at the front in Champagne, simply wished the conflict would involve less paperwork, complaining on more than one occasion of 'this bizarre administrative war, run like clockwork [*réglée comme du papier à musique*]'.[144]

In France, having come through a battle unscathed, Lalu gets a sense of this bureaucratic side of war when he is recruited as a clerk in the regimental field office. He is tasked with writing letters for sepoys who are, like his father, illiterate (only six out of every 100 Punjabis at the time could read and write).[145] When a German plane drops *Flugblätter* with seditious messages into their lines, Lalu's fellow sepoys have no way of reading them and toss them into the fire: '"Paper, paper, nothing else but paper," a sepoy shouted from the Afridi company. "Give us some to brighten this fire with," said Dhayan Singh. And he ran to fetch some.'[146] These are the men who will arrive at Lalu's desk in the regimental office with a request for a letter. For a largely illiterate army, the numbers were surprisingly high: ten to twenty thousand letters would be sent to India from France every week in March and April 1915.[147] Before embarking overseas, this correspondence was first censored, twice, at the regimental field office and at the Indian Base Post Office in Rouen (and later in Boulogne). A rare photograph from the archives of the French Ministry of Defence enables us to catch a fleeting glimpse of the infrastructure put in place: two Indian clerks, dressed in turbans and uniforms, sit at a desk in a field office in front of an abundance of letters, too many to read in much detail (Figure 4.2).[148] A pencil stuck behind his ear, the white officer glancing over the censors' shoulders gives an intimation of the power dynamics at play in such a scene. For Evelyn Berkeley Howell, a former officer in the Indian Civil Service who headed the censorship office – he may even be the officer in this photograph – these letters were documents *to be read*: they were, as he pointed out, 'an interesting psychological study' in that they allowed insight into the morale of the sepoy troops.[149] However, the whole process implied in the photograph also draws the physical forms of writing into sharp focus: an illiterate sepoy dictating his letter to a scribe; a censor handling the fragile, poor-quality paper and crossing out passages; the letter, endowed with a sense of urgency because of the place it originated from, arriving in India after many weeks, perhaps blotted, folded and mud-stained; the recipient staring at the page, keeping it in their hands as if they had hold of a piece of their beloved, but not able to read it themselves. Letters from the front, Santanu Das has shown, were 'both physical trace and report'.[150] In many ways, it is apparent, the war prompted a turn to writing as a material object.

When, on his first day as a clerk, no sepoy arrives to ask Lalu to transcribe a letter, he is ordered to dust the office instead, a task that is interrupted when

Figure 4.2 Hindu soldiers sorting the mail. Service Historique de la Défense, Fonds Rumpf, Vincennes.

he comes across a reproduction of Jean-Auguste-Dominique Ingres's 1856 *La Source*. The painting, at which the sepoy stares 'with wonder and amazement', depicts a naked woman with a pitcher of water overflowing across her shoulder.[151] While perfectly able to read and write, by staring Lalu performs the perceptual act of the illiterate (the title of the reproduction likewise 'did not mean anything to him').[152] Lalu's fascination with the nude, her entire body on full display, underlines his barred access to the mysterious files and folders that circulate around the regimental office. These documents determine the movements and fate of the Indian troops, much like they did for Ford Madox Ford, who, in his account, had drifted to the front 'at the bidding of indifferently written characters on small scraps of paper: WO telegram A/R 2572/26; a yellow railway warrant; a white embarkation order; a pink movement order; a check like a cloakroom ticket ordering the CO of one's Battalion to receive one'.[153] Ford's abundance of papers and Lalu's office documents – the ones that had sent him into the mud of No Man's Land earlier in the novel – suggest an erasure of free will. Lalu is only allowed to clear away regimental files instead of engaging with them, while dusting 'the knick-knacks and the bric-à-brac on the mantelpiece, the clock, the statuettes, the books in an almara with glass doors and, particularly, the shiny splendour of the phonogram'.[154] Unread, paperwork takes its place among the clutter in this room. Instead of contributing to the war in a meaningful way, Lalu cultivates what he thinks of as 'European skill and efficiency in the re-arrangements of the objects d'art in the room'.[155] A far cry from his earlier fight to survive in trench mud, the scene – staring at a nude, dusting files – presents so facetious, so ridiculous a view of war making, precisely in that it leaves the files and folders unread. Bureaucratic documents are material objects to Lalu, as was the land revenue notice to his father. He finds himself in the midst of regimental authority – 'he heard vague stirrings in the inner sanctuaries of the office' – but has no agency, no formal role, no access.[156] If power works its insidious ways through these documents, then Lalu is not privy to these workings, a discrepancy through which Anand articulates a delicately ironic assessment of the colonial soldier's impotence. In this novel, the imperceptibility of power is part of its oppressiveness.

EPILOGUE: RECLAIMING THE LAND IN *THE SWORD AND THE SICKLE*

Mulk Raj Anand came of age in a tense political period, which taught him much, as he once put it, about 'other causes of suffering than my own personal hurts and frustrations'.[157] In the East, victory had not brought an end to hostilities, as the call for self-rule began to resonate loudly in India during these initial post-war years.[158] For the conflict had changed the nature of Europe's empires. Following the Versailles Treaty, disturbances broke out across Asia, Africa and the Middle East, from the May Fourth Movement in China and the Rice Riots in Japan to the Egyptian Revolution. Anand was clear on the motivations for similar disquiet in the Punjab: in exchange for India's war effort, the British government had made a set of promises, most crucially that of nominal independence. 'The sepoys were told, they were fighting for freedom,' Anand put it bluntly, as he looked back in old age, 'but it was not their freedom at all.'[159] In fact, the calls for self-rule that spread through the Global South in the interbellum had additional war-related origins: economic crisis, the continuation of repressive wartime measures (such as the extension of martial law in the form of the Rowlatt Act in 1919) and the memory of coercive recruitment.[160] The breaking point came in April 1919, when British Indian troops fired into a crowd of unarmed civilians in the Jallianwala Bagh, a garden on the site of the Golden Temple in Amritsar, killing 379 worshippers and injuring almost four times as many.[161] The event had huge repercussions, which reverberated through the modernist movement.[162] Living in Amritsar, Anand was arrested for breaking curfew in the days following the massacre and sentenced to seven whips.[163]

These experiences deepened Anand's political beliefs. When Nancy Cunard once remarked to him, in a café on London's Great Russell Street, that there is '[n]othing like a personal insult to make you into a rebel', the Indian author had nodded, much impressed with her perceptive observation, recalling that 'seven stripes of the cane in Amritsar [in] 1919 had made me hate British rule'.[164] Where, before, the teenager had displayed some sympathy for and loyalty to the British, who employed his father, after Jallianwala Bagh, he became a more vocal critic of empire. He developed an interest in the work of activists and freedom fighters such as Lajpat Rai, Annie Besant and Lala Hardyal. In 1921, Anand was briefly imprisoned for his participation in a civil disobedience campaign and, following his father's violent response, fled his home to work at the *Bombay Chronicle*. A few years later at Khalsa College in Amritsar – 'moved', as he recalled in old age, 'by Mrs Besant's talk of freedom struggle' – Anand joined a students' strike and was jailed, again, for a month.[165] The situation became untenable. With funds donated by the poet Muhammad Iqbal, the principal of his college and his mother (who had pawned her jewellery), Anand paid for the boat fare to London. Louis MacNeice first met the Indian exile in those days, outside the British Museum, and described him as 'small and lithe and very handsome', 'a crusader for the Indian Left'.[166]

'[A]lways, before writing,' Anand noted in 1974, 'the experience came first.'[167] Living through the aftermath of war in the Punjab fuelled the political message at the heart of the final novel in his trilogy. The motif of soil again provides a way into these political realities. If, according to Arjun Appadurai, 'we have to follow the things themselves, for their meanings are inscribed in their forms, their uses, their trajectories', then tracking traces of mud through Anand's writings will lead us to *The Sword and the Sickle*, and with it, into India's post-war years.[168] Still dressed in khaki, from the Urdu for 'soil-coloured', Lalu finds himself demobilised at the opening of the novel. He looks as if he has 'just crawled out of a cave in the earth', and all for nothing.[169] Lalu expected a plot of land as a reward for his service, a promise that was often made at the time of recruiting, but rarely fulfilled upon demobilisation.[170] For Saros Cowasjee, it is one of the war's great ironies, 'that these men should fight for a master who first takes away their land and reduces them to serfs, and then urges them into battle with the promise of land as gift!'[171] This failure to deliver a plot of land to an individual sepoy was symptomatic of the much greater failure to deliver home rule for India at large. Both unfulfilled promises made in wartime – for Lalu: 'the right to own their land' and 'the right to be a separate nation' – act as a motivational force for the action in the novel, propelling the plot forward.[172] Throughout, Lalu makes it his mission to challenge the powers-that-be, the British imperialist and the feudal landlord, by joining a peasant movement and advocating land redistribution.[173] As Malcolm Darling put it so aptly in *The Punjab Peasant in Prosperity and Debt*, war had 'stirred the stagnant waters of village life'.[174]

In providing a fictional space for this entangled conflict, *The Sword and the Sickle*, written in London in 1940 but based on the time the author spent living among Indian farmers at Kalākānkar, bears witness to a brief moment in the aftermath of the First World War, when anti-colonial and communist activists joined forces.[175] E. M. Forster, too, remarked on this brief political union, after having stumbled across a colonial government 'frightened of Bolshevism and Gandhi' on his travels in India in 1921–22.[176] Indeed, characters in the novel, Lalu included, take on the proportions of revolutionaries like Brajesh Singh and M. N. Roy, whom Anand much admired. Early in the novel, we come across the demobilised sepoy at a political assembly, held under a banyan tree in the fields behind the bazaar. A handful of local farmers, 'a mass of rugged, heavy-boned rustics in homespuns', are present.[177] Finding the crowd sympathetic, Lalu is encouraged to speak of his war experiences, of how 'trenches were like ditches and the rain fell day and night, till the land was like a marsh' and of how he had been discharged 'without even the mention of a reward, […] no talk of medals or of the promises of land'.[178]

The trenches in France, the fields in the Punjab: moments of affective encounter with the land, its mud staining the body, hold up a mirror to a more profound erasure of the self. As I have argued, Lalu's existence is a matter of mere endurance as a cog in the machine of empire and war. The setting of the initial resistance meeting, under a banyan tree, reinforces this feeling: the tree is a symbol of the men's visceral knowledge of the local landscape, and their claim over it, at a period when they increasingly lost ownership over these fields. To further underscore this sense of loss, Lalu and his uncle – his parents have both died while he was at war – take a stroll around the former family fields, now lost to debts and mortgages:

> The peaceful stillness of desolation lay all about the fields, which undulated into crumbling hills and ravines, except where the fallow land by the lawyer's bungalow was thickly sown with clover. There was no movement in the air and everything seemed to be waiting tense, hot and expectant, as if for the coming of spring.
>
> For a while uncle and nephew walked along, sweating and breathless, each to himself, as both felt nostalgia for the past overcome them on passing through the land they had once tilled together but which was now no longer theirs. Enlarged by the distances he had travelled and detached from his environment, Lalu could not yet believe that his land was not his, while Harnam Singh, who had never dissociated himself from the village, felt not only that the land he had to mortgage and forfeited belonged to him but also that he belonged to the land.[179]

The coming of spring, 'tense, hot and expectant', inspires a spirit of defiance against the fact that 'his land was not his', against the muddy realities this chapter has charted throughout Anand's fiction. Lalu's anti-colonial politics, in *The Sword and the Sickle*, originates from his emotional attachment to the landscape; it is 'entangled', as he describes it, 'among the roots and stakes of the fields'.[180] His peasant movement gains momentum not only through a visceral familiarity with the soil – 'the feel of cool sod on the hands and feet' forms the basis for a politics of resistance – but also, as the novel continues, through an increasing familiarity with paperwork otherwise left unread: a revolutionary newspaper freely distributed to the working classes, a petition to the head of the district, and (in what is perhaps cautiously meant to be read as a metatextual reference) 'a solid indictment of British rule in India, a book, the clear ideas of which would be the chief weapons in the war of Indian independence'.[181]

NOTES

1. For the statistic, see Santanu Das, *India, Empire, and First World War Culture: Writings, Images, and Songs* (Cambridge: Cambridge University Press, 2018), p. 12. 'No army was so hotly pursued by the imperial paparazzi or subjected to such a variety of visual documentation as the Indian sepoys and sowars in France' (p. 126).
2. Mulk Raj Anand, *The Village* (Bombay: Kutub Popular, 1960), p. 77.
3. Anand rubbed shoulders with many modernists, and if he has been the topic of scholarly interest, it has mostly been for these associations. See Gretchen Holbrook Gerzina, 'Bloomsbury and Empire', in *The Cambridge Companion to the Bloomsbury Group*, ed. Victoria Rosner (Cambridge: Cambridge University Press, 2014), pp. 112–27, and Sara Blair, 'Local Modernity, Global Modernism: Bloomsbury and the Places of the Literary', *ELH* 71.3 (2004), 813–38.
4. See Leonard Woolf, *Empire and Commerce in Africa: A Study in Economic Imperialism* (London: Labour Research Department, n.d.). See also *Commodities and Culture in the Colonial World*, ed. Supriya Chaudhuri et al. (Abingdon: Routledge, 2018), p. 1: 'the desire for commodities drove colonial expansion at the same time that colonial expansion fuelled technological innovation.'
5. As Elleke Boehmer claims, 'the Empire enters the nineteenth-century novel chiefly as a commodity, in images of riches and trades', in *Colonial and Postcolonial Literature: Migrant Metaphors* (Oxford: Oxford University Press, 2005), p. 26. See also Elaine Freedgood, *The Ideas in Things: Fugitive Meanings in the Victorian Novel* (Chicago: Chicago University Press, 2006) and John Plotz, *Portable Property: Victorian Culture on the Move* (Princeton: Princeton University Press, 2008).
6. Mulk Raj Anand, *Conversations in Bloomsbury* (London: Wildwood House, 1981), p. 97. Mulk Raj Anand, 'English Novels of the Twentieth Century on India', *The Asiatic Quarterly Review* 39 (1943), 244–57 (p. 244).
7. Anand, *Conversations*, pp. 97–8. Woolf, Anand adds, 'wanted to hint at her own obsession with feelings and in the chaos of the undermind'. This focus has shaped scholarship on Anand's war writing. For one scholar, for instance, 'Anand's subversive forms prompt us to think specifically about Indian shell shock and the Indian shell shocked'. Trevor Dodman, *Shell Shock, Memory, and the Novel in the Wake of World War I* (New York: Cambridge University Press, 2015), p. 148.
8. E. M. Forster, *The Hill of Devi* (London: Penguin, 1965), p. 48.
9. Elleke Boehmer, *Indian Arrivals 1870–1915: Networks of British Empire* (Oxford: Oxford University Press, 2015) and Antoinette Burton, *At the Heart of the Empire: Indians and the Colonial Encounter in Late-Victorian Britain* (Berkeley: University of California Press, 1998). The work of both scholars is

informed by an impulse to study how 'Britain itself has historically been an imperial terrain – a site productive not just of imperial policy or attitudes directed outwards, but of colonial encounters within' (Burton, *Heart of the Empire*, p. 1).
10. For these numbers, see Das, *India, Empire, and First World War Culture*, p. 12.
11. Marleen Fisher, 'Interview with Mulk Raj Anand, 19 May 1973, Khandala', *Journal of Postcolonial Writing* 13.1 (1974), 109–22 (p. 118).
12. Leela Gandhi, *Affective Communities: Anticolonial Thought, Fin-de-Siècle Radicalism, and the Politics of Friendship* (Durham, NC: Duke University Press, 2006).
13. Mulk Raj Anand, *Morning Face* (Bombay: Kutub Popular, 1968), p. 32.
14. Anand, *Conversations*, p. 13: 'I had decided in secret to emulate Joyce's example.' On Woolf reading the manuscript, see p. 96.
15. Mulk Raj Anand, *Seven Summers: The Story of an Indian Childhood* (Bombay: Kutub Popular, n.d.), p. 260. Anand refers to *Seven Ages of Man* as 'autobiographical novels' in Fisher, 'Interview with Anand', p. 112.
16. Anand, *Seven Summers*, p. 169.
17. Ibid., p. 268.
18. Manon Pignot, 'Children', in *The Cambridge History of the First World War*, vol. III: Civil Society, ed. Jay Winter (Cambridge: Cambridge University Press, 2014), pp. 29–45 (p. 36).
19. Anand, *Morning Face*, pp. 38, 64, 133.
20. Ibid., p. 133. Mulk Raj Anand, 'Why I Became a Writer', *Contemporary Indian Literature* 5.11/12 (1965), 13–15 (p. 13).
21. War veterans in Anand's fiction often remember military songs from their time in the First World War. See *Private Life of an Indian Prince* (London: Hutchinson, 1954), p. 319, and *The Sword and the Sickle* (New Delhi: Arnold Heinemann, 1984), p. 161. On the use of these songs for retrieving Indian war experiences, see Das, *India, Empire, and First World War Culture*, pp. 227–38.
22. 'Mulk Raj Anand Remembers', *Indian Literature* 36.2 (1993), 176–86 (p. 182).
23. Anand, *Seven Summers*, p. 211.
24. As late as the 1990s, Anand observed: 'If much of Indian English writing today especially by men appears without substance, it is mainly because the writers live in big towns and have little contact with realities of life on the land.' See 'Mulk Raj Anand Remembers', p. 186.
25. Anand, *Conversations*, pp. 137–8.
26. M. S. Leigh, *The Punjab and the War* (Lahore: Printed by the Superintendent, Governmental Printing, Punjab, 1922), p. 3.
27. Frantz Fanon, *The Wretched of the Earth* (London: Penguin, 2001), p. 34.
28. Anand, *Village*, pp. 12, 16.
29. Ibid., pp. 25–6.
30. Rabindranath Tagore, *Gitanjali (Song Offerings)* (London: India Society, 1912), pp. 5–6. In his famous introduction, William Butler Yeats points out that a 'very young' Tagore 'wrote much of natural objects, he would sit all day in his garden' (p. viii).
31. Anand, *Village*, p. 60.
32. On the motif, see ibid., pp. 31, 97, 101, 104.
33. Ibid., p. 7. Darling identifies four main causes for debt: the small size of holdings; the loss of cattle from drought and disease; ingrained improvidence; and expenditure upon marriage and other ceremonies. See Malcolm Darling, *The Punjab Peasant in Prosperity and Debt* (Oxford: Oxford University Press, 1928). Anand remembers an encounter with a peasant imprisoned because of his debts: *Morning Face*, pp. 158–9.

34. Anand, *Village*, p. 71.
35. Darling, *Prosperity and Debt*, p. 235. In 1939, Anand had refused a job offered by Darling at the BBC Indian Section. However, during the war, he contributed to the BBC as a freelancer.
36. Ibid., p. 279.
37. In *The Village*, Long was 'supposed to have invented a wonderful programme to help the farmers' and often wrote 'articles on Social Reconstruction in the *Civil and Military Gazette*' (pp. 126, 178). See also Anand, *Private Life*, p. 99: 'Haven't you ever read Plato's *Republic* [...]? Sir Malcolm Darling, who did such good work in the Punjab, gave me a copy of this.'
38. George Lamming, *Of Age and Innocence* (London: Allison & Busby, 1981), p. 174.
39. J. R. Ackerley, *Hindoo Holiday: An Indian Journal* (London: Penguin, 2009), p. 12.
40. Chinua Achebe, 'The Novelist as Teacher', in *Morning Yet on Creation Day* (Garden City: Doubleday, 1975), pp. 67–74 (p. 71). See also 'Introduction', in *Empire Writing: An Anthology of Colonial Literature 1870–1918*, ed. Elleke Boehmer (Oxford: Oxford University Press, 2009), pp. xv–xxxvi (p. xxxiv): on 'the problem of generating new self-images through the medium of aesthetic traditions inherited from Europe' and 'the lack of a perceptual framework through which to translate the "subtle charms" of the Australian landscape, to read the "hieroglyphs of haggard gum trees"'.
41. Both poems are included in Boehmer, *Empire Writing*, pp. 69, 71–2.
42. Virginia Woolf, '22 Hyde Park Gate', in *Moments of Being: Autobiographical Writings*, ed. Jeanne Schulkind (London: Pimlico, 2002), pp. 31–42 (p. 31).
43. Saros Cowasjee, *So Many Freedoms: A Study of the Major Fictions of Mulk Raj Anand* (New Delhi: Oxford University Press, 1977), p. 102. At a later stage, Indian men would often be coerced into the army. See Das, *India, Empire, and First World War Culture*, chapter 2, and *Indian Voices of the Great War: Soldiers' Letters, 1914–18*, ed. David Omissi (Basingstoke: Palgrave Macmillan, 1999), p. 16.
44. George Morton-Jack, *The Indian Army on the Western Front: India's Expeditionary Force to France and Belgium in the First World War* (Cambridge: Cambridge University Press, 2014), p. 302.
45. See Das, *India, Empire, and First World War Culture*, p. 85; Omissi, *Indian Voices*, p. 10; Darling, *Prosperity and Debt*, p. xiii: 'As tenacious as [the Punjab farmer] is patient, the more he is buffeted, the harder he works, and, when circumstances are too strong for him, he will often join the army or seek his fortune abroad.'
46. Leigh, *Punjab and the War*, p. 10.
47. See, for instance, *Seven Summers*, p. 120.
48. Anand, *Village*, p. 189.
49. See *Statistics of the Military Effort of the British Empire during the Great War 1914–20* (London: HM Stationery Office, 1920), p. 777, and Leigh, *Punjab and the War*, p. 41.
50. Das, *India, Empire, and First World War Culture*, pp. 77, 57. Grounded in a popular martial race theory of the time, recruiting focused on northern India, where men were known for their military prowess, as opposed to southern India, especially Bengal. Some of these prejudices went back half a century to the Sepoy Uprising of 1857, when most of the Punjab had remained loyal to British rule.
51. Cowasjee, *So Many Freedoms*, pp. 107–8.
52. Leigh, *Punjab and the War*, chapter 6.

53. Kipling, too, mentions the custom in his poetry: 'the black dividing Sea and alien Plain!' ('Christmas in India', 1888).
54. According to Cowasjee, Anand wrote the first draft of this novel in Madrid and Valencia. See *So Many Freedoms*, p. 108. More important, as Das points out, is his timing: 'as Britain entered another world war and Indian troops were summoned again, Anand – while supporting the war effort – boldly joined the critique of the past war to the critique of empire. Back in India, people were wholly divided between the rising force of nationalism and support for the war against fascism [...] Some of this ambivalence inevitably courses through the veins of Anand's First World War sepoys, giving the novel a retrospective political edge and emotional ambivalence absent in much of the Indian literature written in 1914–1918.' See Das, *India, Empire, and First World War Culture*, pp. 344–5.
55. Evelyn Waugh, *Brideshead Revisited* (London: Penguin, 1987), p. 194. See also Das, *India, Empire, and First World War Culture*, p. 345: 'Anand would have known many of the returned soldiers and their stories'; and *Seven Summers*, p. 268: 'I sensed something of the great events which were impending in the world, but mostly through the myths and legends in which mother wrapped them.'
56. Quoted in Dodman, *Shell Shock*, p. 169. In Dodman's reading, Anand 'appropriates, mimics, and revoices prominent period World War I histories written by white British officers of the Indian Army' (p. 151).
57. Das, *India, Empire, and First World War Culture*, p. 343.
58. Guillaume Apollinaire, *Correspondance Générale*, vol. II, ed. Victor Martin-Schmets (Paris: Honoré Champion, 2015), p. 43: to Fernand Fleuret, 10 January 1915.
59. Mulk Raj Anand, *Across the Black Waters* (New Delhi: Orient Paperbacks, 2008), p. 33.
60. Anand, *Seven Summers*, p. 110. 'I tried naively to emulate Europe', he writes in the same novel, 'through an exaggerated respect for hats, top boots, hockey sticks, cricket bats, shorts, trousers, push bikes, cigarettes, books, revolvers and such other gifts of the West which are the true heroes of modern India' (p. 71). See also Anand, *Morning Face*, pp. 115, 331.
61. Virginia Woolf, *To the Lighthouse* (London: Dent, 1967), p. 3.
62. Ibid., p. 7.
63. Anand, *Across the Black Waters*, p. 134. See also p. 76: 'Some food tins, jam jars, cigarette boxes and torn envelopes lay strewn about, from which it seemed that soldiers had rested here on their way to, or back from the front. But such rubbish could be seen anywhere by the canteen of an English regiment in a cantonment in peace time, and was no proof of war.'
64. Ibid., p. 163.
65. Ibid., p. 163.
66. Ibid., p. 11.
67. Ibid., pp. 62, 186.
68. Ibid., p. 186.
69. Edited by David Omissi, these letters survived in the archives precisely because they were censored. Kipling consulted them for *The Eyes of Asia*, a commissioned piece of propaganda in the form of four fictional letters by Indian sepoys, in which the French and Flemish are 'Kings among cultivators'. As to this cultivation: 'their fields are larger than ours, without any divisions, and they do not waste anything except the width of the footpath. [...] I have observed that they have their land always at their hearts and in their mouths, just as in civilized countries. They do not grow more than one crop a year, but this is recompensed to them because their

fields do not need irrigation. The rain in Franceville is always sure and abundant and in excess. They grow all that we grow such as peas, onions, garlic, spinach, beans, cabbages or millet, and their only spice is mustard.' Rudyard Kipling, *The Eyes of Asia* (New York: Doubleday, Page & Co., 1918), p. 30.
70. Omissi, *Indian Voices*, pp. 44–5.
71. Ibid., p. 90.
72. Malcolm Darling, *Wisdom and Waste in the Punjab Village* (Oxford: Oxford University Press, 1934), p. 332. See also *Prosperity and Debt*, p. 158: 'The taste for gardens is spreading and is in part a result of the war, when many a Punjabi enjoyed the luscious fruit of France.'
73. Benjamin Ziemann, 'Agrarian Society', in *The Cambridge History of the First World War*, vol. II: The State, ed. Jay Winter (Cambridge: Cambridge University Press, 2014), pp. 382–407.
74. Paul Fussell, *The Great War and Modern Memory* (New York: Oxford University Press, 1977), p. 37.
75. Morton-Jack, *Indian Army on the Western Front*, p. 204.
76. Ibid., p. 204.
77. Ibid., p. 224. Anand, *Across the Black Waters*, p. 91: 'But why were these trenches so shapeless and irregular? They were so different from the regular trenches built for mimic warfare in the parade grounds at Ferozepur.'
78. Anand, *Across the Black Waters*, p. 105.
79. Virginia Woolf, *A Passionate Apprentice: The Early Journals 1879–1909*, ed. Mitchell A. Leaska (London: Hogarth Press, 1990), p. 396.
80. Anand, *Across the Black Waters*, p. 106.
81. Santanu Das, *Touch and Intimacy in First World War Literature* (Cambridge: Cambridge University Press, 2007), p. 40. The Indian Corps encountered the same issue in Mesopotamia: 'It rains very heavily and the entire surface of the land becomes a quagmire in which the slush is knee deep.' See Omissi, *Indian Voices*, p. 160.
82. Anand, *Across the Black Waters*, p. 107.
83. Ibid., p. 111.
84. Fussell, *Great War and Modern Memory*, p. 231. See also Edna Longley on the war pastoral as oxymoron: 'The Great War, History and the English Lyric', in *The Cambridge Companion to the Literature of the First World War*, ed. Vincent Sherry (Cambridge: Cambridge University Press, 2005), pp. 57–84 (p. 79). Interestingly, Cowasjee refers to *The Village* as a pastoral in *So Many Freedoms*, p. 104.
85. Elizabeth Kolbert, 'Chemical Warfare's Home Front', *New York Review of Books*, <https://www.nybooks.com/articles/2021/02/11/chemical-warfares-home-front/>.
86. Das, *Touch and Intimacy*, p. 37. On trench mud, see also Kate McLoughlin, 'Muddy Poetics: First World War Poems by Helen Saunders and Mary Borden', *Women: A Cultural Review* 26.3 (2015), 221–36.
87. Das, *Touch and Intimacy*, p. 37.
88. Anand, *Across the Black Waters*, p. 127.
89. See for instance the image of the 'dirty native' used to legitimise European intervention in Africa in Stephanie Newell, *Histories of Dirt: Media and Urban Life in Colonial and Postcolonial Lagos* (Durham, NC: Duke University Press, 2020). On race and mud, see also Das, *Touch and Intimacy*, p. 59.
90. Jahan Ramazani, 'Cosmopolitan Sympathies: Poetry of the First Global War', *Modernism/modernity* 23.4 (2016), 855–74 (p. 870).
91. Quoted ibid., pp. 869–70.

92. E. M. Forster, *A Passage to India* (Harmondsworth: Penguin, 1979), p. 31. The comparison between mud and darker races developed into a motif in Forster's writings. It first appears, to the best of my knowledge, in a letter from Egypt: 'what I have seen seems vastly inferior to India, for which I am always longing in the most persistent way, and where I still hope to die. It is only at sunset that Egypt surpasses India – at all other hours it is flat, unromantic, unmysterious, and godless – the soil is mud, the inhabitants are of mud moving, and exasperating in the extreme: I feel as instinctively not at home among them as I feel instinctively at home among Indians.' See *Selected Letters of E. M. Forster*, vol. I: 1879–1920, ed. Mary Lago and P. N. Furbank (London: Collins, 1983), pp. 232–3 (p. 233): to S. R. Masood, 29 December 1915. Anand uses a similar expression, 'mud-smeared people', in *Morning Face*, p. 499.
93. Anand, *Across the Black Waters*, pp. 66, 152, 211.
94. On censorship, see Cowasjee, *So Many Freedoms*, p. 34.
95. *Pound/Lewis: The Letters of Ezra Pound and Wyndham Lewis*, ed. Timothy Materer (London: Faber & Faber, 1985), p. 109.
96. Fussell, *Great War and Modern Memory*, p. 231.
97. Mulk Raj Anand, *Untouchable* (London: Penguin, 2014), p. 137.
98. Ibid., p. 121.
99. Anand, *Across the Black Waters*, p. 128. See also Anand, *Village*, p. 242.
100. Anand, *Across the Black Waters*, p. 126.
101. See also Anand, *Morning Face*, p. 527: 'I heard faint echoes of the voices of Havildar Lachman Singh and Sepoys Kirup and Dhanoo, and Babu Thenoo Ram, who had died abroad. [...] Perhaps the ghosts of these dead ones would come to live around the barracks, because, as mother said, the ghosts remained restlessly wandering on earth and could not rise to heaven or go down to hell if no ceremonies had been performed for their corpses.'
102. Ibid., pp. 89, 82, 83, 243; *Seven Summers*, p. 177; *Untouchable*, pp. 69, 81.
103. Anand, *Morning Face*, p. 372.
104. Morton-Jack, *Indian Army on the Western Front*, p. 292.
105. Sarojini Naidu, *The Broken Wing: Songs of Love, Death and Destiny, 1915–16* (London: William Heinemann, 1917), p. 5.
106. Omissi, *Indian Voices*, p. 73: 'To die in the battlefield is glory. For a thousand years one's name will be remembered.'
107. Ibid., p. 137. See also p. 241. Kipling's fictional letters in *Eyes of Asia* deal with these funeral rites: pp. 21, 28, 68, 100.
108. Joy Damousi, 'Mourning Practices', in *Cambridge History of the First World War*, vol. III, pp. 358–84 (p. 376).
109. The British government ruled it out on the grounds of expense and equality (men with no known graves could not be granted such a privilege). Instead, in a symbolic gesture, one unknown soldier was unearthed, returned to England, and interred in Westminster Abbey. See Jay Winter, *Sites of Memory, Sites of Mourning: The Great War in European Cultural History* (Cambridge: Cambridge University Press, 1995), pp. 22–8.
110. Virginia Woolf, *Freshwater: A Comedy* (London: Hogarth Press, 1976), p. 9.
111. J. Perdriel-Vaissières, *Rupert Brooke's Death and Burial: Based on the Log of the French Hospital Ship DUGUAY-TROUIN*, trans. Vincent O'Sullivan (New Haven: Yale University Press, 1917), pp. 6–9.
112. Virginia Woolf, 'Rupert Brooke', *Times Literary Supplement*, 8 August 1918, p. 371.
113. Rupert Brooke, 'The Soldier', in *The Collected Poems of Rupert Brooke: With a Memoir* (London: Sidgwick & Jackson, 1918), p. 9.

114. Damousi, 'Mourning Practices', p. 378.
115. Longley, 'The Great War, History and the English Lyric', p. 75: 'Most poets were hugely conscious of Hardy.' On Anand and Hardy, see 'Mulk Raj Anand Remembers', p. 178, and Mulk Raj Anand, 'New Bearings in Indian Literature', *The Literary Review* (1961), 453–8 (p. 455).
116. 'Drummer Hodge', in *The Collected Poems of Thomas Hardy* (London: Macmillan, 1962), p. 83. See also Hardy's 1899 poem 'A Christmas Ghost-Story'.
117. *The Collected Letters of Thomas Hardy*, vol. II: 1893–1901, ed. Richard Little Purdy and Michael Millgate (Oxford: Clarendon Press, 1980), p. 242.
118. 'Drummer Hodge', p. 83. John Paul Riquelme, 'The Modernity of Thomas Hardy's Poetry', in *The Cambridge Companion to Thomas Hardy*, ed. Dale Kramer (Cambridge: Cambridge University Press, 1999), pp. 204–23 (p. 211). 'There seems something lasting here ("for ever" and "eternally" both occur in the final stanza), and something uplifting too, a hint that Hodge is coming home in Africa because Africa accepts him, as Nature in its indifference takes up everything.' See R. R. G. Pite, '"Graver things ... braver things": Hardy's War Poetry', in *The Oxford Handbook of British and Irish War Poetry*, ed. Tim Kendall (Oxford: Oxford University Press, 2009), pp. 34–50 (p. 42).
119. Virginia Woolf, *Mrs Dalloway* (London: Penguin, 1996), p. 76. Wilfred Owen, 'A Terre', in *The Complete Poems and Fragments*, vol. I, ed. Jon Stallworthy (London: Chatto & Windus, 2013), pp. 178–80 (p. 179). Thomas Mann, *The Magic Mountain* (New York: A. A. Knopf, 2005), p. 640.
120. T. S. Eliot, *Selected Poems* (London: Faber & Faber, 2002), p. 41.
121. Fussell, *Great War and Modern Memory*, p. 253. Eliot's lilac is a reference to a war poem by Walt Whitman: 'When lilacs last in the door-yard bloom'd [...] / I mourn'd – and yet shall mourn with ever-returning spring.'
122. Mulk Raj Anand, 'Pigeon Indian: Some Notes on Indian-English Writing', *World Literature Written in English* 21.1 (1982), 325–36 (p. 329): 'Some of the Indian words now included in the *Oxford English Dictionary* were originally transported by early Greek and Roman traders, and found their way into medieval English through Greek and Latin. These words have a singing quality about them: *amber, camphor, ginger, indigo, lac, lilac, musk, opal, sandalwood, sugar.*' On the impossibility of rebirth in the modern wasteland, see Vikramaditya Rai, *The Waste Land: A Critical Study* (Delhi: Motilal Banarsidass, 1988), p. 79.
123. Eliot, *Selected Poems*, p. 43.
124. Anand, *Conversations*, p. 48. On Anand and Eliot, see ibid., pp. 43–52, 118–24, 129–32.
125. Fisher, 'Interview with Anand', p. 119.
126. Leonard Woolf, *Diaries in Ceylon 1908–11: Records of a Colonial Administrator and Stories from the East: Three Short Stories on Ceylon* (Colombo: Metro Printers, 1962), p. 67. 'The main battle in imperialism is over land, of course, but when it came to who owned the land, who had the right to settle and work on it, who kept it going, who won it back, and who now plans its future – these issues were reflected, contested, and even for a time decided in narrative.' See Edward Said, *Culture and Imperialism* (New York: Vintage, 1994), pp. xii–xiii.
127. For an example from a similar context, see Kipling's 'Tod's Amendment', in *Plain Tales from the Hills* (Oxford: Oxford University Press, 2009), a story about a land bill in British India. Anand discusses it in a 1943 article, 'English Novels of the Twentieth Century on India'.
128. Radical experimentation would not have worked for the first Indian war novel. See Das, *India, Empire, and First World War Culture*, p. 347.
129. Anand, *Village*, p. 109.

130. Leah Price, 'Introduction: Reading Matter', *PMLA* 121.1 (2006), 9–16 (p. 11).
131. Priyasha Mukhopadhyay, 'Of Greasy Notebooks and Dirty Newspapers: Reading the Illegible in *The Village in the Jungle*', *Journal of Commonwealth Literature* 50.1 (2015), 59–73 (p. 60). See also Priya Joshi, *In Another Country: Colonialism, Culture, and the English Novel in India* (New York: Columbia University Press, 2002) and Priyasha Mukhopadhyay, 'On Not Reading *The Soldier's Pocket-Book for Field Service*', *Journal of Victorian Culture* 22.1 (2017), 40–56: 'How then do we critically locate the unread book, and, more importantly, what can the cultural history of reading gain by taking seriously instances of not reading?' (p. 42).
132. Anand, *Private Life*, p. 136. The prince ultimately signs his state away in another document that looms large through the narrative.
133. For a different context, see Allyson Booth's chapter on maps as abstractions versus the reality of a battlefield in *Postcards from the Trenches: Negotiating the Space between Modernism and the First World War* (New York: Oxford University Press, 1996), p. 91: 'The giant mistake of this plan lies precisely in its theoretical beauty – the assumption that all the barbed wire would be flattened, all the batteries silenced, all the troops entombed. These reductive predictions [...] rely on the same faith in reductive representation, the same distance from physical experience.'
134. Cowasjee, *So Many Freedoms*, p. 65.
135. Fisher, 'Interview with Anand', p. 109.
136. Joshi, *In Another Country*, p. xvii.
137. Anand, 'Pigeon Indian', p. 328. This was something Anand had to learn. When Gandhi (allegedly) read a draft of *Untouchable*, Anand's first novel, he told him not to use 'such heavy words. Write in a simpler language and transliterate what they say.' See 'Mulk Raj Anand Remembers', p. 179.
138. Boehmer, *Empire Writing*, p. xxxii.
139. Anand, *Conversations*, pp. 22, 70.
140. Quoted in Cowasjee, *So Many Freedoms*, p. 16.
141. Anand, *Seven Summers*, pp. 72, 257.
142. Anand, *Village*, p. 173.
143. *The Diary of Virginia Woolf*, vol. I: 1915–19, ed. Anne Oliver Bell (London: Penguin, 1979), p. 56. On Hope Mirrlees's wartime struggles with paperwork, see Annabel Robinson, *The Life and Work of Jane Ellen Harrison* (Oxford: Oxford University Press, 2002), p. 256: 'A "pièce de justification" demands a "permis de séjour" & a permis de séjour un permis d'arriver et de partir & a permis de partir involves a pièce de qualification from yr *patron* as well as the present of yr photograph to several commissionaires de polices. It was like the house that Jack Built & didn't I [Harrison] learn a lot of French.' 'We also had to go to the American embassy to get temporary passports to go back to Paris,' Gertrude Stein recalled. 'We had no papers, nobody had any papers in those days.' See Gertrude Stein, *The Autobiography of Alice B. Toklas* (London: Penguin, 2001), p. 168.
144. *Correspondance*, vol. II, pp. 952–3 (p. 952): to Madeleine Pagès, 14 November 1915.
145. Leigh, *Punjab and the War*, p. 3.
146. Anand, *Across the Black Waters*, p. 221. See also *Sword and Sickle*, pp. 22–3, on *Flugblätter*.
147. Omissi, *Indian Voices*, p. 7.
148. Some witnesses were inventive in evading censorship, for instance by writing with lemon juice instead of ink. Ibid., p. 239.

149. Quoted in Hilary Buxton, 'Imperial Amnesia: Race, Trauma and Indian Troops in the First World War', *Past & Present* 241.1 (2018), 221–58 (p. 228).
150. Das, *India, Empire, and First World War Culture*, p. 207.
151. Anand, *Across the Black Waters*, p. 171.
152. Ibid., p. 171.
153. Ford Madox Ford, 'A Day in Battle: Arms and the Mind', in *The Ford Madox Ford Reader*, ed. Sondra J. Stang (London: Paladin, 1987), pp. 456–61 (p. 458).
154. Anand, *Across the Black Waters*, p. 172.
155. Ibid., p. 173.
156. Ibid., p. 172.
157. Anand, 'Why I Became a Writer', p. 13. See also *Morning Face*, p. 523: 'Somehow, all of us boys seemed to have grown, through the impact of the events in the Punjab, into adults.'
158. The frontier, as scholars have noted, became the new front. On the 'Greater War', see *The Greater War: Other Combatants and Other Fronts, 1914–18*, ed. Jonathan Kraus (London: Palgrave Macmillan, 2014); *Empires at War 1911–23*, ed. Robert Gerwarth and Erez Manela (Oxford: Oxford University Press, 2014); and Paul K. Saint-Amour, *Tense Future: Modernism, Total War, Encyclopaedic Form* (New York: Oxford University Press, 2015).
159. 'Mulk Raj Anand Remembers', p. 183.
160. Ahmad Azhar, 'Punjab Disturbances 1919', in *1914–1918 Online: International Encyclopedia of the First World War*, ed. Ute Daniel et al., <https://encyclopedia.1914-1918-online.net/article/punjab_disturbances_1919> (last updated 30 October 2017). On the continuation of repressive wartime measures, see Anand, *Morning Face*, p. 428; on forced recruiting, see Omissi, *Indian Voices*, pp. 256, 316, 347. E. M. Forster likewise identified forced recruitment into the Egyptian Labour Corps as one of the main motivations for dissent in Egypt in 'The Trouble in Egypt: Treatment of the Fellahin', *Manchester Guardian*, 29 March 1919, p. 8.
161. Kim A. Wagner, '"Calculated to Strike Terror": The Amritsar Massacre and the Spectacle of Colonial Violence', *Past & Present* 233.1 (2016), 185–225. For Wagner, the massacre marks the beginning of a process that concluded with Indian independence in 1947; it is credited 'as the event that galvanized the first major anti-colonial nationalist movement and inexorably set Indian nationalists, including Gandhi, on the path towards independence' (p. 186).
162. Rabindranath Tagore, for instance, famously renounced his knighthood; E. M. Forster received a long letter from Malcolm Darling which prompted him to rewrite the ending to *A Passage to India*. He also wrote a letter about Amritsar (published as 'Hawkeritis' in the *Daily Herald* on 30 May 1919) and a call for the 'dissolution of empire' ('Reflections on India, I: Too Late?', *Nation and Athenaeum*, 21 January 1922, pp. 614–15 (p. 614)). For references to the massacre in *The Sword and the Sickle*, see pp. 10, 142, 263, 329.
163. Not surprisingly, Anand's fiction is filled with scenes of police violence. See, for instance, *Private Life*, pp. 102–10; *Sword and Sickle*, pp. 265–6 and 374–5.
164. Anand, *Conversations*, p. 39. For a fictionalised account of the flogging, see *Morning Face*, pp. 437–67.
165. 'Mulk Raj Anand Remembers', p. 177.
166. Louis MacNeice, *The Strings Are False: An Unfinished Autobiography* (London: Faber & Faber, 1965), p. 209. He found the British ignorant of the situation in the Punjab: 'there is widespread ignorance in this country of the history of British imperialism in India, as it could be told by the subject peoples of Empire.' See *Letters on India* (London: George Routledge & Sons, 1942), p. 29.
167. Fisher, 'Interview with Anand', p. 116.

168. Arjun Appadurai, 'Introduction: Commodities and the Politics of Value', in *The Social Life of Things: Commodities in Cultural Perspective*, ed. Arjun Appadurai (Cambridge: Cambridge University Press, 1986), pp. 3–63 (p. 5).
169. Anand, *Sword and Sickle*, p. 8.
170. Ibid., p. 24. Such rewards are discussed obsessively in Anand's *Across the Black Waters* (pp. 168–71). On land rewards, see Leigh, *Punjab and the War*, p. 283, and Das, *India, Empire, and First World War Culture*, p. 86.
171. Cowasjee, *So Many Freedoms*, p. 111.
172. Anand, *Sword and Sickle*, p. 83.
173. To enable this argument as the background to his novel, Anand moved the scene from the Punjab, where *The Village* was set, to the United Provinces of Agra and Oudh, which contained more landless labourers and farmers. See Cowasjee, *So Many Freedoms*, p. 114.
174. Darling, *Prosperity and Debt*, p. 208. Santanu Das and Saros Cowasjee caution against readily linking these forms of anti-colonial dissent to the Indian war experience – against reading *Across the Black Waters* and *The Sword and the Sickle* in tandem. Anand appears to insist on a connection, writing of a new 'Fate' for India which was 'somehow connected with the war to which he had been and against which everyone was fighting'. Anand, *Sword and Sickle*, pp. 65–6.
175. Anand, *Sword and Sickle*, p. 155: 'surely the struggle of the peasants can go on side by side with the struggle for freedom: in fact the one is not possible without the other.' On this intimate relationship, see Tim Harper, *Underground Asia: Global Revolutionaries and the Assault on Empire* (Cambridge, MA: Harvard University Press, 2021); Das, *India, Empire, and First World War Culture*, pp. 371–8; Mulk Raj Anand, 'India and the People', *The Tribune*, 26 January 1945, p. 15. On the author's stay in Kalākānkar, see 'Mulk Raj Anand Remembers', p. 183.
176. Forster, *Hill of Devi*, p. 72.
177. Anand, *Sword and Sickle*, p. 49.
178. Ibid., p. 52.
179. Ibid., p. 60.
180. Ibid., pp. 213–14.
181. Ibid., pp. 156, 240.

CODA: AT THE MUSEUM

We live in an age of leaflets – and so apparently do our allies and our enemies on the continent and overseas. Most of us do not trouble to preserve such ephemeral documents, but our University Library is an enthusiastic snapper up of such unconsidered trifles. It already possesses a very large collection dealing with Cambridge, started by John Willis Clark, included in his bequest to the University. This collection has been arranged in chronological order, indexed and bound, and is kept up to date. But the Library authorities are particularly anxious to obtain as large a collection as possible of the ephemeral literature of the War, whether it concerns Cambridge or not. Such flying pieces as those which are dropped from aeroplanes or posted on hoardings would be particularly welcome. And let nobody imagine that any printed piece is too trivial for acceptance. It has been abundantly proved that a collection of daily literature of any country is of the greatest value to the historian in after years. All communications should be addressed – The Librarian, University Library, Cambridge.[1]

On 30 January 1915, a few months into the war, readers opened their weekly issue of the *Cambridge Magazine* to a request by the university's librarian, Francis Jenkinson. Titled 'For the Historian of the Future', Jenkinson's short note asked readers to submit their war ephemera for preservation in the library's War Reserve Collection. No printed piece of paper would be too trivial for inclusion: Christmas cards, letters, regimental orders, pamphlets, *Flugblätter*, posters, postcards, trench journals, newspapers, even paper balloons used for distributing propaganda leaflets behind German lines.[2] While the request came rather early in the conflict, in a sense it arrived already too late: Jenkinson regretted not having probed the refugees he met in the first weeks of war for printed materials from Belgium. Similar initiatives on the continent had also been guided by the memory of loss (never systematically collected, most ephemera of the Franco-Prussian War, for instance, had vanished by 1914).[3] With future historians in mind, Cambridge's librarian began collecting with a vengeance, receiving packages from places as far-flung as Gibraltar (a copy of the *Peninsular Post*, 'with its Spanish supplement, which the few English residents in Spain are bringing out as a local counterblast'), Sumatra (enemy propaganda) and Shanghai (a local Chinese periodical entitled *The War*).[4] Arranged, bound, shelved and indexed, Jenkinson's collection – he referred to it intimately as 'my war things' – would count more than 10,000 items by the end of hostilities.[5]

As the war went on, numerous initiatives saw the light of day, rivalling Cambridge's War Reserve Collection in scope. An October 1918 issue of the *Egyptian Mail*, in which E. M. Forster published his wartime journalism, asked for donations for the Imperial War Museum to be submitted to the British Consulate in Alexandria.[6] In an effort to establish a collection representative of a global conflict, the new museum had opened up relations with British embassies abroad for the purpose of acquiring materials, which were often first exhibited locally, drawing crowds of 'ten thousand visitors', as it did in Egypt, to the Municipal Picture Gallery in Alexandria.[7] Two months later, an article in the Anzac magazine *Kia Ora Coo-Ee* attempted to convince the same set of readers to forward their war souvenirs – 'it is the personally-captured thing which, after all, makes the unique museum specimen' – to the War Records Section in Cairo, a collecting field depot for what would later become the Australian War Memorial.[8] The article appeared alongside an advertisement for bound volumes of *Kia Ora Coo-Ee*: 'as a souvenir it will be prized for ever'.[9] Eager responses to such calls for all manner of artefacts, including printed matter, lay at the foundation of national war collections: Britain's Imperial War Museum, Australia's War Museum and France's Musée de la Guerre in 1917, Germany's Kriegsbibliothek in 1921, and Belgium's Koninklijk Museum van het Leger en de Krijgsgeschiedenis in 1923.[10] These nationwide collections were a new phenomenon at the time, broader in scope than the modest war exhibits of the past, which had been restricted to weaponry or associated with particular regiments.[11]

Among the five writers at the heart of this book, Guillaume Apollinaire responded most enthusiastically to a call for materials, this one issued from the Bibliothèque Nationale de France, where Charles de la Roncière was compiling a collection of trench journals.¹² These documents, the French librarian believed, would be useful for future historians to assess, retrospectively, the *état d'esprit* in the trenches.¹³ Late in September 1915, while stationed at the front, Apollinaire forwarded a copy of his unit's trench journal, *Tranchman' Echo*, and his book of poems printed in the field, *Case d'Armons*. 'Only a small number has escaped destruction,' he wrote of *Tranchman' Echo*. 'I send you one of those, the only one I have left.'¹⁴ Apollinaire's war writings were grounded in a similar attempt to keep the flight of years at bay, and he noted in the *Mercure de France* that it was 'vital to put in writing everything that referred to the folklore of the war'.¹⁵ A few months before penning a note to the Bibliothèque Nationale, sensing perhaps that the relationship might not last, he had asked his girlfriend Louise de Coligny-Châtillon to deposit their letters – 'an exquisite monument to my life in 1914–15' – with his concierge in Paris.¹⁶ Early on, the idea had emerged to publish their wartime correspondence in a volume.¹⁷ E. M. Forster likewise posted a letter to a friend, in January 1918, in order that a few moments from his war might be saved from oblivion. 'I want to put a few things on record,' he started, writing from Alexandria. 'Read this letter at your leisure for it is all old news, but news you haven't heard, I think, and pleasant news. My personal interest in it apart, I feel it oughtn't to be lost. [...] Let me know if you get it. And keep it, for one forgets.'¹⁸

'Keep it, for one forgets.' Over the course of writing this book, I spent countless hours digging through Cambridge's War Reserve Collection and Cairo's National Library in search of these elusive print artefacts and the traces of first-hand impressions they contain. In early June 2016, I boarded a train for Paris to examine the already so delicate documents Apollinaire had carefully submitted to the Bibliothèque Nationale a hundred years earlier. There it all still was: the only extant copy of *Tranchman' Echo* (RES 4-LC6-271), a copy of *Case d'Armons* (RES P-YE-51), a rare subscription bulletin for the volume (RES P-YE-514 (bis)) and the poet's letter to de la Roncière. Access to these treasures proved far from self-evident. That June, the Bibliothèque Nationale had been closed, because the nearby Seine had flooded. The last time this had happened – according to urban legend once in a century – was in the winter of 1910, when Apollinaire himself had been forced to flee the rising waters: 'I pack my suitcase and leave, abandoning my books,' he warned readers of *L'Intransigeant*. 'Tonight no one will sleep in the little house at Auteuil.'¹⁹ When I finally had a chance to study Apollinaire's war ephemera, I was reminded by these unforeseen circumstances of how unlikely it was that these documents, coming from the war zone, had survived into the twenty-first century in the first place. The experience was strangely moving. These precariously material artefacts – the stains, the faded ink, the poet's handwriting, the pages yellowed with time – carried traces not only of the war, but of a life that had vanished because of it. Such a visceral response to the material culture of war would occur not more than a handful of times in the span of years of research: standing on a small sluice, near Nieuwpoort, that had played its part in the inundation of the Yser; being gifted a bullet and glass bottle dug up in the fields around Poperinge; staring at a few personal possessions on display in the Tre Sassi Fort, a small war museum I happened upon by accident while hiking, with my brother, through the Italian Dolomites in the summer of 2021. This book is guided by an impulse to understand what modernist writers made of these objects. What kind of history of the modernist engagement with the First World War, I wondered, could be told through artefacts just like these?

As this book has argued, modernist writers turned to material culture to make sense of the war's defining experiences. In their experimental writings, confrontations with vulnerability (Chapter 1), epistemological crisis (Chapter 2), loss (Chapter 3) and power imbalances (Chapter 4) were mediated through inventive, at times visceral engagements with helmets, shells, trench art, shop signs, monuments and mud, but also trench journals, postcards, military dictionaries, memorial volumes, land deeds and office files. The First World War fuelled a fascination not only with material culture in modernist literature, but with the materiality of modernism's own medium, as objects of writing became so uniquely and curiously shaped by the ongoing conflict. As object, the text, too, was used, and misused, to mediate the war's experiences: the precarious life of the trenches modelled in the precarious form of *Case d'Armons* (Chapter 1); the global front's representational crisis imprinted on to misspelled shop signs and censored newspaper pages (Chapter 2); a foreshortened life replaced by, and recuperated through, the bound memorial volume (Chapter 3); and the sepoy's profound erasure of the self emblematised in office files left unread (Chapter 4). If, to the modernist, the work performed by these material and print artefacts was often subversive, then they acknowledged that these same artefacts were simultaneously accorded *different* meanings and recruited to tell *other* versions of the war experience. One context in which this was the case was the museum. Even in wartime, the five writers featured in this book remained avid museum-goers: Apollinaire visited the local Musée des Beaux-Arts while in training at the barracks in Nîmes; Forster worked as a catalogue compiler and night-time watchman in the National Gallery in the early war days (where he received instructions 'to attack a petrol bomb with sand instead of water'); Mirrlees dodged zeppelins to study art at the Louvre; Woolf was a regular at the National Gallery and Victoria & Albert Museum; and Anand, living in Bloomsbury in the 1920s, questioned the provenance of the British Museum's collections, packed with loot from earlier imperial conflicts.[20] Their excitement when museums fully reopened after the Armistice, with the most valuable possessions emerging from subterranean storage, was tangible. Mirrlees witnessed it and wrote the moment into *Paris: A Poem*: 'In the

Louvre / The Pietà of Avignon, / L'Olympe, / Giles, / Mantegna's Seven Deadly Sins, / The Chardins; / They arise, serene and unetiolated, one by one from / their subterranean sleep of five long years.'[21]

Modernist responses to the establishment of war museums, after these 'five long years', were more divided. As Ruth Hoberman argued, in *Museum Trouble: Edwardian Fiction and the Emergence of Modernism*, the modern museum was 'a contested and conflicted site'.[22] In Britain, public museums witnessed a heyday in the years following the war, with numbers rising from sixty such institutions in 1850 to more than 500 in 1928.[23] Among them was the Imperial War Museum, founded in 1917 and opened to the public, in the Crystal Palace in London, three years later (Figure 5.1). Its collection at the time displayed some of the objects at the core of *Modernism, Material Culture and the First World War*: Adrian helmets (UNI11315), shop and trench signs (FEQ66), the original Cenotaph made from wood (now lost), a cross from a war grave (EPH8612), mud-stained trench boots (EQU3888) and models of mudscapes (Q15996). Some early visitors must already have had some familiarity with the war's material culture, if not through first-hand experience, then through souvenirs, images disseminated through the popular press, or visits to the model trench in Kensington Gardens and the ruined French village in Trafalgar Square. However, for many others, the Imperial War Museum made possible the first visceral sense of contact with objects that had actually

Figure 5.1 Visitors at the new war museum at Crystal Palace, May 1921. Imperial War Museum (Q 17028).

been to war. Locking arms, visitors bent over display cases or stared at paintings: in an early photograph, medals, John Singer Sargent's *Gassed* and Jacob Epstein's *The Tin Hat*, which was cast from a real trench helmet, were among the objects that drew crowds to the Crystal Palace. In the first two years, 2.5 million visitors were received at the Imperial War Museum, followed by an average 250,000 visitors every year for most of the decade.[24]

If modernist writers such as E. M. Forster or Virginia Woolf were not as easily charmed, it was because they understood that these museums instrumentalised objects to frame a particular version of the war experience. Displaced, institutionalised and recontextualised, helmets and trench models became museum pieces. Forster once commented on this process. Reporting for the *Nation and Athenaeum* on the British Empire exhibition, which he visited a week before it officially opened in 1924, the novelist stumbled upon a model of the Mosque of Wazir Khan at Lahore, made by students of a local art school. Unlike many of the exhibits already on display, the model was still being unpacked: 'this was so lovely and stood so incidentally and accidentally upon a table, that it had all the magic of a real building, met by chance among squalid or pretentious streets. When I see it next, it will probably be glassed, docketed, and have lost its preternatural charm.'[25] What made the model so striking – 'delicate, touching' – was the way it had been met by accident instead of as a museum piece incorporated into the exhibit's fold: not yet put at a physical remove, not yet elevated for contemplation, not yet labelled and made to signify.[26] The mosque may have, unexpectedly, evoked fond memories of Forster's own travels in the Punjab in 1912. Casually placed on a table, it could still be touched, generating, as Hope Mirrlees once put it, 'a sudden physical conviction (like fingering for the first time the antiquity one had so often gazed at through the glass case in the museum)'.[27] Many such moments of embodied contact informed the history of modernist engagement with war objects explored in this book, from Madeleine Pagès's 'shock', all the way from Oran, at receiving *Case d'Armons* in the mail, to the bodies of women bent over the graves of their dead husbands and sons in Hope Mirrlees's *Paris: A Poem* and Virginia Woolf's *Jacob's Room*. The glass case, the label, the physical remove instead of the affective thrill: 'The moment you put a picture into a Palace of Art', as Forster concluded his review in the *Nation and Athenaeum*, 'it wilts like a cut flower.'[28]

The same is true of the military equipment Virginia Woolf had found in the United Services Museum in Whitehall in the mid-1920s – 'cannon and torpedos and gun-carriages and helmets and spurs and faded uniforms and the thousand other objects which piety and curiosity have saved from time and treasured and numbered and stuck in glass cases forever'.[29] That the context of these objects matters is clear from early responses to John Singer Sargent's *Gassed*, a gigantic painting of blindfolded soldiers being led across the battlefield, which took pride of place in the new Imperial War Museum. E. M.

Forster first saw it in the Royal Academy, hung between two of Sargent's high-society portraits, Viscountess Cowdray and Mrs Langman. Such positioning illustrates what Jennifer Wellington, in *Exhibiting War*, terms 'deliberate editorial action': *Gassed* loses a measure of its biting critique by dint of association with these domestic portraits, yielding, in the process, a cleaner and more glorifying picture of war than perhaps intended (a reality all the more problematic given the wartime history of using exhibits as propaganda and recruitment tools).[30] 'Many ladies and gentlemen fear that Romance is passing out of war with the sabres and the chargers,' Forster observed. 'Sargent's masterpiece reassures them. He shows that it is possible to suffer with a quiet grace under the new conditions, and Lady Cowdray and the Hon. Mrs Langman, as they looked over the twenty feet of canvas that divided them, were still able to say, "How touching", instead of "How obscene".'[31] Woolf was compelled to draw similar conclusions when she spotted the painting at the Royal Academy.[32] On another occasion in the National Gallery – a summer's day late in the war – she had felt uncomfortable with its rooms devoted to battle pictures and its life-size portrait of Lord Kitchener, noting in a letter to her sister that 'the atmosphere of picture galleries, always gloomy, is worse than ever now, when the glory of war has to be taught'.[33] For the first time on a nationwide scale, a particular version of the war – one that glorifies sacrifice yet neglects its harsher realities – was framed around objects on display, while Woolf and Forster must have remembered a different experience. Their writings, by contrast, turned to these objects, from shop signs to tombstones, to articulate a critique of war.

And yet, the modernist authors in this book had affectively charged responses to these museum pieces, much as I would be struck by Apollinaire's print artefacts at the Bibliothèque Nationale almost a century later. The key, perhaps, was distance, in the way the First World War is distant for us now – a gap in time that is negotiated, at times even overcome, through objects. Apollinaire, for instance, wrote affectionately about a small Napoleon museum run by a ten-year-old in the Rue de Poissy in Paris, and about a much larger museum, in Châteauroux, which owned Napoleon's sabre from the Battle of Aboukir but which had failed to acquire the camp bed in which the emperor had died in St Helena.[34] E. M. Forster stopped on that island once, en route to South Africa in 1929, to see Napoleon's house. His *Guide to Alexandria* likewise directs visitors to a quiet convent in the city, where they would find the tombstones of three forgotten British soldiers – movingly referenced by name in the guide: Arthur Brice, Thomas Hamilton Scott, Henry Gosle – who fell in the Napoleonic Wars.[35] Virginia Woolf, in turn, spent a cold morning, in March 1926, at the naval museum at Greenwich:

> I played with my mind watching what it would do, – & behold if I didn't almost burst into tears over the coat Nelson wore at Trafalgar with the

medals which he hid with his hand when they carried him down, dying, lest the sailors might see it was him. There was too, his little fuzzy pigtail, of golden greyish hair tied in black; & his long white stockings, one much stained, & his white breeches with the gold buckles, & his stock – all of which I suppose they must have undone & taken off as he lay dying. Kiss me Hardy &c – Anchor, anchor, – I read it all when I came in, & could swear I was there on the Victory.

'So the charm worked in that case,' Woolf concluded.[36]

Why had the charm worked in the Greenwich museum? Why Napoleon and Nelson, but not Kitchener? The question is impossible to answer now. But these anecdotal moments at the museum show that the modernists were both attentive to the institutional uses and misuses First World War objects were put to *and* receptive to the emotional responses Napoleonic War objects evoked. The politics behind Napoleon's camp bed and Nelson's coat had perhaps faded, so that only the suggestion of a vanished life remained: these objects *resonated* in the 1920s, in Stephen Greenblatt's familiar use of the word, 'not only as witnesses to the violence of history but as signs of use, marks of the human touch'.[37] The bed and the coat had stood the test of time, a surprising feat, given their precarious nature as objects. Encountering them in museums, where they lay forgotten, meant sensing a visceral proximity to these dead men and recovering something of the lingering, far-away past in the process. As E. M. Forster wrote, sometime in the war, the museum-goer 'should visit certain definite objects, and then come away – a golden rule indeed in all museums. He might then find that a scrap of the past has come alive.'[38]

NOTES

1. 'For the Historian of the Future', *Cambridge Magazine*, 30 January 1915, p. 209.
2. Mark Nicholls, 'A Reason for Remembering: Francis Jenkinson and the War Reserve Collection', *Transactions of the Cambridge Bibliographical Society* 11.4 (1999), 497–515.
3. Susanne Brandt, 'The Memory Makers: Museums and Exhibitions of the First World War', *History and Memory* 6.1 (1994), 95–122 (p. 108).
4. Nicholls, 'A Reason for Remembering', pp. 502–7.
5. Quoted from Jenkinson's diaries, ibid., p. 500.
6. 'Donations for the Imperial War Museum', *Egyptian Mail*, 16 October 1918, p. 2.
7. 'The Imperial War Museum', *Palestine News*, 29 August 1918, p. 10. For these relations, see Gaynor Kavanagh, 'Museum as Memorial: The Origins of the Imperial War Museum', *Journal of Contemporary History* 23.1 (1988), 77–97 (p. 85).
8. H. W. Dinning, 'The War Museum', *Kia Ora Coo-Ee*, 4 December 1918, p. 10. See also Frank Reid, 'Souvenir Hunters: Collecting Curios in the Firing Line', *Kia Ora Coo-Ee*, 15 March 1918, p. 14.
9. Dinning, 'The War Museum', p. 10.
10. See Jay Winter, *Sites of Memory, Sites of Mourning: The Great War in European Cultural History* (Cambridge: Cambridge University Press, 1995), pp. 80–1, and

Brandt, 'The Memory Makers', p. 113. The Belgian museum started from the collection of a small museum at Sainte-Adresse, in Normandy, the seat of the Belgian government in exile.
11. See Alys Cundy, 'The Imperial War Museum and the Material Culture of the First World War, 1917–2014', in *The Edinburgh Companion to the First World War and the Arts*, ed. Ann-Marie Einhaus and Katherine Isobel Baxter (Edinburgh: Edinburgh University Press, 2017), pp. 402–18 (p. 406). See also Jennifer Wellington, *Exhibiting War: The Great War, Museums and Memory in Britain, Canada and Australia* (Cambridge: Cambridge University Press, 2017), p. 2.
12. Etienne-Alain Hubert, 'Poilus, Envoyez vos Journaux à la BN', *Petit Journal*, 19 June 1915, n.p.
13. Quoted ibid.
14. Guillaume Apollinaire, *Correspondance Générale*, vol. II, ed. Victor Martin-Schmets (Paris: Honoré Champion, 2015), pp. 765–6: to Charles de la Roncière, 20 September 1915.
15. Guillaume Apollinaire, 'Contribution à l'Étude des Superstitions et du Folklore du Front', in *Œuvres en Prose Complètes*, vol. I, ed. Michel Décaudin (Paris: Gallimard, 1977), pp. 1,381–5 (p. 1,382).
16. Apollinaire, *Correspondance*, vol. II, pp. 213–14 (p. 214): to Lou, 17 March 1915.
17. The title would be *Lettres à Lou* or *Correspondance avec l'ombre de mon amour*; neither volume ever materialised. See ibid., pp. 240–2, 247–9. Apollinaire also started, and quickly abandoned, a war memoir, *Souvenirs de la Grande Guerre*, in October 1915. See Laurence Campa, *Guillaume Apollinaire* (Paris: Gallimard, 2013), p. 515.
18. *Selected Letters of E. M. Forster*, vol. I: 1879–1920, ed. Mary Largo and P. N. Furbank (London: Collins, 1983), pp. 280–2 (p. 280): to Florence Barger, 6 January 1918.
19. Guillaume Apollinaire, 'Impressions d'un Inondé', in *Œuvres en Prose Complètes*, vol. III, ed. Pierre Caizergues and Michel Décaudin (Paris: Gallimard, 1993), pp. 407–9 (p. 409).
20. Forster, *Selected Letters*, vol. I, pp. 213–15 (p. 214): to Malcolm Darling, 6 November 1914. On modernism and the museum, see Rupert Arrowsmith, *Modernism and the Museum: Asian, African, and Pacific Art and the London Avant-Garde* (Oxford: Oxford University Press, 2011); Ruth Hoberman, *Museum Trouble: Edwardian Fiction and the Emergence of Modernism* (Charlottesville: University of Virginia Press, 2011); and Catherine E. Paul, *Poetry in the Museums of Modernism: Yeats, Pound, Moore, Stein* (Ann Arbor: University of Michigan Press, 2002).
21. Hope Mirrlees, *Paris: A Poem* (London: Faber & Faber, 2020), p. 8. See also *The Diary of Virginia Woolf*, vol. I: 1915–19, ed. Anne Olivier Bell (London: Penguin, 1979), p. 138: 'The Academy is storing its precious pictures, only 18 in number, in some Tube. They are told to expect immense bombs at the end of the month, which will dig 20 feet deep, & then explode.'
22. Hoberman, *Museum Trouble*, p. 25.
23. Ibid., p. 10.
24. Brandt, 'The Memory Makers', p. 112.
25. E. M. Forster, 'The Birth of an Empire', in *Abinger Harvest* (London: Edward Arnold & Co., 1946), pp. 44–7 (p. 47).
26. Ibid., p. 47.
27. Hope Mirrlees, 'Listening to the Past', in *Collected Poems*, ed. Sandeep Parmar (Manchester: Carcanet, 2011), pp. 85–9 (p. 85).
28. Forster, 'The Birth of an Empire', p. 47.

29. Virginia Woolf, 'Waxworks at the Abbey', in *The Essays of Virginia Woolf*, vol. IV: 1925–28, ed. Andrew McNeillie (London: Hogarth Press, 1994), pp. 540–2 (p. 540).
30. Wellington, *Exhibiting War*, p. 5.
31. E. M. Forster, 'Me, Them and You', in *Abinger Harvest*, pp. 27–30 (p. 29).
32. Virginia Woolf, 'The Royal Academy', in *The Essays of Virginia Woolf*, vol. III: 1919–24, ed. Andrew McNeillie (London: Hogarth Press, 1988), pp. 89–95.
33. Woolf, *Diary*, vol. I, p. 168. See also *The Letters of Virginia Woolf*, vol. II: 1912–22, ed. Nigel Nicolson and Joanna Trautmann (London: Chatto & Windus, 1980), pp. 258–61 (p. 260): to Vanessa Bell, 15 June 1918.
34. Guillaume Apollinaire, 'Les Reliques de Napoléon: Une Ville Désappointée', in *Œuvres en Prose*, vol. III, pp. 417–18; 'Un Petit Musée', in *Œuvres en Prose Complètes*, vol. II, ed. Pierre Caizergues and Michel Décaudin (Paris: Gallimard, 1991), p. 686.
35. E. M. Forster, *Alexandria: A History and a Guide* and *Pharos and Pharillon*, ed. Miriam Allott (Cairo: American University of Cairo Press, 2004), p. 89.
36. *The Diary of Virginia Woolf*, vol. III: 1925–30, ed. Anne Olivier Bell and Andrew McNeillie (London: Penguin, 1982), p. 72.
37. Stephen Greenblatt, 'Resonance and Wonder', in *Exhibiting Cultures: The Poetics and Politics of Museum Display*, ed. Ivan Karp and Steven Lavine (Washington, DC: Smithsonian Institute, 1991), pp. 42–56 (p. 44).
38. Forster, *Alexandria*, p. 91.

BIBLIOGRAPHY

Achebe, Chinua, 'The Novelist as Teacher', in *Morning Yet on Creation Day* (Garden City: Doubleday, 1975), pp. 67–74.
Ackerley, J. R., *Hindoo Holiday: An Indian Journal* (London: Penguin, 2009).
Adamson, Walter L., *Embattled Avant-Gardes: Modernism's Resistance to Commodity Culture in Europe* (Berkeley: University of California Press, 2007).
Adéma, Marcel, *Guillaume Apollinaire* (Paris: La Table Ronde, 1968).
Adéma, Marcel, *Guillaume Apollinaire le mal-aimé* (Paris: Plon, 1952).
Adéma, Marcel and Michel Décaudin, eds, *Album Apollinaire* (Paris: Gallimard, 1971).
Aldington, Richard, *Death of a Hero* (London: Penguin, 2013).
Allard, Roger, 'Untitled', *SIC*, January–February 1919, pp. 281–2.
Anand, Mulk Raj, *Across the Black Waters* (New Delhi: Orient Paperbacks, 2008).
Anand, Mulk Raj, *Conversations in Bloomsbury* (London: Wildwood House, 1981).
Anand, Mulk Raj, 'E. M. Forster: A Personal Recollection', *The Journal of Commonwealth Literature* 18.1 (1983), 80–3.
Anand, Mulk Raj, 'English Novels of the Twentieth Century on India', *The Asiatic Quarterly Review* 39 (1943), 244–57.
Anand, Mulk Raj, 'India and the People', *The Tribune*, 26 January 1945, p. 15.

Anand, Mulk Raj, *Letters on India* (London: George Routledge & Sons, 1942).
Anand, Mulk Raj, *Morning Face* (Bombay: Kutub Popular, 1968).
Anand, Mulk Raj, 'Mulk Raj Anand Remembers', *Indian Literature* 36.2 (1993), 176–86.
Anand, Mulk Raj, 'New Bearings in Indian Literature', *The Literary Review* (1961), 453–8.
Anand, Mulk Raj, 'Pigeon Indian: Some Notes on Indian-English Writing', *World Literature Written in English* 21.1 (1982), 325–36.
Anand, Mulk Raj, *Private Life of an Indian Prince* (London: Hutchinson, 1954).
Anand, Mulk Raj, *Seven Summers: The Story of an Indian Childhood* (Bombay: Kutub Popular, n.d.).
Anand, Mulk Raj, *The Sword and the Sickle* (New Delhi: Arnold Heinemann, 1984).
Anand, Mulk Raj, *Untouchable* (London: Penguin, 2014).
Anand, Mulk Raj, *The Village* (Bombay: Kutub Popular, 1960).
Anand, Mulk Raj, 'Why I Became a Writer', *Contemporary Indian Literature* 5.11/12 (1965), 13–15.
Apollinaire, Guillaume, 'Agréments de la Guerre en Avril', in *Œuvres en Prose*, vol. III, pp. 223–7.
Apollinaire, Guillaume, 'Alan Seeger', *Bulletin des Écrivains*, September 1916, p. 3.
Apollinaire, Guillaume, 'Aphorismes Touchant le Fantassin du Front', in *Œuvres en Prose*, vol. III, p. 240.
Apollinaire, Guillaume, 'Art et Curiosité: Les Commencements du Cubisme', in *Œuvres en Prose*, vol. II, pp. 1,514–16.
Apollinaire, Guillaume, 'L'Art Vivant et la Guerre', in *Œuvres en Prose*, vol. II, pp. 857–8.
Apollinaire, Guillaume, 'Le Burin', in *Œuvres en Prose*, vol. II, p. 1,317.
Apollinaire, Guillaume, *Calligrammes: Poems of Peace and War, 1913–16*, trans. A. H. Greet (Berkeley: University of California Press, 1980).
Apollinaire, Guillaume, 'Le Caporal Larguier', in *Œuvres en Prose*, vol. III, p. 221.
Apollinaire, Guillaume, 'Carte Postale', in *Œuvres Poétiques*, p. 297.
Apollinaire, Guillaume, 'Le Cas de Richard Mutt', in *Œuvres en Prose*, vol. II, pp. 1,378–80.
Apollinaire, Guillaume, 'Le Casque des Agents', in *Œuvres en Prose*, vol. III, p. 1,095.
Apollinaire, Guillaume, 'Le Chapeau Haut-de-Forme', in *Œuvres en Prose*, vol. III, p. 1,063.
Apollinaire, Guillaume, 'Contribution à l'Étude des Superstitions et du Folklore du Front', in *Œuvres en Prose*, vol. I, pp. 1,381–5.

Apollinaire, Guillaume, *Correspondance Générale*, vols. I–III, ed. Victor Martin-Schmets (Paris: Honoré Champion, 2015).
Apollinaire, Guillaume, 'La Cravate et la Montre', in *Œuvres Poétiques*, p. 192.
Apollinaire, Guillaume, *The Cubist Painters*, trans. Peter Read (Midsomer Norton: Artists Bookworks, 2002).
Apollinaire, Guillaume, 'Curiosités du Front', *Brise d'Entonnoirs*, November–December 1916, pp. 1–2.
Apollinaire, Guillaume, 'Curiosities from the Front', intr. and trans. Cedric Van Dijck, *PMLA* 134.3 (2019), 555–61.
Apollinaire, Guillaume, 'Gazette Cormon-Collin-Flameng', in *Œuvres en Prose*, vol. III, pp. 260–4.
Apollinaire, Guillaume, 'La Ghirba', in *Œuvres en Prose*, vol. II, p. 1,413.
Apollinaire, Guillaume, 'L'Hellespontienne', in *Œuvres en Prose*, vol. III, p. 221.
Apollinaire, Guillaume, 'Histoire d'une Gazette du Front', in *Œuvres en Prose*, vol. III, pp. 247–50.
Apollinaire, Guillaume, 'Il y a', in *Œuvres Poétiques*, pp. 280–1.
Apollinaire, Guillaume, 'Impressions d'un Inondé', in *Œuvres en Prose*, vol. III, pp. 407–9.
Apollinaire, Guillaume, 'Les Journaux de Tranchée Italiens', in *Œuvres en Prose*, vol. II, pp. 1,383–4.
Apollinaire, Guillaume, 'Lacerba', in *Œuvres en Prose*, vol. II, p. 822.
Apollinaire, Guillaume, 'Littérateurs-Soldats', in *Œuvres en Prose*, vol. III, p. 221.
Apollinaire, Guillaume, 'La Littérature Tchèque et la Censure Autrichienne', in *Œuvres en Prose*, vol. II, pp. 1,353–4.
Apollinaire, Guillaume, 'Die Moderne Malerei', in *A Cubism Reader: Documents and Criticism, 1906–14*, ed. Mark Antliff and Patricia Leighten, trans. Jane Marie Todd (Chicago: University of Chicago Press, 2008), pp. 471–6.
Apollinaire, Guillaume, *Œuvres en Prose Complètes*, vol. I, ed. Michel Décaudin (Paris: Gallimard, 1977).
Apollinaire, Guillaume, *Œuvres en Prose Complètes*, vol. II, ed. Pierre Caizergues and Michel Décaudin (Paris: Gallimard, 1991).
Apollinaire, Guillaume, *Œuvres en Prose Complètes*, vol. III, ed. Pierre Caizergues and Michel Décaudin (Paris: Gallimard, 1993).
Apollinaire, Guillaume, *Œuvres Poétiques*, ed. André Billy, Marcel Adéma and Michel Décaudin (Paris: Gallimard, 1959).
Apollinaire, Guillaume, 'Ouvrages sur la Guerre Actuelle', in *Œuvres en Prose*, vol. II, pp. 1,182–3.
Apollinaire, Guillaume, 'Le Papier', in *Œuvres en Prose*, vol. III, p. 516.

Apollinaire, Guillaume, 'La Peinture Moderne', in *Œuvres en Prose*, vol. II, pp. 501–5.
Apollinaire, Guillaume, 'Un Petit Musée', in *Œuvres en Prose*, vol. II, p. 686.
Apollinaire, Guillaume, 'Petites Annonces', in *Œuvres en Prose*, vol. III, pp. 281–4.
Apollinaire, Guillaume, 'La Pochette de la Marraine', in *Œuvres en Prose*, vol. II, p. 1,373.
Apollinaire, Guillaume, *The Poet Assassinated*, trans. Matthew Josephson (New York: Broom, 1923).
Apollinaire, Guillaume, 'Les Poètes de ma Batterie', in *Œuvres en Prose*, vol. III, pp. 228–31.
Apollinaire, Guillaume, 'Les Reliques de Napoléon: Une Ville Désappointée', in *Œuvres en Prose*, vol. III, pp. 417–18.
Apollinaire, Guillaume, *Selected Poems*, trans. Martin Sorrell (Oxford: Oxford University Press, 2015).
Apollinaire, Guillaume, *Selected Writings of Guillaume Apollinaire*, trans. Roger Shattuck (New York: New Directions, 1971).
Apollinaire, Guillaume, 'Superstitions de Guerre', in *Œuvres en Prose*, vol. III, p. 492.
Apollinaire, Guillaume, 'Sur la Mort de René Dalize', in *Œuvres en Prose*, vol. III, pp. 255–9.
Apollinaire, Guillaume, 'Tour', in *Œuvres Poétiques*, p. 200.
Apollinaire, Guillaume, 'Le Tunnel sous la Manche', in *Œuvres en Prose*, vol. III, p. 582.
Apollinaire, Guillaume, 'Vieux Papiers', in *Œuvres en Prose*, vol. III, p. 1,050.
Apollinaire, Guillaume and Gaston Picard, 'M Guillaume Apollinaire et la Nouvelle École Littéraire' (interview), in *Œuvres en Prose*, vol. II, pp. 988–91.
Appadurai, Arjun, 'Introduction: Commodities and the Politics of Value', in *The Social Life of Things: Commodities in Cultural Perspective*, ed. Arjun Appadurai (Cambridge: Cambridge University Press, 1986), pp. 3–63.
Arbouin, Gabriel, 'Devant l'Idéogramme d'Apollinaire', in *A Cubism Reader: Documents and Criticism, 1906–14*, ed. Mark Antliff and Patricia Leighten, trans. Jane Marie Todd (Chicago: University of Chicago Press, 2008), pp. 652–7.
Arrowsmith, Rupert, *Modernism and the Museum: Asian, African, and Pacific Art and the London Avant-Garde* (Oxford: Oxford University Press, 2011).
Audoin-Rouzeau, Stéphane, *Men at War, 1914–18: National Sentiment and Trench Journalism in France during the First World War* (Oxford: Berg, 1995).

Auslander, Leora and Tara Zahra, eds, *Objects of War: The Material Culture of Conflict and Displacement* (Ithaca: Cornell University Press, 2018).

Azhar, Ahmad, 'Punjab Disturbances 1919', in *1914–1918 Online: International Encyclopedia of the First World War*, ed. Ute Daniel et al., <https://encyclopedia.1914-1918-online.net/article/punjab_distur bances_1919> (last updated 30 October 2017).

Barthes, Roland, *The Rustle of Language*, trans. Richard Howard (Berkeley and Los Angeles: University of California Press, 1989).

Bayly, Christopher, *Empire and Information: Intelligence Gathering and Social Communication in India, 1780–1870* (Cambridge: Cambridge University Press, 1996).

Beasley, Rebecca, 'Modernism's Translations', in *The Oxford Handbook of Global Modernisms*, ed. Mark Wollaeger (Oxford: Oxford University Press, 2012), pp. 551–70.

Becker, Annette, 'Art, Material Life and Disaster: Civilian and Military Prisoners of War', in *Matters of Conflict: Material Conflict, Memory and the First World War*, ed. Nicholas J. Saunders (London: Routledge, 2004), pp. 26–34.

Becker, Annette, 'The Avant-Garde, Madness and the Great War', *Journal of Contemporary History* 35.1 (2000), 71–84.

Becker, Annette, *La Grande Guerre d'Apollinaire: Un Poète Combattant* (Paris: Texto, 2014).

Beil, Christine, *Der Ausgestellte Krieg: Präsentationen des Ersten Weltkriegs 1914–39* (Tübingen: Tübinger Vereinigung für Volkskunde, 2005).

Bell, Vanessa, *Sketches in Pen and Ink: A Bloomsbury Notebook*, ed. Lia Giachero (London: Hogarth Press, 1997).

Benjamin, Walter, *Selected Writings*, vol. I, ed. Marcus Paul Bullock et al. (Cambridge, MA: Belknap Press, 1996).

Benjamin, Walter, 'The Storyteller: Observations on the Works of Nikolai Leskov', in *Selected Writings*, vol. III: 1935–38, trans. Edmund Jephcott et al., ed. Howard Eiland and Michael W. Jennings (Cambridge, MA: Harvard University Press, 2002), pp. 143–66.

Bennett, Jane, *Vibrant Matter: A Political Ecology of Things* (Durham, NC: Duke University Press, 2010).

Berthier, René, 'Espoir en Guillaume Apollinaire', *SIC*, August 1916, p. 10.

Billy, André, *Apollinaire Vivant* (Paris: Éditions de la Sirène, 1923).

Billy, André, *Avec Apollinaire: Souvenirs Inédits* (Paris: La Palatine, 1966).

Billy, André, 'Guillaume Apollinaire', *SIC*, January 1919, pp. 284–6.

Blair, Sara, 'Local Modernity, Global Modernism: Bloomsbury and the Places of the Literary', *ELH* 71.3 (2004), 813–38.

Boehmer, Elleke, *Colonial and Postcolonial Literature: Migrant Metaphors* (Oxford: Oxford University Press, 2005).

Boehmer, Elleke, ed., *Empire Writing: An Anthology of Colonial Literature 1870–1918* (Oxford: Oxford University Press, 2009).

Boehmer, Elleke, *Indian Arrivals 1870–1915: Networks of British Empire* (Oxford: Oxford University Press, 2015).

Bohn, Willard, *Apollinaire and the International Avant-Garde* (Albany: State University of New York Press, 1997).

Bohn, Willard, 'Apollinaire and the New Spirit: *Le Festin d'Ésope* (1903), *Les Soirées de Paris* (1912–14), and *L'Élan* (1915–16)', in *The Oxford Critical and Cultural History of Modernist Magazines*, vol. III, ed. Peter Brooker et al. (Oxford: Oxford University Press, 2013), pp. 120–42.

Bohn, Willard, 'Picasso, Gertrude Stein, and Guillaume Apollinaire', in *The Cambridge History of Modernism*, ed. Vincent Sherry (Cambridge: Cambridge University Press, 2017), pp. 626–45.

Bohn, Willard, *Reading Apollinaire's* Calligrammes (London: Bloomsbury, 2019).

Bonikowski, Wyatt, *Shell Shock and the Modernist Imagination: The Death Drive in Post-World War I British Fiction* (Abingdon: Routledge, 2016).

Booth, Allyson, *Postcards from the Trenches: Negotiating the Space between Modernism and the First World War* (New York: Oxford University Press, 1996).

Bornstein, George, *Material Modernism: The Politics of the Page* (Cambridge: Cambridge University Press, 2001).

Boudar, Gilbert and Pierre Caizergues, eds, *La Bibliothèque de Guillaume Apollinaire*, vol. II (Paris: Éditions du Centre Nationale de la Recherche Scientifique, 1987).

Bourke, Joanna, *Dismembering the Male: Men's Bodies, Britain and the Great War* (London: Reaktion, 1996).

Bradbury, Malcolm, 'The Denuded Place: War and Form in *Parade's End* and *USA*', in *The First World War in Fiction*, ed. Holger Klein (London: Macmillan, 1976), pp. 193–209.

Braddock, Jeremy, *Collecting as Modernist Practice* (Baltimore: Johns Hopkins University Press, 2012).

Bradshaw, David, '"Vanished, Like Leaves": The Military, Elegy and Italy in *Mrs Dalloway*', *Woolf Studies Annual* 8 (2002), 107–25.

Brandt, Susanne, 'The Memory Makers: Museums and Exhibitions of the First World War', *History and Memory* 6.1 (1994), 95–122.

Breunig, Leroy C., ed., *The Cubist Poets in Paris: An Anthology* (Lincoln: University of Nebraska Press, 1995).

Briggs, Julia, *Reading Virginia Woolf* (Edinburgh: Edinburgh University Press, 2006).

Briggs, Martin, *Through Egypt in War-Time* (London: Fisher Unwin, 1918).

Brooke, Rupert, *The Collected Poems of Rupert Brooke: With a Memoir* (London: Sidgwick & Jackson, 1918).
Brown, Bill, 'Introduction: Textual Materialism', *PMLA* 125.1 (2010), 24–8.
Brown, Bill, *A Sense of Things: The Object Matter of American Literature* (Chicago: University of Chicago Press, 2003).
Buitenhuis, Peter, *The Great War of Words: Literature as Propaganda 1914–18 and After* (London: B. T. Batsford, 1989).
Burton, Antoinette, *At the Heart of the Empire: Indians and the Colonial Encounter in Late-Victorian Britain* (Berkeley: University of California Press, 1998).
Bush, Christopher, *Ideographic Modernism: China, Writing, Media* (New York: Oxford University Press, 2010).
Buxton, Hilary, 'Imperial Amnesia: Race, Trauma and Indian Troops in the First World War', *Past & Present* 241.1 (2018), 221–58.
Caizergues, Pierre, 'Apollinaire Journaliste: Textes Retrouvés et Textes Inédits avec Présentation et Notes', II (doctoral thesis, University of Paris III, 1977), Service de Reproduction des Thèses, University of Lille III, 1979.
Campa, Laurence, *Guillaume Apollinaire* (Paris: Gallimard, 2013).
Caracciolo, Marco, 'Leaping into Space: The Two Aesthetics of *To the Lighthouse*', *Poetics Today* 31.2 (2010), 251–84.
Carrington, Dora, *Letters and Extracts from her Diaries* (London: Jonathan Cape, 1970).
Cavafy, C. P., *C. P. Cavafy: Selected Poems*, ed. and trans. Avi Sharon (London: Penguin, 2008).
Cendrars, Blaise, *Œuvres Complètes*, vol. VIII (Paris: Denoël, 1964).
Chantler, Ashley and Rob Hawkes, eds, *War and the Mind: Ford Madox Ford's* Parade's End, *Modernism and Psychology* (Edinburgh: Edinburgh University Press, 2015).
Chaudhuri, Supriya et al., eds, *Commodities and Culture in the Colonial World* (Abingdon: Routledge, 2018).
Child, Harold Hannyngton, 'Kew Gardens', *Times Literary Supplement*, 29 May 1919, p. 293.
Childs, Peter, '*A Passage to India*', in *The Cambridge Companion to E. M. Forster*, ed. David Bradshaw (Cambridge: Cambridge University Press, 2007), pp. 188–208.
Cohen, Scott, 'The Empire from the Street: Virginia Woolf, Wembley, and Imperial Monuments', *Modern Fiction Studies* 50.1 (2004), 85–109.
Collier, Patrick, *Modern Print Artefacts: Textual Materiality and Literary Value in British Print Culture, 1890–1930s* (Edinburgh: Edinburgh University Press, 2016).
Cork, Richard, *A Bitter Truth: Avant-Garde Art and the Great War* (New Haven and London: Yale University Press in association with Barbican Art Gallery, 1994).

Cowasjee, Saros, *So Many Freedoms: A Study of the Major Fictions of Mulk Raj Anand* (New Delhi: Oxford University Press, 1977).
Cundy, Alys, 'The Imperial War Museum and the Material Culture of the First World War, 1917–2014', in *The Edinburgh Companion to the First World War and the Arts*, ed. Ann-Marie Einhaus and Katherine Isobel Baxter (Edinburgh: Edinburgh University Press, 2017), pp. 402–18.
Cuny, Noëlle and Xavier Kalck, eds, *Modernist Objects: Literature, Art, Culture* (Clemson: Clemson University Press, 2020).
Damousi, Joy, 'Mourning Practices', in *The Cambridge History of the First World War*, vol. III: Civil Society, ed. Jay Winter (Cambridge: Cambridge University Press, 2014), pp. 358–84.
Darling, Malcolm, *The Punjab Peasant in Prosperity and Debt* (Oxford: Oxford University Press, 1928).
Darling, Malcolm, *Wisdom and Waste in the Punjab Village* (Oxford: Oxford University Press, 1934).
Das, Santanu, *India, Empire, and First World War Culture: Writings, Images, and Songs* (Cambridge: Cambridge University Press, 2018).
Das, Santanu, *Touch and Intimacy in First World War Literature* (Cambridge: Cambridge University Press, 2007).
Daugherty, Beth Rigel, 'Letters from Readers to Virginia Woolf', *Woolf Studies Annual* 12 (2006), 1–212.
Debon, Claude, *Calligrammes dans Tous ses États – Édition Critique du Receuil de Guillaume Apollinaire* (Paris: Éditions Calliopées, 2008).
Debon, Claude and Peter Read, eds, *Les Dessins de Guillaume Apollinaire* (Paris: Buchet-Chastel, 2008).
Demeester, Karen, 'Trauma and Recovery in Virginia Woolf's *Mrs Dalloway*', *Modern Fiction Studies* 44.3 (1998), 649–73.
Demoor, Marysa, 'From Epitaph to Obituary: The Death Politics of T. S. Eliot and Ezra Pound', *Biography* 28.2 (2005), 255–75.
Dinning, H. W., 'The War Museum', *Kia Ora Coo-Ee*, 4 December 1918, p. 10.
Dobson, Eleanor, *Writing the Sphinx: Literature, Culture and Egyptology* (Edinburgh: Edinburgh University Press, 2020).
Dodman, Trevor, *Shell Shock, Memory, and the Novel in the Wake of World War I* (New York: Cambridge University Press, 2015).
'Donations for the Imperial War Museum', *Egyptian Mail*, 16 October 1918, p. 2.
Dos Passos, John, *The Best Times: An Informal Memoir* (London: André Deutsch, 1968).
Drucker, Johanna, *The Visible Word: Experimental Typography and Modern Art, 1909–23* (Chicago: University of Chicago Press, 1994).
Dulab, Mohammed, 'Arabic Made Easy', *Alpha/Omega*, May 1917, pp. 11–13.

Editorial, *The Gnome*, March 1917, p. 2.
Ekstein, Modris, *Rites of Spring: The Great War and the Birth of the Modern Age* (Boston: Houghton Mifflin, 2000).
Eliot, T. S., *Collected Poems 1909–35* (London: Faber & Faber, 1936).
Eliot, T. S., *Selected Poems* (London: Faber & Faber, 2002).
Éluard, Paul, *Lettres de Jeunesse* (Paris: Seghers, 1962).
Fahmy, Khaled, 'The Egyptian Revolution of 1919: The Birth of a Nation', unpublished keynote lecture, 'The Great Theft of History: World War One and the Prelude to Revolution', London, 27 March 2019.
Fahmy, Ziad, *Ordinary Egyptians: Creating the Modern Nation through Popular Culture* (Palo Alto: Stanford University Press, 2011).
Fanon, Frantz, *The Wretched of the Earth* (London: Penguin, 2001).
Faulkner, William, *As I Lay Dying* (London: Vintage, 2004).
Favret, Mary A., 'Everyday War', *ELH* 72.3 (2005), 605–33.
Fernald, Anne, *Virginia Woolf: Feminism and the Reader* (New York: Palgrave Macmillan, 2006).
Fisher, Marleen, 'Interview with Mulk Raj Anand, 19 May 1973, Khandala', *Journal of Postcolonial Writing* 13.1 (1974), 109–22.
Flaubert, Gustave, *Madame Bovary* (Harmondsworth: Penguin, 1971).
Fletcher, Angus, 'Ezra Pound's Egypt and the Origin of the "Cantos"', *Twentieth-Century Literature* 48.1 (2002), 1–21.
'For the Historian of the Future', *Cambridge Magazine*, 30 January 1915, p. 209.
Ford, Ford Madox, 'A Day in Battle: Arms and the Mind', in *The Ford Madox Ford Reader*, ed. Sondra J. Stang (London: Paladin, 1987), pp. 456–61.
Forster, Charles, *The Monuments of Egypt and their Vestiges of Patriarchal Traditions* (London: Richard Bentley, 1853).
Forster, E. M., *Abinger Harvest* (London: Edward Arnold, 1961).
Forster, E. M., *Alexandria: A History and a Guide* and *Pharos and Pharillon*, ed. Miriam Allott (Cairo: American University of Cairo Press, 2004).
Forster, E. M., 'Army English', *Egyptian Mail*, 12 January 1919, p. 2.
Forster, E. M., *Aspects of the Novel* (Harmondsworth: Penguin, 1970).
Forster, E. M., 'The Birth of an Empire', in *Abinger Harvest* (London: Edward Arnold & Co., 1946), pp. 44–7.
Forster, E. M., 'Canopus, Menouthis, Aboukir. By the Rev. Father J. Faivre, S. J.', *Egyptian Mail*, 29 December 1918, p. 2.
Forster, E. M., 'Diana's Dilemma', *Egyptian Mail*, 26 August 1917, p. 2.
Forster, E. M., 'The Egyptian Labour Corps', *The Times*, 8 November 1919, p. 8.
Forster, E. M., 'Eliza in Egypt: Alexandria in 1799', *Egyptian Gazette*, 5 April 1917, p. 5.
Forster, E. M., 'Gippo English', *Egyptian Mail*, 16 December 1917, p. 2.

Forster, E. M., *The Government of Egypt: Recommendations by a Committee of the International Section of the Labour Research Department, with Notes on Egypt by E. M. Forster* (London: Labour Research Department, 1920).
Forster, E. M., 'Hawkeritis', *Daily Herald*, 30 May 1919, p. 4.
Forster, E. M., 'Higher Aspects', *Egyptian Mail*, 5 May 1918, p. 2.
Forster, E. M., *The Hill of Devi* (London: Penguin, 1965).
Forster, E. M., *Howards End* (Harmondsworth: Penguin, 1971).
Forster, E. M., 'In the Rue Lepsius', *Listener* 46, 5 July 1951, pp. 28–9.
Forster, E. M., 'John McNeill Has Come', *Egyptian Mail*, 10 February 1918, p. 2.
Forster, E. M., Letter to *The Times*, 14 July 1959, p. 9.
Forster, E. M., 'The Lost Guide', in *Alexandria: A History and a Guide* and *Pharos and Pharillon*, ed. Miriam Allott (Cairo: American University of Cairo Press, 2004), pp. 351–9.
Forster, E. M., 'Me, Them and You', in *Abinger Harvest* (London: Edward Arnold & Co., 1946), pp. 27–30.
Forster, E. M., 'Memoir to Mohammed El Adl', in *Alexandria: A History and a Guide* and *Pharos and Pharillon*, ed. Miriam Allott (Cairo: American University of Cairo Press, 2004), pp. 329–46.
Forster, E. M., 'A Musician in Egypt', *Egyptian Mail*, 21 October 1917, p. 2.
Forster, E. M., 'The Objects', *Athenaeum*, 7 May 1920, pp. 599–600.
Forster, E. M., *A Passage to India* (Harmondsworth: Penguin, 1979).
Forster, E. M., 'Pericles in Paradise', *PMLA* 134.2 (2019), 359–65.
Forster, E. M., 'Pharos (Part III)', *Athenaeum*, 12 December 1919, pp. 1,030–1.
Forster, E. M., 'Photographic Egypt', *Egyptian Mail*, 13 January 1918, p. 2.
Forster, E. M., 'Reflections on India, I: Too Late?', *Nation and Athenaeum*, 21 January 1922, pp. 614–15.
Forster, E. M., 'Review of Kew Gardens', *Daily News*, 31 July 1919, p. 2.
Forster, E. M., 'The Scallies', *Egyptian Mail*, 18 November 1917, p. 2.
Forster, E. M., *Selected Letters of E. M. Forster*, vol. I: 1879–1920, ed. Mary Lago and P. N. Furbank (London: Collins, 1983).
Forster, E. M., *Selected Letters of E. M. Forster*, vol. II, 1921–70, ed. Mary Lago and P. N. Furbank (London: Collins, 1985).
Forster, E. M., 'The Solitary Place', *Egyptian Mail*, 10 March 1918, p. 2.
Forster, E. M., 'The Trouble in Egypt: Treatment of the Fellahin', *Manchester Guardian*, 29 March 1919, p. 8.
Forster, E. M., *The Uncollected Egyptian Essays of E. M. Forster*, ed. Hilda D. Spear and Aly Abdel-Moneim (Dundee: Blackness Press, 1988).
Forster, E. M. and George Valassopoulos, 'The Poetry of C. P. Cavafy', *Athenaeum*, 9 May 1919, pp. 247–8.
'Four Young Poets', *Times Literary Supplement*, 23 January 1919, p. 40.

Frayn, Andrew, 'Introduction: Modernism and the First World War', *Modernist Cultures* 12.1 (2017), 1–15.
Freedgood, Elaine, *The Ideas in Things: Fugitive Meanings in the Victorian Novel* (Chicago: Chicago University Press, 2006).
Freedman, Ralph, *Rainer Maria Rilke: Der Meister* (Frankfurt and Leipzig: Insel Verlag, 2002).
Freud, Sigmund, 'Mourning and Melancholia', in *The Standard Edition of the Complete Psychological Works of Sigmund Freud*, vol. XIV, trans. James Strachey (London: Hogarth Press and the Institute of Psycho-Analysis, 1957), pp. 243–58.
Friedman, Alan Warren, *Fictional Death and the Modernist Enterprise* (Cambridge: Cambridge University Press, 1995).
Froula, Christine, *Virginia Woolf and the Bloomsbury Avant-Garde: War, Civilization, Modernity* (New York: Columbia University Press, 2005).
Furbank, P. N., *E. M. Forster: A Life*, vols. I–II (London: Secker & Warburg, 1978).
Fussell, Paul, *The Great War and Modern Memory* (New York: Oxford University Press, 1977).
Gandhi, Leela, *Affective Communities: Anticolonial Thought, Fin-de-Siècle Radicalism, and the Politics of Friendship* (Durham, NC: Duke University Press, 2006).
Garcia, Edgar, *Signs of the Americas: A Poetics of Pictography, Hieroglyphs and Khipu* (Chicago: University of Chicago Press, 2020).
Gasston, Aimée, *Modernist Short Fiction and Things* (London: Palgrave Macmillan, 2021).
Gaudier-Brzeska, Henri, 'Vortex (Written from the Trenches)', *Blast*, 1915, pp. 33–4.
Gerwarth, Robert and Erez Manela, eds, *Empires at War 1911–23* (Oxford: Oxford University Press, 2014).
Gerzina, Gretchen Holbrook, 'Bloomsbury and Empire', in *The Cambridge Companion to the Bloomsbury Group*, ed. Victoria Rosner (Cambridge: Cambridge University Press, 2014), pp. 112–27.
Gillespie, Diane F., 'A City in the Archives: Virginia Woolf and the Statues of London', in *Woolf and the City: Selected Papers of the Nineteenth Annual Conference on Virginia Woolf*, ed. E. F. Evans and S. E. Cornish (Clemson: Clemson University Press, 2010), pp. 55–62.
Glendinning, Victoria, *Leonard Woolf: A Biography* (New York: Free Press, 2006).
Gordon, Lyndall, *Virginia Woolf: A Writer's Life* (London: Virago Press, 2006).
'Grande Importance de Pâte à Copier', *Mercure de France*, 1 October 1915, pp. 397–8.

Green, Barbara, 'Feminist Things', in *Transatlantic Print Culture, 1880–1940: Emerging Media, Emerging Modernisms*, ed. Ann Ardis and Patrick Collier (Basingstoke: Palgrave Macmillan, 2008), pp. 66–79.

Greenblatt, Stephen, 'Resonance and Wonder', in *Exhibiting Cultures: The Poetics and Politics of Museum Display*, ed. Ivan Karp and Steven Lavine (Washington, DC: Smithsonian Institute, 1991), pp. 42–56.

Greenwood, Jeremy, *Omega Cuts* (Woodbridge: Wood Lea Press, 1998).

Griffiths, N., 'Editorial', *Sphinx*, 19 December 1914, p. 2.

Grossi, Erica, 'The Photo Albums of the First World War: Composing and Practising the Images of the Time of Destruction', in *War Time: First World War Perspectives on Temporality*, ed. Louis Halewood, Adam Luptak and Hanna Smyth (Abingdon: Routledge, 2019), pp. 132–52.

Haag, Michael, *Alexandria: City of Memory* (New Haven: Yale University Press, 2004).

Halim, Hala, *Alexandrian Cosmopolitanism: An Archive* (New York: Fordham University Press, 2013).

Hammill, Faye and Mark Hussey, *Modernism's Print Cultures* (London: Bloomsbury, 2016).

Harding, Jason and John Nash, eds, *Modernism and Non-Translation* (Oxford: Oxford University Press, 2019).

Hardy, Thomas, *The Collected Letters of Thomas Hardy*, vol. II: 1893–1901, ed. Richard Little Purdy and Michael Millgate (Oxford: Clarendon Press, 1980).

Hardy, Thomas, *The Collected Poems of Thomas Hardy* (London: Macmillan, 1962).

Hardy, Thomas, *Jude the Obscure* (London: Penguin, 1998).

Harper, Tim, *Underground Asia: Global Revolutionaries and the Assault on Empire* (Cambridge, MA: Harvard University Press, 2021).

Hemingway, Ernest, *A Farewell to Arms* (London: Arrow Books, 2004).

Hemingway, Ernest, *A Moveable Feast* (London: Jonathan Cape, 1964).

Henkin, David M., *City Reading: Written Words and Public Spaces in Antebellum New York* (New York: Columbia University Press, 1998).

Hoberman, Ruth, *Museum Trouble: Edwardian Fiction and the Emergence of Modernism* (Charlottesville: University of Virginia Press, 2011).

Hoberman, Ruth, 'Woolf and Commodities', in *Virginia Woolf in Context*, ed. Bryony Randall (Cambridge: Cambridge University Press, 2012), pp. 449–60.

Howarth, Peter, *The Cambridge Introduction to Modernist Poetry* (Cambridge: Cambridge University Press, 2012).

Hubert, Etienne-Alain, 'Poilus, Envoyez vos Journaux à la BN', *Petit Journal*, 19 June 1915, n.p.

Hughes-Wilson, John, in association with the Imperial War Museum, *A History of the First World War in 100 Objects* (London: Cassell, 2014).

Hulme, T. E., *Further Speculations by T. E. Hulme*, ed. Sam Hynes (Minneapolis: University of Minnesota Press, 1955).

Hussey, Mark, *Virginia Woolf and War: Fiction, Reality, and Myth* (Syracuse: Syracuse University Press, 1991).

Hynes, Samuel, *A War Imagined: The First World War and English Culture* (London: Pimlico, 1992).

'The Imperial War Museum', *Palestine News*, 29 August 1918, p. 10.

Inglis, K. S., 'The Homecoming: The War Memorial Movement in Cambridge, England', *Journal of Contemporary History* 27.4 (1992), 583–602.

James, Henry, 'Henry James's First Interview', in *Henry James on Culture: Collected Essays on Politics and the American Social Scene*, ed. Pierre A. Walker (Lincoln: University of Nebraska Press, 1999), pp. 138–45.

Jameson, Fredric, *The Political Unconscious: Narrative as a Socially Symbolic Act* (Ithaca: Cornell University Press, 1981).

Jones, David, *In Parenthesis* (London: Faber & Faber, 2010).

Jongeneel, Els, 'Les Combats d'Orphée: La Poésie de Guerre de Guillaume Apollinaire', *RELIEF: Revue Électronique de Littérature Française* 8.2 (2014), 1–14.

Joshi, Priya, *In Another Country: Colonialism, Culture, and the English Novel in India* (New York: Columbia University Press, 2002).

Jusanis, Gregory, 'Farewell to the Classical: Excavations in Modernism', *Modernism/modernity* 11.1 (2004), 37–53.

Kavanagh, Gaynor, 'Museum as Memorial: The Origins of the Imperial War Museum', *Journal of Contemporary History* 23.1 (1988), 77–97.

Kelly, Alice, *Commemorative Modernisms: Women Writers, Death and the First World War* (Edinburgh: Edinburgh University Press, 2020).

Kipling, Rudyard, *The Eyes of Asia* (New York: Doubleday, Page & Co., 1918).

Kipling, Rudyard, *Plain Tales from the Hills* (Oxford: Oxford University Press, 2009).

Kolbert, Elizabeth, 'Chemical Warfare's Home Front', *New York Review of Books*, <https://www.nybooks.com/articles/2021/02/11/chemical-warfares-home-front/>.

Kraus, Jonathan, ed., *The Greater War: Other Combatants and Other Fronts, 1914–18* (London: Palgrave Macmillan, 2014).

Krockel, Carl, *War Trauma and English Modernism: T. S. Eliot and D. H. Lawrence* (London: Palgrave, 2011).

Lafon, Alexandre, 'War Losses (France)', in *1914–1918 Online: International Encyclopedia of the First World War*, ed. Ute Daniel et al., <https://

encyclopedia.1914-1918-online.net/article/war_losses_france> (last updated 8 October 2014).

Lamming, George, *Of Age and Innocence* (London: Allison & Busby, 1981).

Larabee, Mark D., *Front Lines of Modernism: Remapping the Great War in British Fiction* (Basingstoke: Palgrave Macmillan, 2011).

Lawrence, D. H., *Kangaroo* (London: Martin Secker, 1923).

[Lawrence, T. E.], 'Release of Damascus (from a correspondent beyond the Jordan)', *Palestine News*, 10 October 1918, p. 6.

Leed, Eric, *No Man's Land: Combat and Identity in World War I* (New York: Cambridge University Press, 2009).

Lefebvre, Henri, *Critique de la Vie Quotidienne*, vol. II (Paris: L'Arche, 1961).

Lefebvre, Henri, *Everyday Life in the Modern World*, trans. Sacha Rabinovitch (London: Penguin, 1971).

Lehmann, John, *Thrown to the Woolfs* (London: Weidenfeld & Nicolson, 1978).

Leigh, M. S., *The Punjab and the War* (Lahore: Printed by the Superintendent, Governmental Printing, Punjab, 1922).

Levenback, Karen, *Virginia Woolf and the Great War* (Syracuse: Syracuse University Press, 1999).

Levenson, Michael, *A Genealogy of Modernism: A Study of English Literary Doctrine, 1908–22* (New York: Cambridge University Press, 1986).

Lewis, Wyndham, *Blasting and Bombardiering* (Berkeley and Los Angeles: University of California Press, 1967).

Lilienfeld, Jane, 'Woolf: War and Peace', in *Virginia Woolf in Context*, ed. Bryony Randall (Cambridge: Cambridge University Press, 2012), pp. 159–69.

Longley, Edna, 'The Great War, History and the English Lyric', in *The Cambridge Companion to the Literature of the First World War*, ed. Vincent Sherry (Cambridge: Cambridge University Press, 2005), pp. 57–84.

'Lost Mails', *Egyptian Mail*, 22 October 1918, p. 2.

Loy, Mina, *The Last Lunar Baedeker* (Manchester: Carcanet, 1985).

Macaulay, Rose, *The Writings of E. M. Forster* (Letchworth: Garden City Press, 1938).

Mack, John, *The Art of Small Things* (Cambridge, MA: Harvard University Press, 2009).

Mackay, Marina, *Modernism, War, and Violence* (London: Bloomsbury, 2017).

McLoughlin, Kate, *Authoring War: The Literary Representation of War from the Iliad to Iraq* (Cambridge: Cambridge University Press, 2011).

McLoughlin, Kate, 'Muddy Poetics: First World War Poems by Helen Saunders and Mary Borden', *Women: A Cultural Review* 26.3 (2015), 221–36.

MacNeice, Louis, *The Strings Are False: An Unfinished Autobiography* (London: Faber & Faber, 1965).
'Mainly about People', *Sphinx*, 16 June 1923, p. 14.
Mann, Thomas, *The Magic Mountain* (New York: A. A. Knopf, 2005).
Mao, Douglas, *Solid Objects: Modernism and the Test of Production* (Princeton: Princeton University Press, 1998).
Mao, Douglas and Rebecca L. Walkowitz, 'The New Modernist Studies', *PMLA* 123.3 (2008), 737–48.
Marcus, Laura, 'Virginia Woolf and the Hogarth Press', in *Modernist Writers and the Marketplace*, ed. Ian Willison, Warrick Gould and Warren Chernaik (New York: St. Martin's Press, 1996), pp. 133–42.
Marshall, J. E., *The Egyptian Enigma 1890–1928* (London: John Murray, 1928).
Materer, Timothy, ed., *Pound/Lewis: The Letters of Ezra Pound and Wyndham Lewis* (London: Faber & Faber, 1985).
Mathews, Timothy, *Reading Apollinaire: Theories of Poetic Language* (Manchester: Manchester University Press, 1987).
Mellor, Leo, *Reading the Ruins: Modernism, Bombsites and British Culture* (Cambridge: Cambridge University Press, 2011).
Metzinger, Jean, 'Cubisme et Tradition', in *A Cubism Reader: Documents and Criticism, 1906–14*, ed. Mark Antliff and Patricia Leighten, trans. Jane Marie Todd (Chicago: University of Chicago Press, 2008), pp. 123–37.
Mirrlees, Hope, *A Fly in Amber: Being an Extravagant Biography of the Romantic Antiquary Sir Robert Bruce Cotton* (London: Faber & Faber, 1962).
Mirrlees, Hope, 'Listening to the Past', in *Collected Poems*, ed. Sandeep Parmar (Manchester: Carcanet, 2011), pp. 85–9.
Mirrlees, Hope, *Paris: A Poem* (London: Faber & Faber, 2020).
Mitchell, Timothy, *Colonising Egypt* (Berkeley: University of California Press, 1991).
Morey, Peter, 'Postcolonial Forster', in *The Cambridge Companion to E. M. Forster*, ed. David Bradshaw (Cambridge: Cambridge University Press, 2007), pp. 254–73.
Morton-Jack, George, *The Indian Army on the Western Front: India's Expeditionary Force to France and Belgium in the First World War* (Cambridge: Cambridge University Press, 2014).
Mukhopadhyay, Priyasha, 'Of Greasy Notebooks and Dirty Newspapers: Reading the Illegible in *The Village in the Jungle*', *Journal of Commonwealth Literature* 50.1 (2015), 59–73.
Mukhopadhyay, Priyasha, 'On Not Reading *The Soldier's Pocket-Book for Field Service*', *Journal of Victorian Culture* 22.1 (2017), 40–56.
Musil, Robert, 'Monuments', in *Posthumous Papers of a Living Author* (London: Penguin, 1995), pp. 64–8.

Naidu, Sarojini, *The Broken Wing: Songs of Love, Death and Destiny, 1915–16* (London: William Heinemann, 1917).

Nelson, Robert, 'Soldier Newspapers: A Useful Source in the Social and Cultural History of the First World War', *War in History* 17.2 (2010), 167–91.

'New Books and Reprints', *Times Literary Supplement*, 6 May 1920, p. 286.

Newell, Stephanie, *Histories of Dirt: Media and Urban Life in Colonial and Postcolonial Lagos* (Durham, NC: Duke University Press, 2020).

Nicholls, Mark, 'A Reason for Remembering: Francis Jenkinson and the War Reserve Collection', *Transactions of the Cambridge Bibliographical Society* 11.4 (1999), 497–515.

Noble, Joan Russell, ed., *Recollections of Virginia Woolf* (London: Peter Owen, 1972).

Lord Northcliff, Alfred Harmsworth, *At the War* (London: Hodder & Stoughton, 1916).

Olson, Stanley B., 'The History of the Hogarth Press: 1917–23; A Biographical Study with Critical Discussion of Selected Publications' (unpublished doctoral thesis, Royal Holloway College, 1972).

Omissi, David, ed., *Indian Voices of the Great War: Soldiers' Letters, 1914–18* (Basingstoke: Palgrave Macmillan, 1999).

Orwell, George, 'Politics and the English Language', in *The Collected Essays, Journalism and Letters of George Orwell: In Front of Your Nose, 1945–50*, ed. Sonia Orwell and Ian Angus (New York: Harcourt, Brace & World, 1968), pp. 127–40.

Oulanne, Laura, *Materiality in Modernist Short Fiction: Lived Things* (New York: Routledge, 2021).

Outka, Elizabeth, *Consuming Traditions: Modernity, Modernism, and the Commodified Authentic* (New York: Oxford University Press, 2009).

Owen, Wilfred, *The Complete Poems and Fragments*, vol. I, ed. Jon Stallworthy (London: Chatto & Windus, 2013).

Owen, Wilfred, *Wilfred Owen: Collected Letters*, ed. Harold Owen and John Bell (London: Oxford University Press, 1967).

Pagès, Madeleine, 'Préface à l'Édition de 1952', in *Lettres à Madeleine: Tendre comme le Souvenir*, ed. Laurence Campa (Paris: Gallimard, 2005), pp. 27–34.

'The "Palestine News" in Manchester', *Egyptian Mail*, 30 May 1918, p. 2.

'Paris: A Poem by Hope Mirrlees, London: The Hogarth Press', *Times Literary Supplement*, 6 May 1920, p. 10.

Parkinson, Richard B., 'The Use of Old Objects: Ancient Egypt and English Writers around 1920', in *Ancient Egypt in the Modern Imagination*, ed. Eleanor Dobson and Nichola Tonks (London: Bloomsbury, 2020), pp. 199–211.

Paul, Catherine E., *Poetry in the Museums of Modernism: Yeats, Pound, Moore, Stein* (Ann Arbor: University of Michigan Press, 2002).

Perdriel-Vaissières, J., *Rupert Brooke's Death and Burial: Based on the Log of the French Hospital Ship DUGUAY-TROUIN*, trans. Vincent O'Sullivan (New Haven: Yale University Press, 1917).

Perloff, Marjorie, *The Futurist Moment: Avant-Garde, Avant Guerre, and the Language of Rupture* (Chicago: University of Chicago Press, 1986).

Pignot, Manon, 'Children', in *The Cambridge History of the First World War*, vol. III: Civil Society, ed. Jay Winter (Cambridge: Cambridge University Press, 2014), pp. 29–45.

Pite, R. R. G., '"Graver things ... braver things": Hardy's War Poetry', in *The Oxford Handbook of British and Irish War Poetry*, ed. Tim Kendall (Oxford: Oxford University Press, 2009), pp. 34–50.

Plotz, John, *Portable Property: Victorian Culture on the Move* (Princeton: Princeton University Press, 2008).

Posman, Sarah et al., eds, *The Aesthetics of Matter: Modernism, the Avant-Garde, and Material Exchange* (Berlin: De Gruyter, 2013).

Potter, Jane, 'For Country, Conscience and Commerce: Publishers and Publishing, 1914–1918', in *Publishing in the First World War: Essays in Book History*, ed. Mary Hammond and Shafquat Towheed (Basingstoke: Palgrave Macmillan, 2007), pp. 11–26.

Potter, Jane, 'Materiality', in *The Edinburgh Companion to First World War Periodicals*, ed. Marysa Demoor, Cedric Van Dijck and Birgit Van Puymbroeck (Edinburgh: Edinburgh University Press, 2023), pp. 17–31.

Pound, Ezra, *Gaudier-Brzeska: A Memoir* (Hessle: Marvell Press, 1960).

Pound, Ezra, *Hugh Selwyn Mauberley* (London: Ovid Press, 1920).

Pound, Ezra, *Ripostes of Ezra Pound* (London: Stephen Swift, 1912).

Price, Leah, 'Introduction: Reading Matter', *PMLA* 121.1 (2006), 9–16.

Proust, Marcel, *In Search of Lost Time: In the Shadows of Young Girls in Flower*, trans. James Grieve (London: Penguin, 2002).

Pryor, Sean, 'A Poetics of Occasion in Hope Mirrlees's *Paris*', *Critical Quarterly* 61.1 (2019), 37–53.

Rai, Vikramaditya, *The Waste Land: A Critical Study* (Delhi: Motilal Banarsidass, 1988).

Ramazani, Jahan, 'Cosmopolitan Sympathies: Poetry of the First Global War', *Modernism/modernity* 23.4 (2016), 855–74.

Rasmussen, Anne, 'The Spanish Flu', in *The Cambridge History of the First World War*, vol. III, ed. Jay Winter (Cambridge: Cambridge University Press, 2014), pp. 334–57.

Read, Peter, *Apollinaire and Cubism* (Midsomer Norton: Artists Bookworks, 2002).

'The Register of Um-Nefer: A Remarkable M.S.', *The Gnome*, November 1916, p. 6.

Reid, Fiona, 'War Psychiatry and Shell Shock', in *1914–1918 Online: International Encyclopedia of the First World War*, ed. Ute Daniel et al., <https://encyclopedia.1914-1918-online.net/article/war_psychiatry_and_shell_shock> (last updated 11 December 2019).

Reid, Frank, 'Souvenir Hunters: Collecting Curios in the Firing Line', *Kia Ora Coo-Ee*, 15 March 1918, p. 14.

René-Maurel, Jean, 'Guillaume Apollinaire à la Caserne', *Mercure de France*, December 1918, pp. 560–2.

Rilke, Rainer Maria, *Auguste Rodin*, trans. Jessie Lemont (New York: Sunwise, 1919).

Riquelme, John Paul, 'The Modernity of Thomas Hardy's Poetry', in *The Cambridge Companion to Thomas Hardy*, ed. Dale Kramer (Cambridge: Cambridge University Press, 1999), pp. 204–23.

Robinson, Annabel, *The Life and Work of Jane Ellen Harrison* (Oxford: Oxford University Press, 2002).

Said, Edward, *Culture and Imperialism* (New York: Vintage, 1994).

Saint-Amour, Paul, 'Afterword: Deep War Time', *Modernism/modernity* Print Plus 5.2 (2020), <https://modernismmodernity.org/forums/posts/stamour-deep-war-time>.

Saint-Amour, Paul K., *Tense Future: Modernism, Total War, Encyclopaedic Form* (New York: Oxford University Press, 2015).

Salmon, André, 'Histoire Anecdotique du Cubism', in *A Cubism Reader: Documents and Criticism, 1906–14*, ed. Mark Antliff and Patricia Leighten, trans. Jane Marie Todd (Chicago: University of Chicago Press, 2008), pp. 357–69.

Sassoon, Siegfried, *War Poems of Siegfried Sassoon* (Mineola: Dover, 2004).

Saunders, Nicholas J., 'Material Culture and Conflict: The Great War, 1914–2003', in *Matters of Conflict: Material Culture, Memory and the First World War*, ed. Nicholas J. Saunders (London: Routledge, 2004), pp. 5–25.

Saunders, Nicholas J., ed., *Matters of Conflict: Material Culture, Memory and the First World War* (London: Routledge, 2004).

Saunders, Nicholas J., *Trench Art: Materialities and Memories of War* (London: Routledge, 2003).

Saunders, Nicholas J. and Paul Cornish, eds, *Modern Conflict and the Senses* (London: Routledge, 2017).

Scarry, Elaine, *The Body in Pain: The Making and Unmaking of the World* (Oxford: Oxford University Press, 1988).

Scarry, Elaine, *Dreaming by the Book* (Princeton: Princeton University Press, 2001).

Scates, Bruce and Rebecca Wheatley, 'War Memorials', in *The Cambridge History of the First World War*, vol. III: Civil Society, ed. Jay Winter (Cambridge: Cambridge University Press, 2014), pp. 528–56.

Schotter, Jessie, *Hieroglyphic Modernisms: Writing and New Media in the Twentieth Century* (Edinburgh: Edinburgh University Press, 2017).

Schwartz, Kathryn, 'A New History of Print in Ottoman Cairo', Ottoman History Podcast, hosted by Nir Shafir, 15 July 2016, <http://www.ottomanhistorypodcast.com/2016/07/print-cairo.html>.

Shaheen, Mohammed, *E. M. Forster and the Politics of Imperialism* (London: Palgrave Macmillan, 2004).

Shattuck, Roger, *The Banquet Years: The Origins of the Avant-Garde in France 1885 to World War I* (New York: Anchor Books, 1958).

Shears, Jonathon and Jen Harrison, eds, *Literary Bric-à-Brac and the Victorians: From Commodities to Oddities* (Abingdon: Routledge, 2016).

Sheehan, Paul, *Modernism and the Aesthetics of Violence* (Cambridge: Cambridge University Press, 2013).

Sheffield, Gary, *The First World War in 100 Objects: The Story of the Great War Told Through the Objects That Shaped It* (London: André Deutsch, 2013).

Sherry, Vincent, *The Great War and the Language of Modernism* (New York: Oxford University Press, 2003).

Shone, Richard, *Bloomsbury Portraits: Vanessa Bell, Duncan Grant and their Circle* (New York: E. P. Dutton, 1976).

Silver, Kenneth E., *Esprit de Corps: The Art of the Parisian Avant-Garde and the First World War, 1914–1925* (Princeton: Princeton University Press, 1989).

Silver, Sean, *The Mind Is a Collection: Case Studies in Eighteenth-Century Thought* (Philadelphia: University of Pennsylvania Press, 2015).

Spencer, Toby, *British Culture and the First World War: Experience, Representation and Memory* (London: Bloomsbury, 2014).

S. S. [Socrates Spiro], 'Arabic Made Easy', *Kia Ora Coo-Ee*, 15 October 1918, p. 13.

S. S. [Socrates Spiro], 'Cairo Street Cries', *Kia Ora Coo-Ee*, 15 July 1918, p. 17.

Stape, J. H., *An E. M. Forster Chronology* (London: Macmillan, 1993).

Stape, J. H., ed., *Virginia Woolf: Interviews and Recollections* (London: Palgrave Macmillan, 1995).

Statistics of the Military Effort of the British Empire during the Great War 1914–20 (London: HM Stationery Office, 1920).

Stein, Gertrude, *The Autobiography of Alice B. Toklas* (London: Penguin, 2001).

Stevenson, Randall, *Literature and the Great War: 1914–18* (Oxford: Oxford University Press, 2014).

Steward, Jessie, *Jane Ellen Harrison: A Portrait from Letters* (London: Merlin Press, 1959).
Stewart, Susan, *On Longing: Narratives of the Miniature, the Gigantic, the Souvenir, the Collection* (Durham, NC: Duke University Press, 1992).
Swanwick, Michael, *Hope-in-the-Mist: The Extraordinary Career and Mysterious Life of Hope Mirrlees* (Montclair: Temporary Culture, 2009).
Tagore, Rabindranath, *Gitanjali (Song Offerings)* (London: India Society, 1912).
Tate, Trudi, *Modernism, History and the First World War* (Penrith: Humanities Ebooks, 2013).
Taylor-Batty, Juliette, *Multilingualism in Modernist Fiction* (London: Palgrave Macmillan, 2013).
Tearle, Oliver, *The Great War,* The Waste Land *and the Modernist Long Poem* (London: Bloomsbury, 2019).
Towheed, Shafquat and Edmund King, eds, *Reading and the First World War: Readers, Texts, Archives* (Basingstoke: Palgrave Macmillan, 2015).
Tranchman' Echo: Journal Mondain Paraissant à Chaque Cuite du Rédacteur 3, June 1915.
Trumpener, Katie, 'Memories Carved in Granite: Great War Memorials and Everyday Life', *PMLA* 115.5 (2000), 1,096–103.
Van Puymbroeck, Birgit and Cedric Van Dijck, 'Apollinaire's Trench Journalism and the Affective Public Sphere', *Texas Studies in Literature and Language* 60.3 (2018), 269–92.
Wagner, Kim A., '"Calculated to Strike Terror": The Amritsar Massacre and the Spectacle of Colonial Violence', *Past & Present* 233.1 (2016), 185–225.
Walker, Julian, *Words and the First World War: Language, Memory, Vocabulary* (London: Bloomsbury, 2017).
Wallach, Yair, *A City in Fragments: Urban Text in Modern Jerusalem* (Palo Alto: Stanford University Press, 2020).
Waugh, Evelyn, *Brideshead Revisited* (London: Penguin, 1987).
Waugh, Evelyn, *A Little Learning: An Autobiography* (London: Penguin, 2019).
'Week in Books', *Newsweek*, 22 April 1933, p. 32.
Wellington, Jennifer, *Exhibiting War: The Great War, Museums and Memory in Britain, Canada and Australia* (Cambridge: Cambridge University Press, 2017).
White, Horatio S., *Willard Fiske, Life and Correspondence: A Biographical Study* (New York: Oxford University Press, 1925).
'The Wholesome Tongue', *Egyptian Mail*, 12 January 1919, p. 2.
Williams, Raymond, *The Politics of Modernism: Against the New Conformists* (London: Verso, 1994).

Williams, Raymond, 'When Was Modernism?', in *The Politics of Modernism: Against the New Conformists* (London: Verso, 1994), pp. 31–6.
Willis Jr, J. H., *Leonard and Virginia Woolf as Publishers: The Hogarth Press, 1917–41* (Charlottesville: University Press of Virginia, 1992).
Wills, Clair, 'On Hope Mirrlees', *London Review of Books*, 10 September 2020, pp. 36–7.
Winter, Jay, 'Shell-Shock and the Cultural History of the Great War', *Journal of Contemporary History* 35.1 (2000), 7–11.
Winter, Jay, *Sites of Memory, Sites of Mourning: The Great War in European Cultural History* (Cambridge: Cambridge University Press, 1995).
Winter, Jay, *War Beyond Words: Languages of Remembrance from the Great War to the Present* (Cambridge: Cambridge University Press, 2017).
Wittman, Laura, 'Memorials: Embodiment and Unconventional Mourning', in *The Edinburgh Companion to the First World War and the Arts*, ed. Ann-Marie Einhaus and Katherine Isobel Baxter (Edinburgh: Edinburgh University Press, 2017), pp. 149–65.
Wollaeger, Mark, *Modernism, Media, and Propaganda: British Narrative from 1900 to 1945* (Princeton: Princeton University Press, 2006).
Wood, H. F., *Egypt under the British* (London: Chapman & Hall, 1896).
Woolf, Leonard, *Beginning Again: An Autobiography of the Years 1911 to 1918* (London: Hogarth Press, 1964).
Woolf, Leonard, *Diaries in Ceylon 1908–11: Records of a Colonial Administrator and Stories from the East: Three Short Stories on Ceylon* (Colombo: Metro Printers, 1962).
Woolf, Leonard, *Downhill All the Way: An Autobiography of the Years 1919–39* (New York: Harcourt, Brace & World, 1967).
Woolf, Leonard, *Empire and Commerce in Africa: A Study in Economic Imperialism* (London: Labour Research Department, n.d.).
Woolf, Leonard, *Letters of Leonard Woolf*, ed. Frederic Spotts (London: Weidenfeld & Nicolson, 1989).
Woolf, Leonard, *Sowing: An Autobiography of the Years 1880–1904* (London: Hogarth Press, 1960).
Woolf, Leonard and James Strachey, eds, *Virginia Woolf and Lytton Strachey: Letters* (New York: Harcourt, Brace & Co., 1956).
Woolf, Leonard and Virginia, *Two Stories* (Richmond: Hogarth Press, 1917).
Woolf, Virginia, '22 Hyde Park Gate', in *Moments of Being: Autobiographical Writings*, ed. Jeanne Schulkind (London: Pimlico, 2002), pp. 31–42.
Woolf, Virginia, 'Abbeys and Cathedrals', in *Essays*, vol. V, pp. 301–6.
Woolf, Virginia, 'The Art of Fiction', in *Essays*, vol. IV, pp. 599–603.
Woolf, Virginia, 'A Cambridge V.A.D.', in *Essays*, vol. II, pp. 112–14.
Woolf, Virginia, 'Craftsmanship', in *Essays*, vol. VI, pp. 91–102.

Woolf, Virginia, *The Diary of Virginia Woolf*, vol. I: 1915–19, ed. Anne Olivier Bell (London: Penguin, 1979).
Woolf, Virginia, *The Diary of Virginia Woolf*, vol. II: 1920–24, ed. Anne Olivier Bell and Andrew McNeillie (London: Penguin, 1981).
Woolf, Virginia, *The Diary of Virginia Woolf*, vol. III: 1925–30, ed. Anne Olivier Bell and Andrew McNeillie (London: Penguin, 1982).
Woolf, Virginia, *The Essays of Virginia Woolf*, vol. I: 1904–12, ed. Andrew McNeillie (London: Hogarth Press, 1986).
Woolf, Virginia, *The Essays of Virginia Woolf*, vol. II: 1912–18, ed. Andrew McNeillie (London: Hogarth Press, 1987).
Woolf, Virginia, *The Essays of Virginia Woolf*, vol. III: 1919–24, ed. Andrew McNeillie (London: Hogarth Press, 1988).
Woolf, Virginia, *The Essays of Virginia Woolf*, vol. IV: 1925–28, ed. Andrew McNeillie (London: Hogarth Press, 1994).
Woolf, Virginia, *The Essays of Virginia Woolf*, vol. V: 1929–32, ed. Stuart N. Clarke (London: Hogarth Press, 2009).
Woolf, Virginia, *The Essays of Virginia Woolf*, vol. VI: 1933–41, ed. Andrew McNeillie (London: Hogarth Press, 1987).
Woolf, Virginia, *Freshwater: A Comedy* (London: Hogarth Press, 1976).
Woolf, Virginia, 'I Am Christina Rossetti', in *Essays*, vol. V, pp. 208–17.
Woolf, Virginia, *Jacob's Room* (Oxford: Oxford World's Classics, 2008).
Woolf, Virginia, *Jacob's Room*, ed. Stuart N. Clarke and David Bradshaw (Cambridge: Cambridge University Press, 2020).
Woolf, Virginia, *The Letters of Virginia Woolf*, vol. II: 1912–22, ed. Nigel Nicolson and Joanna Trautmann (London: Chatto & Windus, 1980).
Woolf, Virginia, *The Letters of Virginia Woolf*, vol. VI: 1936–41, ed. Nigel Nicolson and Joanna Trautmann (London: Chatto & Windus, 1983).
Woolf, Virginia, 'The Lives of the Obscure', in *Essays*, vol. IV, pp. 118–45.
Woolf, Virginia, 'The Modern Essay', in *Essays*, vol. IV, pp. 216–27.
Woolf, Virginia, 'Modern Fiction', in *Essays*, vol. IV, pp. 157–65.
Woolf, Virginia, 'Modern Novels', in *Essays*, vol. III, pp. 30–6.
Woolf, Virginia, *Monday or Tuesday* (Richmond: Hogarth Press, 1921).
Woolf, Virginia, *Mr Bennett and Mrs Brown* (London: Hogarth Press, 1924).
Woolf, Virginia, 'Mr Sassoon's Poems', in *Essays*, vol. II, pp. 119–22.
Woolf, Virginia, *Mrs Dalloway* (London: Penguin, 1996).
Woolf, Virginia, *Mrs Dalloway's Party: A Short Story Sequence*, ed. Stella McNichol (London: Hogarth Press, 1973).
Woolf, Virginia, 'The New Crusade', in *Essays*, vol. II, pp. 201–3.
Woolf, Virginia, 'The Old Order', in *Essays*, vol. II, pp. 167–76.
Woolf, Virginia, 'On Not Knowing French', in *Essays*, vol. V, pp. 3–9.
Woolf, Virginia, 'On Not Knowing Greek', in *Essays*, vol. IV, pp. 38–53.

Woolf, Virginia, *A Passionate Apprentice: The Early Journals 1879–1909*, ed. Mitchell A. Leaska (London: Hogarth Press, 1990).
Woolf, Virginia, 'The Perfect Language', in *Essays*, vol. II, pp. 114–19.
Woolf, Virginia, 'Phases of Fiction', *Essays*, vol. V, pp. 40–88.
Woolf, Virginia, 'Reading', in *Essays*, vol. III, pp. 141–61.
Woolf, Virginia, *A Room of One's Own* and *Three Guineas* (London: Penguin, 2000).
Woolf, Virginia, 'The Royal Academy', in *Essays*, vol. III, pp. 89–95.
Woolf, Virginia, 'Rupert Brooke', *Times Literary Supplement*, 8 August 1918, p. 371.
Woolf, Virginia, 'Rupert Brooke', in *Essays*, vol. I, pp. 277–84.
Woolf, Virginia, 'A Sketch of the Past', in *Moments of Being: Autobiographical Writings*, ed. Jeanne Schulkind (London: Pimlico, 2002), pp. 78–160.
Woolf, Virginia, 'Solid Objects', in *The Mark on the Wall and Other Short Fiction* (Oxford: Oxford World's Classics, 2001), pp. 54–9.
Woolf, Virginia, 'Street Haunting', in *Essays*, vol. IV, pp. 480–91.
Woolf, Virginia, 'The Sun and the Fish', in *Essays*, vol. IV, pp. 519–24.
Woolf, Virginia, *To the Lighthouse* (London: Dent, 1967).
Woolf, Virginia, 'An Unwritten Novel', in *The Mark on the Wall and Other Short Fiction* (Oxford: Oxford World's Classics, 2001), pp. 18–29.
Woolf, Virginia, 'Waxworks at the Abbey', in *Essays*, vol. IV, pp. 540–2.
W. S. C., 'Death of Mr Rupert Brooke: Sunstroke at Lemnos', *The Times*, 26 April 1915, p. 5.
Yourcenar, Marguerite, *Œuvres Romanesques* (Paris: Gallimard, 1989).
Ziemann, Benjamin, 'Agrarian Society', in *The Cambridge History of the First World War*, vol. II: The State, ed. Jay Winter (Cambridge: Cambridge University Press, 2014), pp. 382–407.
Zwerdling, Alex, '*Jacob's Room*: Woolf's Satiric Elegy', *ELH* 48.4 (1981), 894–913.
Zwerdling, Alex, *Virginia Woolf and the Real World* (Berkeley: University of California Press, 1986).

INDEX

Ackerley, J. R., 133, 136
agriculture, 130, 133–40, 145
aeroplane / aviation, 18, 21, 27, 33, 61, 64, 73–6, 149, 164
Aldington, Richard, 4
Amritsar, 5, 131–2, 143, 151–2
Anand, Mulk Raj, 1–12, 128–54, 167
  Across the Black Waters, 11, 128, 131–43, 148
  Morning Face, 132, 143
  Private Life of an Indian Prince, 147
  Seven Summers, 132, 136, 138–9
  The Sword and the Sickle, 11, 128, 152–4
  The Village, 10, 128–9, 131–43, 144, 147, 148
  Untouchable, 142, 161
Apollinaire, Guillaume, 1–2, 6, 8–11, 16–40, 55, 72, 108, 138, 146, 149, 165–70
  '1915', 9, 19, 36–9, 40
  Alcools, 16, 21, 24, 25
  Calligrammes, 36

Case d'Armons, 9, 17, 18–19, 34–40, 48, 49, 166–7, 169
'Curiosities from the Front', 18, 19, 29–30, 32, 33, 40
'La Vie Anecdotique', 21, 32
Médaillon Toujours Fermé, 40
'Postcard', 9, 18–19, 36–40
The Cubist Painters, 22–3
The Poet Assassinated, 32, 35
'There's/There are', 19, 26, 27, 38, 40
Tranchman' Echo, 19, 33–5, 40, 166
archive, 34, 36, 90, 107, 139, 149, 164–6
Arts à Paris, 19, 33
Athenaeum, 69, 108, 169

Battles
  Aboukir, 170
  Cambrai, 112
  Champagne (Second), 23, 25, 26
  Festubert, 130, 132, 137–8
  Gallipoli, 56, 83, 94, 144

Battles (cont.)
  Gaza (First), 52
  Loos, 130, 137
  Marne, 105
  Messines, 132
  Mons, 114
  Neuve Chapelle, 130, 137
  Passchendaele, 114
  Verdun, 144
  Ypres (First), 25, 130, 137
Benjamin, Walter, 24, 49, 51, 61
Berthier, René, 35, 37, 40
Bibliothèque Nationale de France, 34, 128, 165–6, 170
Billy, André, 19, 30, 33, 35, 38, 46
body, 6, 11, 52, 92–3, 95–8, 101–3, 106, 133–5, 140–3, 153, 169
  corpse, 71, 105–6, 132, 143–6
Boer War, 145
book (as object), 1–2, 6, 9, 10, 18–19, 32–40, 57–60, 70–1, 77, 93, 103–15, 146–51
Braque, Georges, 19, 21
Brise d'Entonnoirs, 30, 33
Brooke, Rupert, 10, 12, 68, 93, 94, 96, 111–15, 127, 144
Bulletin des Armées de la République, 28, 32, 36, 39, 40
Bulletin des Écrivains, 33
bureaucratic paperwork, 9, 11, 104, 128, 131, 146–51, 154, 167

calligram / picture-poem, 17–18, 23–4, 30, 32, 35, 72, 108
Cambridge, 53, 64, 94–9, 104, 112–14, 120, 122, 164–6
Cambridge Magazine, 164–5
Carrington, Dora, 12, 118, 120, 122
Cavafy, C. P., 12, 53, 69–71, 73
Cendrars, Blaise, 24, 31, 108
censorship, 2, 8–11, 32, 34, 39, 51, 52, 65–7, 69, 73, 75, 77, 149, 157, 161, 167
China, 19–20, 72–3, 151, 165
Cocteau, Jean, 19, 108

collage, 8–10, 19, 22–3, 36–9, 49, 67, 110, 146
commodity, 1, 29, 130, 138–9
cross, 30, 31, 88–9, 102–3, 113, 144, 168
Cubism, 17, 18, 19–24, 39, 41
curiosity, 1, 16–40, 112

Darling, Malcolm, 135, 137, 140, 152, 155, 156, 162
debris, 1, 5, 9, 24, 27, 29, 34
de Coligny-Châtillon, Louise ('Lou'), 19, 25, 27, 36, 43, 166, 172
de la Roncière, Charles, 34, 165–6
dictionary, 9, 52–60, 63, 65, 70, 76–7, 99, 130, 160, 167
Duchamp, Marcel, 22
Duhamel, Georges, 21, 42
Dutt, Toru, 12, 136, 145

Edwardian literature (Bennett, Galsworthy, Wells), 2–3, 5, 130, 168
Egyptian Gazette, 55–7, 65, 70, 80
Egyptian Mail, 6–8, 10, 53, 56–8, 61–5, 69, 73, 76–7, 165
El Adl, Mohammed, 54, 79, 85
Eliot, T. S., 5, 11, 12, 69, 148
  Coriolan, 5
  'The Waste Land', 52, 108, 124, 145–6
Epstein, Jacob, 31, 169
Excelsior, 21, 31, 33, 36

Festin d'Ésope, 21, 33
Ford, Ford Madox, 3–4, 6, 12, 31, 50–1, 150
Forster, E. M., 1–2, 5–12, 50–78, 98, 110, 119, 129–30, 133, 135, 142, 148, 149, 153, 165–71
  Alexandria, 10, 53, 59–60, 70–2, 76, 170–1
  A Passage to India, 12, 50, 77, 133, 135, 142
  'Army English', 63–6

A Room with a View, 59
'Gippo English', 61–3, 66
Howards End, 72
Pharos and Pharillon, 77
The Hill of Devi, 135
'The Story of a Panic', 59
Where Angels Fear to Tread, 59
Freud, Sigmund, 91, 103
Frisian horse, 9, 18, 32, 35, 40, 46
Fry, Roger, 95, 110, 114
furniture, 2–3, 19–20, 25–6, 67–8, 95, 130, 150–1

Gaudier-Brzeska, Henri, 29, 31, 72, 99, 116, 121
Gnome, 55, 73–5, 85
gravestone / tombstone, 1–2, 10, 69, 88–115, 121, 143–4, 170
Guardian (*Manchester Guardian*), 7

Hardy, Thomas, 11, 53, 97, 119, 145–6
Harrison, Jane Ellen, 104, 121–2, 161
Hemingway, Ernest, 4, 27, 39
Heron Press, 114
Hogarth Press, 8, 10, 11, 36, 77, 93, 94, 103–15, 138, 146

Imagism, 72
Intransigeant, 19, 25, 27, 166
Iqbal, Muhammad, 148, 152

James, Henry, 50–2, 112, 121
Jones, David, 38, 138

Kia Ora Coo-Ee, 55, 57, 165
Kitchener, Lord, 170–1
Kollwitz, Käthe, 12, 106, 123

language
  and army, 38, 51, 62–4, 67
  and empire, 51, 132, 145, 148
  as play, 54, 58, 62
  in crisis, 50–2, 61–78, 139, 167
Lawrence, D. H., 4, 81, 98

Lawrence, T. E., 7, 55, 81
leaflet, 88, 90, 164–5
Léger, Fernand, 5, 18
Lewis, Wyndham, 3, 46, 142

Mansfield, Katherine, 69, 95, 103, 109, 113–14, 124
  Prelude, 109, 113, 124
Martineau, Henri, 21, 23
medal, 5, 129, 153, 169, 171
Mercure de France, 12, 18, 21, 25, 27, 29, 31–4, 46, 49, 166
Mirrlees, Hope, 1–2, 6, 8, 10–11, 88–115, 146, 148, 166–9
  A Fly in Amber, 108
  Paris: A Poem, 8, 10, 92–3, 103–10, 112, 166–9
  'Listening to the Past', 105
  Madeleine, 103
monument / memorial 1–2, 5, 9–10, 52–3, 67–75, 77, 88–115, 144, 166–7
  Albert Memorial (London), 125
  book as memorial, 111–15, 167
  cenotaph, 90, 113, 168
  Cleopatra's Needle, 70–1
  Cookham War Memorial, 88–90, 98
  Elgin Marbles, 98, 99, 101, 103
  Grave of the Unknown Warrior (Westminster Abbey), 144, 159
  Parthenon / Acropolis, 98–103, 111–12
  Pompey's Pillar, 70–1
  Victoria Memorial (London), 90
  Wellington Monument (Hyde Park), 101
mud, 1–2, 6, 10–11, 25, 30, 39, 96, 99–102, 105, 122, 128–54, 167–9
museum, 11, 19, 53, 105, 164–71
  Anti-War Museum (Berlin), 30–1
  Australian War Memorial, 56, 165
  British Museum, 70, 75, 86, 98, 101, 103, 152, 167
  Graeco-Roman Museum (Alexandria), 59, 70

museum (*cont.*)
  Imperial War Museum (London), 68, 165, 168–9
  Louvre, 104–5, 167–8
  Musée de la Guerre, 165
  Musée des Beaux-Arts (Nîmes), 167
  Museum voor Leger en Krijgsgeschiedenis (Brussels), 165
  National Gallery (London), 50, 167, 170
  Naval Museum (Greenwich), 170–1
  Royal Academy, 170
  United Services Museum (Whitehall), 169
  Victoria & Albert Museum, 129, 167
Musil, Robert, 90–1, 107

Naidu, Sarojini, 133, 143
Napoleon, 30, 54, 60, 101, 170–1
Nelson, Horatio, 98, 170–1

Owen, Wilfred, 4, 68, 145

Pagès, Madeleine, 16–18, 26, 27, 29, 31–5, 39, 40, 169
Palestine News, 7–8, 55
paper shortage, 2, 8, 10, 36, 104, 109–10
periodical (as object), 7–9, 18–19, 23, 34, 58, 65, 75, 167
photograph, 19–20, 26, 31, 56, 67–8, 73, 88, 95, 99, 101, 108, 128–9, 149, 169
Picasso, Pablo, 19, 21–3, 39, 42, 45
Poems by C. N. Sidney Woolf, 10, 93, 111–14
postcard, 8–9, 19, 23, 32, 36–40, 121, 165, 167
poster, 8, 32, 61, 108, 165
Pound, Ezra, 3, 12, 71–3, 99, 121, 142, 146

propaganda, 39, 52, 61–4, 77, 122, 165, 170
Proust, Marcel, 27, 92, 97, 116, 129

Read, Herbert, 129, 148
Red Cross, 11, 51, 62–3, 73
'Register of Um-Nefer: A Remarkable M.S.', 73–6
Reims Cathedral, 25, 32, 99, 121
Rilke, Rainer Maria, 5, 97
Rire aux Éclats, 33

Sargent, John Singer, 169–70
Sassoon, Siegfried, 4, 50, 142
shell / shrapnel, 1, 5–6, 17–18, 26–32, 39, 113, 139–41, 167
shell shock, 4, 13, 113, 154
signboard, 10, 52–4, 60–7, 73, 76–8, 107, 167, 168
soil / earth, 5, 10–11, 30, 51, 93, 102–3, 128–71
souvenir, 1, 5, 9, 16, 17, 27–31, 34, 68, 130, 165–8
Spanish Civil War, 114, 138
Spencer, Stanley, 12, 88–92, 98
Sphinx, 55, 57, 65
Spiro, Socrates, 12, 57–8, 60, 80
Soirées de Paris, 22–4, 32, 33, 43
statue, 6, 9, 10, 17, 19, 25, 68, 71, 88–115, 150
Stein, Gertrude, 4, 12, 19, 24, 27, 30, 72, 85, 104, 161
Stephen, Thoby, 94, 112–15
Stevens, Wallace, 3, 129

Tagore, Rabindranath, 12, 134, 162
Times, 55, 56, 65, 92, 114
Times Literary Supplement, 2, 3, 93, 95, 97, 103–4, 108, 110, 114–15, 144
translation, 53, 57, 58, 62–3, 69, 75–6, 77, 136
travel guide, 9, 53–60, 69–72, 76–7, 99, 165–6, 170–1
trench art, 6, 9, 17, 18, 27–30, 167

trench press, 9, 11, 18, 30, 33–4, 55, 58, 73–5, 165–7

Ulysses, 37–9, 98, 103
uniform, 1, 5, 17, 19, 26, 30–1, 46, 68, 99–100, 138–9, 149, 169–71
   (Adrian) helmet, 1–2, 5–6, 18, 27, 30–1, 40, 45–6, 167–9
   Bleu Horizon, 30, 105, 123
   boots, 96–7, 102, 138, 168
   equipment, 1, 30–1, 143, 169–70
   (trench) coat, 5, 26, 99, 101, 138, 170–1

Vermorel sprayer, 5, 17, 30, 45
Versailles Conference and Treaty, 104, 122, 129, 151
Vorticism, 29, 99

War Office, 13, 51, 143, 149
watch, 5, 22, 24
Waugh, Evelyn, 4, 29, 81, 114, 138
weaponry, 5, 29, 32, 99–100, 141, 165, 169
West, Rebecca, 4
Woolf, Leonard, 55, 93–6, 108–9, 112–14, 130, 146, 148

Woolf, Virginia, 1–12, 54, 61, 69, 76–7, 88–115, 130, 132, 136, 139, 140, 144, 146, 148, 167–71
   'Abbeys and Cathedrals', 101
   'A Sketch of the Past', 98, 120
   Freshwater, 144
   Jacob's Room, 9, 10, 88–115, 169
   Kew Gardens, 10, 93, 103, 109–10
   'Modern Novels', 2–3, 5
   Monday or Tuesday, 109
   'Mr Bennett and Mrs Brown', 3, 5, 12
   Mrs Dalloway, 4, 100, 101, 145
   'Mrs Dalloway in Bond Street', 92
   'On Not Knowing French', 76
   'Phases of Fiction', 3
   'Solid Objects', 100
   'Street Haunting', 113
   'Thoughts on Peace in an Air Raid', 98
   Three Guineas, 31, 98, 120
   To the Lighthouse, 75, 119, 130, 139
Yeats, W. B., 133, 155
Ypres (Ieper), 6, 25, 68, 99, 130, 137

EU representative:
Easy Access System Europe
Mustamäe tee 50, 10621 Tallinn, Estonia
Gpsr.requests@easproject.com

www.ingramcontent.com/pod-product-compliance
Lightning Source LLC
Chambersburg PA
CBHW051124160426
43195CB00014B/2334